*Spiritual Encounters with Unusual
Light Phenomena: Lightforms*

Religion, Education and Culture

Series Editors:
William K. Kay (Bangor University, UK)
Leslie J. Francis (University of Warwick, UK)
and Jeff Astley (Durham University, UK)

This series addresses issues raised by religion and education within contemporary culture. It is intended to be of benefit to those involved in professional training as ministers of religion, teachers, counsellors, psychologists, social workers or health professionals while contributing to the theoretical development of the academic fields from which this training is drawn.

Spiritual Encounters with Unusual Light Phenomena: Lightforms

MARK FOX

UNIVERSITY OF WALES PRESS
CARDIFF
2008

British Library Cataloguing-in-Publication Data
A catalogue record for this book is available from the British Library.

ISBN 978-0-7083-2157-7

www.wales.ac.uk/press

The right of Mark Fox to be identified as author of this work has been asserted by him in accordance with sections 77 and 79 of the Copyright, Designs and Patents Act 1988.

Printed in Wales by Dinefwr Press, Llandybïe

Dedicated to the memory of my mother, Irene Fox.
She gave light to all who knew and loved her.

Contents

Acknowledgements

I should like to thank the following people, without whom this book could not have been written: Professor Paul Badham, Dr Wendy Dossett and Peggy Morgan, past and present directors of the Religious Experience Research Centre, for access to such a large amount of archival material. I hope that this book has gone some way to repaying their trust and kindness. Val Camroux and Selina Stewart for ensuring that my college timetable always gave me the opportunity to write; Professor Leslie Francis and Canon Michael Perry, members of the steering group, for friendly and helpful advice; Tracey Kesterton, for support and encouragement; Jennifer Randell, for editing – and thereby greatly improving – the text; and Anne Watkins at the Religious Experience Research Centre for kind advice, particularly whilst I was researching the life of Sir Alister Hardy and the history of Lampeter.

Author's note

Numbers in brackets throughout the text refer to the numbers of the accounts as they are found in the archive. All accounts have been reproduced as written, including errors and/or irregularities of spelling, grammar and punctuation, unless otherwise indicated.

Lightforms – a mystery posed

Lightforms

A teacher, settling her terminally ill aunt for the night and appalled at the prospect of nursing yet another relative through a terrible illness, is suddenly startled to see a strange and wonderful light in the corner of the bedroom she and her aunt share. It grows in size and brilliance and she feels overwhelmed by a comforting presence that she associates with it. It seems to be giving her the strength she needs to go on. Many years later she will remark that she has never since that time felt such a feeling of peace and comfort as she did on that night. There is a sequel to her experience. The following night she settles her aunt down again and this time notices that *she* is gazing at the very corner of the room where the mysterious light appeared the night before. Questioning her aunt about what she is seeing, she receives the reply: 'I'm not telling you, it's a secret.' The aunt dies a few days later but the teacher never forgets her experience. Reading of an appeal for experiences like hers in a newspaper many years later, she writes it down and sends it in, even enclosing a diagram of the layout of the room in order to show how she could not have mistaken what she saw for any ordinary outside light on that memorable occasion.

A freshly bereaved widower begins to hear a series of voices shortly after his wife's death. One day he hears her say, 'Take me to him', and shortly afterwards beautiful pale blue lights begin to appear throughout his flat in whatever room he happens to be. One night a golden flame of light appears near the ceiling, then vanishes. The blue lights remain, however, and he is somewhat baffled as to what they might mean. Pondering the significance of his light experiences some years after they began he is particularly puzzled by the voices that seemed to presage them, for he is profoundly deaf and cannot hear normal conversation. He heard the voices clearly, however. Later, he too responds to a newspaper request for experiences like his by writing them down and sending them in.

A nineteen-year-old girl, standing in the beautiful garden of her parents' home in Sussex, suddenly notices a 'silent change' steal across the peaceful landscape. The grass suddenly seems to shine with an inner radiance, along with everything else in her field of vision. Not daring to move, she feels uplifted and thankful to be experiencing such an extraordinary living light. Her senses seem to have become more acute and she feels as if she can even hear the leaves growing. All the colours seem enhanced and brighter. She receives the impression that she is suddenly looking into the absolute nature of things, seeing reality as it *really* is. Several years later she reads a magazine interview with a man who has dedicated his life to studying experiences like hers, and she writes it down and sends it to him.

Suffering terribly from acute food poisoning, a man racked with terrible stomach pains suddenly and inexplicably awakes to what he will later describe as a 'spirit of well being'. He finds himself standing in some kind of cave or tunnel, and ahead of him he sees a kind of disc of light, like a door or opening to the outside: wherever 'outside' is. He looks down and realizes that he is clad in some sort of loose white robe. Incredibly, his left arm, lost in an accident many years before, now seems to be intact. He moves reluctantly towards the door of light when he suddenly hears a voice crying loudly: 'Go back, there is much for you to do!' The power in the voice gives him the strength to stop, and he begins to back away from the door. All at once he is back on the couch again, where he had been sitting only moments before, now racked with the agonizing stomach pains once more. Later, having recovered, he will hear a radio programme about a man who is setting up a special research unit to study experiences like his and an appeal for accounts at the end of the programme includes the address to send them to. He writes up his own experience and sends it in. It is 1971 and the research unit is entering its third year and it has already amassed 3,000 accounts, many like his.

Attending a performance by the Hallé Orchestra of Beethoven's Choral Symphony, an emotionally distressed and depressed woman prays to be taken out of the 'black pit' of her own mind. Suddenly she feels surrounded by a rush of light that lifts her and both surrounds her and wells up within her. With the light comes a feeling of bliss 'a million times stronger' than anything she has ever experienced. She feels a strange cool breeze playing over her, and experiences a 'whirling sensation' that leaves her feeling as if she is hovering a foot or so above her body. Later she will attend a talk in her local church hall given by a man who is collecting and analysing experiences like hers as part of an ongoing series of studies of spiritual and religious experiences. She writes her incredible account down and sends it to him.

A mystery posed

What are we to make of experiences like these? What is their nature? Where do they come from? What do they mean? Different as they at first appear, might they actually share a common source? If so, can we explain that source scientifically and rationally? Or should we reject such 'conventional' explanations, and look instead to a higher, stranger, supernatural source: a spiritual world, perhaps, coexisting alongside our own but capable of 'breaking through' to it on certain special occasions? These are just some of the questions raised by each of the unusual experiences of light that I have just presented – experiences that form the basis of this book and which I have termed 'Lightforms'.

This book grew out of a discovery of almost 400 accounts of unusual experiences of light, nearly all unpublished, and gathered over a period of more than thirty years. These accounts include descriptions of experiences that today we might describe as 'angelic experiences' and 'near-death experiences', unusual episodes that have aroused much debate and controversy, and remain, for many, deeply mysterious and deserving of deeper analysis and exploration than they have so far received. In addition, however, the collection that forms the basis of this study also includes other encounters with unusual lights that are little discussed and barely known in the literature. Amongst these are people's descriptions of being caught in beams and shafts of light, of being wrapped or filled with light, of seeing unusual flashes of light, of suddenly seeing the whole landscape alive and transfused with supernatural light, and of seeing lights that appear to them while they are wide awake and far from death; lights that sometimes communicate with and comfort them, frequently at times of great stress and crisis.

What are we to make of experiences like these? Should we just dismiss them as fraud, fabrication and/or hallucination? Such an approach may appear attractive to sceptics. It is difficult, however, to invoke it as an explanation for many or even the vast majority of accounts that form this study of lightforms because, as we shall see, most come from sane, sensible, level-headed people who have reflected upon their experiences for many years and who, in some cases, have gone to great lengths themselves to consider – and ultimately disregard – all 'conventional' explanations for them.

Doubly difficult for the sceptics is the fact that a significant proportion of these experiences share a number of common traits and patterns, despite the diversity of descriptions and the fact that a great many of the persons reporting their experiences were widely separated in time and space when they occurred. How best to account for such consistency, such patterning? This is a question that runs like a thread throughout this book: raising, as it does, the possibility that a common core or source may underlie the various descriptions of light that are presented in it. Talk of such a possible 'common core' is of more than merely academic interest. If we were to try and dismiss experiences such as those with which this chapter began as mere hallucination and fantasy we would surely expect a wide variety of descriptions, from the mundane to the outrageous. As we shall see, however, a statistically significant percentage of all of the various different 'types' of light episodes recounted throughout the study resemble each other in a number of crucial ways. How can this be? Is the human mind somehow constructed to hallucinate and to fantasize in a number of set ways? Or may it be the case that a common, transcendent other-worldly source is responsible for a large number of unusual encounters with light and therefore responsible for their consistency and sharing of common features?

Lightforms in context

Early chapters of this study address two further crucial questions. Readers may already be wondering where a cache of almost 400 largely unpublished and remarkable accounts of light, some over thirty years old, has come from. If they are all as dramatic as those with which we began, why have they not been seen, published and discussed before? This is a good question, and chapter 1 will be concerned to answer it.

As that chapter will show, the lightforms study needs to be set in the context of the history of the archive from which its material was taken.

For this, too, is a fascinating story, revolving, as it does, around the life and vision of a brilliant and unusual man who devoted much of his life to collecting unusual spiritual, religious and paranormal experiences and to analysing them and making their existence more widely known. That this man was a marine biologist seems perverse until it is realized what he was attempting to do. His name was Alister Hardy and his vision was to reconcile the 'worlds' of science and the spirit in such a way that evolutionary theory and spiritual experience could be seen to complement, not contradict, each other. In the process, he amassed a diverse range of highly unusual experiences, largely as a result of appeals in newspapers, magazines and on radio and television.

At present, the collection of accounts of unusual experiences that Hardy began to establish numbers almost 6,000 items, and is housed at the University of Wales, Lampeter. Chapter 1 will give an indication of just how rich, mysterious and diverse that collection has now become. Despite sharing his work with co-researchers, the vast majority of accounts sent to Hardy and his successors have remained unpublished and largely unexamined. It is partly to alert readers and researchers to the existence of this remarkable treasure trove of the spiritual, the unusual and the uncanny that chapter 1 is written. It also serves to put this study in a focused, historical context.

Chapter 2 is concerned with context too, attempting to locate this study of unusual lights cross-culturally. To do this, it ranges widely across the world's religions and spiritual traditions in search of experiences that include manifestations of spiritual and mystic lights. There we will encounter the experiences of shamans across various cultures, ecstatic experiences associated with kundalini yoga, the Buddhist experience of shunyata, descriptions of light from the Upanishads, dramatic conversion visions, apparitions of the Virgin Mary, appearances of Jesus and startling encounters with angels and the 'being of light' reported often in near-death experiences. Throughout, the chapter will seek to discern and present any patterns that underlie the diversity of experiences being examined.

Sharing the mystery

Part II of this book, the lightforms study proper, seeks to test whether or not any kind of pattern can be discerned within the nearly 400 accounts of light that form its basis. It presents a large number of these accounts under the categories that close reading revealed them to have fallen into, and analyses and comments in detail upon them. All of the chapters in part II include remarkable and fascinating examples of particular 'types' of light experience, of which some in particular can be given special advance mention here. Chapter 3, for example, presents and explores a small but highly significant number of *shared* experiences of unusual light. Students of religious, spiritual and paranormal experience will immediately recognize the significance of these, firstly because of their relative rarity (most spiritual, religious and paranormal experiences occur to single individuals, frequently when they are alone) and secondly because of the opportunities shared experiences present for verification. For these reasons, despite only containing ten cases, the 'shared' category is given particular attention at the beginning of part II.

Alister Hardy began collecting accounts for his archive – originally named the 'Religious Experience Research Unit' (RERU) – in 1969. By 1971 he had amassed around 3,000 of them. As chapter 1 will show, despite a wide variety of interests, he was sometimes unwilling or simply unable to investigate in detail every account sent to him, leaving that for others who came after him. Whilst he showed some interest in out-of-body experiences, what have come to be known as 'near-death experiences'(NDEs) do not appear to have interested him, and he was content simply to acknowledge them and to file them when they were sent to him.

The result of this is interesting in the extreme, because in the first five or six years of Hardy's research unit's life a significant number of persons at or near the point of death were to undergo – and later to send to Hardy – accounts of highly unusual experiences that took place at the extremes of their illnesses and sometimes during actual episodes of temporary clinical death. These are, of course, the occasions for the occurrence of what are today known as near-death experiences. This term, however, did not exist before 1975, when it was coined by Raymond Moody in his ground-breaking and best-selling study *Life after Life*. Before that time such experiences were rarely discussed, and were virtually unknown. Today, by contrast, there can be few people in the West who do not know that out-of-body experiences, feelings of bliss and peace, tunnels, lights, encounters with deceased relatives and reluctant returns to life are frequently reported near the point of clinical death. Any accounts of such experiences written and sent to Alister Hardy's unit between 1969 and 1974 therefore assume a particular importance. We can see, for example, if any pre-1975 accounts match to any significant extent the myriad accounts of NDEs reported and publicized since that time. This gives us a unique opportunity to examine a group of similar experiences that we can be reasonably assume were not influenced to any significant extent by expectation, publicity-seeking, wishful thinking or imagination fuelled by popular media coverage. The result will be of special interest to those with a particular interest in near-death experiences, for any collection of prè-1975 cases offers a virtually unparalleled 'control' group of NDEs that cannot have arisen from the attention that was focused on them in the last quarter of the twentieth century and on into the twenty-first.

Drawing conclusions

Part III is concerned to draw conclusions, and it is here perhaps that its most controversial and thought-provoking claims are to be found. As the reader will see, the unusual experiences of light that form the basis of the book permit of no easy, straightforward explanations. Considering, and ultimately discarding, interpretations of these remarkable experiences in terms of things such as mental instability, stress, drugs, migraine, epilepsy and other abnormal mental processes, it draws the intriguing conclusion that in an age where science claims to be able to explain so much, it cannot explain what has happened to many of the persons whose testimonies we have examined. In short: we are drawn to a final recognition that these unusual experiences of light may permit us brief but tantalizing glimpses of the intrusion of another world into our own: a world from which peace, love, joy, comfort, hope and light may flow in order to illuminate our darkest hours.

Part biography, part history, part investigation, part discovery, the ground that I cover has determined that the subject-matter is diverse enough to be all-encompassing, yet focused enough to enable certain, highly specific conclusions to be drawn. Both academics and general readers should find much here to interest them. The age of many of the accounts – which describe experiences stretching from the early years of the twenty-first century back to the early years of the twentieth – the shared accounts, and the pre-Moody NDEs, might be expected to have a particular appeal to specialists working in the field. This is not, however, a book written solely for them. The pleasure of simply sitting and reading the remarkable experiences that are reproduced in these pages may well be deemed to have repaid the price of admission, for specialists and non-specialists alike.

Part I

1

A sacred 'something': the spiritual odyssey of Sir Alister Hardy*

A secret in the heart of Wales

Lampeter – or, to give the town its Welsh name, Llanbedr Pont Steffan – nestles in the hills in the middle of lush, green west Wales, north of the Forest of Brechfa, west of the Cambrian mountains, on the very edge of what is sometimes referred to as the 'green desert'. This small, Welsh-speaking market town seems to the casual visitor to be far away from civilization. Yet the popular coastal holiday resort of Aberaeron is only 12 miles away, and less than an hour's drive leads to the impressive National Library of Wales.

People have lived around Lampeter for thousands of years, the earliest evidence being the prehistoric stone circle at Altgoch and a scattering of Bronze Age and Roman remains. There is something enchanting, almost mystical about the town and its surroundings. There are reports of strangely coloured lights in the surrounding hills, particularly around Tregaron bog. Some locals acknowledge this while others remain tight-lipped, choosing perhaps to keep the area's secrets close.

Lampeter escaped the 1904–5 Welsh Religious Revival but is nevertheless crammed with chapels and churches. By far the largest institution in the town, however, is its university. Founded as St David's College in 1822 and known today as the University of Wales, Lampeter, it is the oldest university institution in England and Wales apart from Oxford and Cambridge. Its original building, next to the

---

* Unless cited otherwise, the material in this chapter comes almost entirely from information housed at the RERC's archive at the University of Wales, Lampeter. John Keeble's largely unpublished work on the life of Hardy is housed there and proved to be of exceptional use. The ex-director Peggy Morgan and librarian Anne Watkins were also of great help.

remains of an old motte and bailey castle, was modelled on the older Oxford colleges, with an enclosed, grassed quadrangle embraced by the founding institution of St David's. Today the University of Wales, Lampeter is the smallest university in Britain, but its size belies its excellent academic reputation. Unsurprisingly, given the rich religious and spiritual heritage of the surrounding area, subjects such as philosophy and theology have also gained a growing and acknowledged academic respect in recent years.

Perhaps this is why in the summer of 2000 it became the home of the Religious Experience Research Centre (RERC). Originally housed at Manchester College, Oxford, by the time it arrived in Lampeter the centre held almost 6,000 accounts of spiritual, religious and paranormal experiences, many unexamined and most entirely unpublished. Amongst these 6,000 accounts are a large number of accounts of unusual light, and these are the subject-matter and central focus of this book. As will become clear as this chapter unfolds, these cannot be properly explored or understood without first pausing to consider the history of the RERC and its founder, Sir Alister Hardy.

A sacred 'something'

Who was Hardy? In many ways he was a man ahead of his time: a charismatic, unusual, original and fascinating character whom history seems to have almost entirely overlooked. Yet his achievements were many and varied. Almost a hundred years ago, for example, when many people were arguing that scientific discoveries spelled the end of anything spiritual or 'supernatural', Hardy disagreed. Instead – and he was to argue this throughout his life – he sought a reconciliation between the worlds of science and spirit. Far from *disproving* a spiritual 'something' to life, he argued, evolution actually *required* it, for it has enabled us to adapt and survive in ways that would have been impossible without it. It was religion itself, he argued, that often stopped people from appreciating the spiritual dimension to life. It is tempting see Hardy as an early twenty-first-century thinker and writer rather than what he was: a man who was born in the nineteenth century and whose feet were planted firmly in the twentieth.

Born in 1896, from a very early age Hardy was clearly aware of a spiritual 'presence' in his life, but he gives repeated indications in his writings that this was not something he saw as the exclusive preserve of any one religion, and not even as something that needed to be looked for in religion at all. His own unpublished autobiography records how he loved to walk in the countryside as a boy, wandering along river banks near his Northamptonshire home 'at times almost with a feeling of ecstasy'. So overwhelming at times were his feelings of gratitude for the beauties of nature that

> Just occasionally when I was sure no-one could see me, I became so overcome with the glory of the natural scene that for a moment or two I fell on my knees in prayer – not prayer asking for anything, but thanking God, who felt very real to me, for the glories of his kingdom and for allowing me to feel them.

Hardy's use of the word 'God' is interesting here, for he would often attempt to avoid it in his writings because of the sometimes misleading impressions that the word 'God' carried. Indeed, 'God' was to remain for Hardy much more a mystical or supernatural presence in life accessible to all rather than Something or Somebody wrapped up in centuries of creed, dogma and tradition. In 1914, having been called up to fight in the First World War, he made a special vow 'to what I called God' that, if he survived, he would devote his life to the task of reconciling the worlds of biology and the spirit. By 1917, he was writing:

> How soon, alas, does industrial materialism draw the blinds and shut out the light . . . The Church *has* failed – it appeals not to those who really make up the nation but to the superstitious, narrow-minded, the lovers of tradition and outward show. Something must happen – life cannot drift on as it has done for so long. A few days ago I went with a kindred spirit to Durham Cathedral to hear 'His Grace the Archbishop of Canterbury' preach – I was bitterly disappointed.

By 1925 – and by the time he had begun to think seriously about his project to reconcile the worlds of science and spirit – he could write: 'There is no fear now of my burying myself in any church – that idea has gone, bust, swept away for ever.' Indeed, his writings are full of little 'parables' and aphorisms that attest to his complete disillusionment with 'conventional' religion. Around the same time as he could write of his 'swept-away' notions of being 'buried in church', for example, he was also planning and partly writing a book about a group of men moving from church to church, seeking God, and coming away disgusted each time. In between visits, they go out into the woods and here at last find the very presence they were seeking in the churches – feelings that Hardy himself had powerfully felt when walking the Northamptonshire river banks and ones that he summed up for the BBC in an interview that he gave well into his seventies:

Like the people who write to me, I, too, have the sense of being in touch with something bigger than myself. My own religious experiences have been Wordsworthian in feel – the feeling of exaltation at seeing sunlight through young lime trees, for example. I am frankly religious. Of course I don't think of God as an old gentleman out there. I do go to church services but they are not necessary to my religion.

If Hardy's religious and spiritual 'yearnings' were somewhat unorthodox and unconventional, his scientific concerns were more in keeping with the times. Yet even here he showed himself on numerous occasions to be at odds with the 'establishment': especially regarding his interest in subjects such as telepathy and prayer. In 1914, as a young man of eighteen, he went up to Exeter College, Oxford to take a diploma in forestry. However, the outbreak of war was to disrupt his studies. Having made his 'vow' to God, he was posted to the First Northern Cyclist Battalion whose task was to ensure the Lincolnshire coast was defended against enemy attack. Whilst doing his wartime duties, Hardy became increasingly interested in the still fledgeling field of the paranormal.

Exploring strange seas

During 1916 and 1917 Hardy attended séances. In addition, as part of his wartime service, Hardy was posted to a Camouflage School in London and it was whilst he was here that he had an unusual experience that was to fuel a lifelong interest in the possibility of telepathy. During his London posting he became friendly with a medium, a Mrs Wedgewood, widow of Arthur Wedgewood, a leading member of the London Spiritualist movement. Meanwhile, his task at the Camouflage School was to research and develop what came to be known as the 'dazzle effect', an attempt to confuse the enemy regarding the size and distance of English ships by painting them with strange designs and colours. Recalling a day when he had been experimenting with various 'dazzle effect' designs before meeting Mrs Wedgewood for dinner, Hardy was to recall later:

> I had taken a large sheet of white cardboard and then painted it all over with a most vivid pink distemper. I was then going to cut it up into all sorts of shapes to use in our experiments, but I found it took much longer to dry than I expected so that I had it in front of me and kept looking at it to see if it was ready for some considerable time before I actually cut it up. Again I am quite certain that no one could have told Mrs Wedgewood what I had

been doing, for no one at the camouflage school knew her or knew that I was going out to dinner with her. I had not sat down at the dinner table with her for more than a moment or two when she suddenly said 'Oh what have you been doing? I see a large pink square on the table in front of you . . .' From that time on I must admit that I was myself, in my heart of hearts, convinced that telepathy was real; at the same time I knew that my account was not scientifically good evidence and could not convince others.

After the war, Hardy returned to Oxford to take up a place on an honours course in zoology. At the same time he saw and applied for a scholarship in Naples to study marine creatures. Needing some rare worms for his application that had not been seen in Britain for almost forty years, he went to Brightlingsea in Essex, the last place the worms had been spotted. Finding some of the specimens he needed very late in the day, he realized that he could not get back to Oxford and so stayed in the town's Anchor Hotel. That night, as his biographer John Keeble describes it, Hardy was awoken by revellers:

> He was astonished to find himself looking across the room at tiny lights of various colours dancing within a small space. The small space was in fact the jar in which he had stored his worms. The water in the jar contained microscopic organisms that were luminous.

This was plankton, and Hardy's fascination with plankton was to continue throughout his life. In the years following the war it was even seriously suggested that plankton – drifting microscopic plants and animals that provide food for much larger marine life – could be harvested to help combat food shortages. In 1957 Hardy would receive a knighthood at Buckingham Palace for services to the fishing industry, including research into the mysterious, luminous field of seaborne food that had so astonished him that night at Brightlingsea.

Already by 1919, with Hardy not yet twenty-five years old, we see the interests that were to dominate his life clearly in place. On the one hand we see the marine biologist, at home in the world of science and seeking to carve out a career there. On the other we see the mystic, open to the presence of the spiritual but alienated from the religious orthodoxies of his day. And somewhere between the two we see the maverick: not afraid to tackle controversial subjects such as telepathy, nor afraid of attempting to build a bridge between the seemingly unbridgeable worlds of science and the spirit. Perhaps in seeking to build such a bridge he was seeking some reconciliation within himself. Or perhaps he was early on seeking to resolve some of the contradictions of the age in which he lived: contradictions that still in many ways remain within our own.

Voyages of discovery

In the immediate post-war years, however, it was the scientist in Hardy that had the upper hand. There were only three students in his zoology class at Oxford and one of those was Sylvia Garstang who would later become his wife. His future father-in-law, Walter Garstang, himself a renowned zoologist, early on warned the young Alister Hardy that if he really wanted to pursue his more unconventional interests he should first set about making his name in more conventional fields – and this he duly did. He won the scholarship to Naples, returned to embark on research in the North Sea and quickly established himself in the field of marine biology. He worked in the Fisheries Department of the Ministry of Agriculture and Fisheries and was appointed chief zoologist on Captain Scott's old ship *Discovery*, which set sail for the Antarctic in 1925. Hardy was to be away at sea until 1928, marrying Sylvia Garstang the following year.

Before leaving, however, Hardy did something that showed that he had not forgotten the vow he had made in 1914. Giving his address as RRS *Discovery*, c/o Foreign Fleet Division, London, he lodged a request with a press-cutting agency to collect and save for his return any newspaper cuttings concerning subjects 'dealing with or referring even remotely to: Religion, God, Faith, Prayer, Relations or antagonism of Religion and Science [and] Anything in fact of a religious or spiritual nature'. Underneath this, Hardy added a list of things he did *not* want to receive, which included 'Ecclesiastical or church notices or news, reports of services or sermons (unless arousing public interest or controversy), obituary or other notes on the lives of ministers of any denomination, or dealing with psychic research, spiritualism and kindred subjects (unless in a religious connection)'.

Much later in his life, Hardy would expand on this request, writing that in September 1925, three months before the *Discovery* expedition finally got under way after lengthy delays, 'My attention had been arrested by a description of a religious experience in the daily press. How often, I wondered, did such reports occur and pass unnoticed?' Clearly Hardy intended to find out, and by lodging the request with the agency he started in motion a series of varied appeals for religious experiences that would eventually yield almost 6,000 accounts. The request not to receive anything 'dealing with psychic research, spiritualism and kindred subjects' is puzzling, considering how much of his later life would be devoted to the exploration of phenomena such as telepathy. From comments made in later years, however, it is clear that Hardy was attempting to avoid the issue of human survival after death, deeming it to be something that fell outside the field of his already wide inquiry. In the event, he was to receive many accounts bearing directly on this subject, including reports of apparitions and near-death experiences together with a diverse range of other 'paranormal' events. It is to his credit that he replied to and filed away everything he received, even if it was clear that it was not necessarily what he was looking for. Indeed, he would later write that 'the mine of our material awaits a host of researchers', and to this day many of the accounts that Hardy collected throughout his life remain largely unexamined and unpublished, including most of those that make up this study.

What Hardy *was* looking for at this time would become clearer as the years passed, when his method of describing the sorts of religious experiences he was seeking became more refined. As would become evident, he was in a key sense looking for reports from persons who had a continuous, ongoing sense of the presence of Something or Someone else in their lives: rather like his own Northamptonshire experiences, but *continuously*. In the event, he received much more than this, drawing the observation of one commentator that ultimately he became 'like a fisherman casting his net upon the water, but instead of coming up with a few well-defined fish, [finding] he had caught a great array of glittering creatures that did not seem to fit his preconceived grouping' (Maxwell and Tschudin 1990: 6).

None of this was evident in 1925, however. In fact, he found the first batch of press cuttings that were sent to him to be wholly unsatisfactory for the purposes of his research. Next, he tried appealing for experiences in thirty religious journals, but received barely 200 replies that were once again unusable. It seemed that people had difficulty understanding what sort of thing he was after. In addition, as he was later to comment, 'a high percentage of replies were from the elderly and a very large proportion of these were female,' making them unsuitable for use in any statistically rigorous or significant contexts.

More successful was his ongoing scientific career. Whilst two children were born to him and Sylvia – in 1931 and 1934 – Hardy was gradually achieving recognition in the field of natural history and zoology. In 1942 he became Regius Professor of Natural History at the University of Aberdeen. In 1946 he took up the Linacre Chair of

Zoology at Oxford: a post he held until 1961. The knighthood arrived towards the end of his tenure of the Oxford chair. He had indeed heeded the advice of his father-in-law to make his way in a suitably 'orthodox' field in order to pursue his other interests.

Science and the spirit

In 1950 Hardy gave a talk about monsters to the Bodley Club at Merton College, Oxford. Nothing would please him more, he said, than somebody finding something in Loch Ness. However, he argued, there were even greater mysteries to be explored. In the following year he gave the Essex Hall Lecture to members of the Unitarian and Free Christian Churches entitled 'Science and the quest for God' and made clear exactly what these mysteries were and how he was seeking to explore them. The lecture reveals where Hardy's thinking about science and spirituality had led him by this time. He argued that a proper scientific study of people's religious experiences is certainly possible and that theology itself might develop as a science, once it was freed from the 'shackles' of dogma and religion. Above all, he argued, the study of religious experience might help bridge the gap between science and religion, enabling us to recognize that our ability to have profound spiritual experiences has actually helped us to evolve and to survive as a species. It is clear that he wanted to place the spiritual and religious experiences of ordinary men and women at the very foundation of his attempt to reconcile the 'worlds' of biology and the spirit. This would also have the added effect of showing that such experiences still occur: despite the mechanistic world-view of science that repeatedly declares such things to be plainly impossible, outdated and 'mythological'.

Another way of showing that the scientific world-view is too narrow, he argued, is to pay close attention to the findings of psychical research, which, he said 'has now yielded definite proof of the existence of what is usually called telepathy: the communication of one mind with another by means other than through the ordinary senses'. Whilst the recognition that telepathy exists is 'one of the most revolutionary biological discoveries ever made', he argued, it is also 'of tremendous importance to religion'. Expanding on this idea, and asserting that the ability to communicate between two human minds might point to the possibility of a human mind communicating with something far greater, he declared:

It is within the realm of extra-sensory perception that I believe what we call prayer may be found to lie. Not petitionary prayer for the alteration of physical events, such as rain, or even personal safety, but prayer to receive help and guidance for a better way of life.

Finally, he posed a crucial question:

Can there possibly be a greater quest than the securing of evidence which will demonstrate beyond all reasonable doubt the existence of an extra-sensory world about us in which our consciousness is somehow in touch with something greater than our individual selves – some power from which we can receive strength and support? Could not the results of research reveal to others what to some is a profound conviction?

Even at the age of fifty-five, it is clear that Hardy envisaged extensive future research that would provide answers to the profound questions that he consistently posed, and he would repeatedly return to these questions in the years ahead. In 1953, for example, in an address to the British Society for Psychical Research (BSPR) entitled 'Biology and psychical research', he argued that currently anecdotal reports of allegedly psychic phenomena such as telepathy required controlled scientific experiments in order to be taken seriously by the scientific establishment. Indeed, Hardy was an ardent supporter of the BSPR's rigorously scientific approach to things like telepathy, and he temporarily assumed the presidency of the Society between 1965 and 1968. In his presidential address to the society on 5 May 1966, entitled 'Psychical research and civilization' he even went so far as to assert: 'I believe that a vigorously conducted programme of psychical research is more likely than any other human activity to overthrow materialism as a widely accepted doctrine, especially if it is broadened, as I think it should be, to include the systematic study of religious experience.'

This quotation is revealing in that it makes clear how widely Hardy was prepared to cast his net in search of data to study. It also reveals him to be once again a man ahead of his time. Few theologians and religious scholars even in the twenty-first century are prepared to take many paranormal claims like telepathy seriously: here was Hardy, in 1966, prepared to embrace *both* religious *and* paranormal experiences and to consider them side by side.

Towards the goal

From the late 1950s through to the mid-1960s Hardy continued to pursue his interests in the twin realms of biology and the spirit. Towards the end of this period one crucial goal, the establishment of a serious centre for the scientific study of religious and spiritual experience, had begun to move closer. For this, of course, he needed accounts of experiences to study. He had repeated his appeal for press cuttings relating to such experiences, first launched in 1925, in the years 1935 and 1945. The 1945 appeal proved so disappointing, however, that he did not repeat it in 1955. Meanwhile, in 1963 and 1965 Aberdeen University invited him to give two series of the Gifford Lectures, named after Lord Gifford, a Scottish judge who had left endowments to four universities for the express purpose of financing research into the areas that so fascinated Hardy. In both sets of lectures he returned again and again to the need for a systematic study of religious and spiritual experience, declaring in the first lecture series: 'Much I am sure could be done to collect, from all sorts of sources, evidence to support the view that there is something here which is really fundamental and of overwhelming importance to mankind', and adding: 'We must have more studies of the nature of religious experience and more research into the psychic side of man. Let us go forward to reclaim the ground that has been lost in the world through a false belief that science points only to materialism.' Significantly, Hardy directed that the royalties from the 1966 publication of the second series of lectures should be earmarked for the financing of a centre devoted to the studies he was advocating. That goal was moving closer.

In 1967 he began a series of studies designed to determine once and for all whether telepathy could be proved scientifically. These involved the testing of 200 people over a seven-week period at Caxton Hall in London. As with so many other such experiments both before and after Hardy's, the outcome of his study was mixed. On the one hand, he was forced to write to paranormal researcher Guy Lyon Playfair: '[Y]ou will see that a very large number of experiments we did, in the hope of getting better evidence for telepathy, failed and show the extraordinary importance of what appears to be chance coincidence . . .'. He was also forced to admit in the same letter that whereas at one time he had thought telepathy proved beyond doubt, now, after several more years of study, he had concluded that 'it had not been demonstrated experimentally as I thought . . .'.

On the other hand, the Caxton Hall experiments had thrown up some statistical anomalies that indicated that *something* strange was going on. In later years, alluding to this, he would make the quite remarkable claim that telepathy experiments might be revealing that some people are in fact *luckier* than others. Talking in September 1970 to a conference of the Parapsychological Foundation being held that year in France, for example, he spoke of studies like those at Caxton Hall in the following way, posing the question:

> Is it possible that what all these experiments are really demonstrating is a scientific measurement of what we in our ignorance call luck; that some people are in fact much luckier, whatever that may really mean, at card guessing than others? This is a shocking thing to be said by a scientist, and I hope it will never get into the popular press, but the point I want to make is that this should in fact be no more shocking to the scientific position of today than alleged demonstration of card-guessing clairvoyance.

This virtually unique 'take' on what the unusual statistical anomalies involved in telepathy studies might mean is thought-provoking in the extreme. To date there has been little or no attempt to follow it up and it stands as yet another example of Hardy's maverick spirit and deeply inquiring mind. And despite the disclaimer that what he was saying was 'a shocking thing to be said by a scientist', it is clear that as he approached and passed his seventieth year Alister Hardy was a scientist used to saying such things.

The RERU

In 1968, as Hardy entered his seventy-second year, he was also on the verge of what, for many, was to be his lifetime's greatest achievement. In this year he began to gather around him the people who would advise him on the setting-up of a centre to study religious and spiritual experiences. The choices he made at this time reveal his ability to move in many different academic 'worlds'. From the field of parapsychology he brought in R. H. Thouless, equally at home in the field of the psychology of religion, and H. H. Price, a philosopher of renown who held a great interest in religious experience and the possibility of the soul's immortality. Also from the world of philosophy Hardy chose the renowned figure of Basil Mitchell, and from psychology he chose Michael Argyle, whose studies within psychology and the psychology of religion would span over fifty years. Indeed,

Michael Argyle would sit on a research committee attached to Hardy's research centre until shortly before his death in 2002 and had a sustained interest in the study of religious experience throughout his life.

For the site of his centre Hardy chose Manchester College, Oxford. He had first become associated with the college because of his Unitarian connections and had in time been made honorary president, and so it was here, in 1969, that the centre – named the Religious Experience Research Unit (RERU) – finally opened. Hardy had remembered his vow of 1914, and with his characteristic determination and patience had finally achieved the platform from which to launch his project for a 'spiritual biology'. From his own later recollections it seems clear that, for him, more than 'mere' diligence and perseverance had been involved, however. As he was to write, 'Ever since making the vow I have had the curious feeling that all the events in my life have been arranged as if by some benign power.' Whatever the full reasons – visible or hidden – by 1969 a shop at 24 Holywell had been made available for the RERU's work and it was time for research to begin in earnest. Two rooms had been made available, and the funding of the work was aided by private charities, individual donors and the founder's own funds.

A hint of Hardy's own ambitions for the RERU can be found in a letter he wrote on 26 May 1969:

> I am not at the unit going to be concerned with experiences that point to contact with individuals who have passed on, important as these experiences are . . . I am primarily concerned in my unit with the collection of evidence of people's experiences of being in touch with some transcendental element beyond the self which I believe is the basis of all religion. I want to set going a unit that will build up such a collection of evidence from these that it must in time convince the intellectual world that here is something of overwhelming importance and a part of the natural history of man.

No 'manifesto' for the unit's future could express Hardy's aims better than he expresses them here himself, and it was not long before he set about the task of collecting the sorts of accounts of experience that he was looking for. Before the year was out he had made the first of several newspaper appeals for accounts, in the *Guardian* of 20 September 1969 at the end of an interview conducted by Geoffrey Moorhouse. Other appeals quickly followed, in *The Observer* and *The Times*. In 1971, one appeal in the *Daily Mail* alone brought in over

1,000 accounts. By now, perhaps chastened by the failures of his earlier appeals for experiences via press-cutting agencies, Hardy had become much more adept at describing the sorts of experiences he wanted. The appeal in *The Observer* of 8 March 1970, for instance, described an experience of Beatrice Webb who:

> [W]as conscious of experiencing a sense of reverence or awe – an apprehension of a power and purpose outside herself – which she called 'feeling' and which was sometimes induced by appreciation of great music or corporate worship. But her experience went further than this nebulous, fleeting 'feeling' – because as a result of it she achieved a religious interpretation of the universe which satisfied and upheld her and enabled her to seek continuous guidance in prayer.

From this description it is clear that what Hardy was looking for was the sort of *continuous* awareness of God, experienced by – but not necessarily confined to – mystics, poets or even saints. The appeal continued:

> Professor Hardy proposes, if readers will kindly cooperate, to study and compare as many personal records of such experiences as possible. He invites all who have been conscious of, and perhaps influenced by, some such power, whether they call it God or not, to write a simple and brief account of these feelings and their effects. They should include particulars of age, sex, nationality, religious upbringing and other factors thought to be relevant . . . They will be regarded as strictly confidential and names will be suppressed in any published accounts of the research.

Commenting on the responses to these early appeals some years later, Hardy was to note:

> In spite of our saying this, examples of the more ecstatic, dramatic types of experience were sent in in fair numbers from the very beginning. Perhaps the use of the term 'religious experience' in the name of our Unit tended to give the impression that we were only concerned with particular isolated unusual experiences rather than with a continuing feeling of a transcendental reality or of a divine presence.

Indeed, so concerned was Hardy that the term 'religious experience' might be misunderstood that he contemplated replacing it with 'spiritual awareness'. In the end, however, conscious of standing in a continuous academic tradition of the study of religious experience that included figures such as Edwin Starbuck and the great William James, he allowed the phrase 'religious experience' to remain. It remains to this day in the name of the centre that he founded.

In addition to the numerous newspaper appeals during these early years of the RERU, a special request for accounts was also launched via a pamphlet entitled *Research into Religious Experience – How You Can Take Part*. Again, Hardy attempted to clarify with this what sorts of experiences he was looking for, writing that in addition to what he termed 'dramatic isolated experiences' he was also seeking 'accounts of that continuing sense of spiritual awareness which many people feel makes a difference to their lives'. In the event, he would receive far more accounts describing the former and rather fewer describing the latter.

Unusual experiences

The following extracts, selected from amongst the earliest accounts received by the unit, give just a hint of what people began to send. To be sure, there *were* a number of descriptions of the continuous, ongoing, presence of a spiritual awareness. Of this, one respondent wrote:

> I think from my childhood I have always had the feeling that the true reality is not to be found in the world as the average person sees it. There seems to be a constant force at work from the inside trying to push its way to the surface of consciousness. The mind is continually trying to create a symbol sufficiently comprehensive to contain it, but this always ends in failure. There are moments of pure joy with a heightened awareness of one's surroundings, as if a great truth had been passed across. (651)

Another wrote:

> I find it difficult to describe my experience, only to say that it seems to be outside of me and enormous and yet at the same time I am part of it, everything is. It is purely personal and helps me to live and to love others. It is difficult to describe, but in some way because of this feeling I feel united to all people, to all living things. Of recent years the feeling has become so strong that I am now training to become a social worker because I find that I must help people: in some way I feel their unhappiness as my own. (663)

And another wrote:

> As far back as I can remember I have never had a sense of separation from the spiritual force I now choose to call God . . . From the age of about 6 to 12 in places of quiet and desolation this feeling of 'oneness' often passed to a state of 'listening'. I mean by 'listening' that I was suddenly alerted to something that was going to happen. What followed was a feeling of tremendous exaltation in which time stood still. (786)

However, this represents only a very small sample of what was sent. For in addition to experiences like these, a diverse range of very different, dramatic, spontaneous and sometimes radically life-changing spiritual experiences were submitted to the unit in its earliest years. Many of these, far from describing a continuous presence in the lives of their writers, described single episodes: recalled in later years either because they were simply unforgettable or because of the subsequent effects they had on the lives of those who had experienced them.

There were, for example, a number of testimonies received by the unit that attempted to describe single episodes in which God or some kind of supernatural presence became suddenly very real to people. One ex-soldier wrote:

> In 1943, at the age of 28, I was a sergeant in the British Army of the Middle East enjoying leave in Palestine. I made Jerusalem my centre . . . Bitterly disappointed [after being hurried with tourists through the Church of the Holy Sepulchre] I made my solitary way across the Brook Kedron and ascended the other side towards Gethsemane, hardly knowing or caring where I went. I sat down in the Garden, which was completely deserted. Gradually peace returned to me, and I was suddenly conscious of a Presence. For how long I sat there I do not know, but this I know: Our Lord was surely present with me. I left the Garden of Gethsemane with a serene feeling of happiness. (311)

Sometimes the feelings that accompanied these experiences were described in very positive ways – feelings of peace, love, joy and happiness particularly frequently. The following experience is typical of these:

> One night I suddenly had an experience as if I was buoyed up by waves of utterly sustaining power and love. The only words that came near to describing it were 'underneath are the everlasting arms', though this sounds like a picture, and my experience was not a picture but a feeling . . . This I am sure has affected my life as it has made me know the love and sustaining power of God. *It came from outside and unasked.* (356; emphasis in the original)

Sometimes the experiences were overwhelming in their intensity, leaving the lives of experients changed for ever. The following subject, for example, likens her experience to the conversion of the apostle Paul, writing:

> I had an experience seven years ago that changed my whole life. I had lost my husband six months before and my courage at the same time. I felt life

would be useless if fear were allowed to govern me. One evening, with no preparation, as sudden and dynamic as the revelation to Saul of Tarsus, I knew that I was in the presence of God, and that he would never leave me nor forsake me and that he loved me with a love beyond imagination – no matter what I did. In that minute of time my life was changed. I feared nothing, and knew he was always with me. (676)

Sometimes, experiences were described that were simple, tender, touching and moving. The following account, from a mother who had lost her daughter, is typical of these:

My daughter Joan was killed by a car when she was 7 years old. She and I were very close and I was grief-stricken. She was lying in her coffin in her bedroom. I fell on my knees by the bedside. Suddenly I felt as if something a bit behind me was so overcome with pity that it was consolidating itself. Then I felt a touch on my shoulder lasting only an instant, and I knew there was another world. (165)

Certainly Hardy received many accounts describing events that were comparable to other 'types' of religious experiences reported in many other cultures and contexts. One type that he received many times in the early years was the *mystical* experience – a sudden awareness of the interconnectedness and unity of all things. The following example is typical of these:

One day years ago I went for a walk in the fields with my dog. My mind suddenly started thinking about the beauty around me, and I considered the marvellous order and timing of the growth of each flower, herb and the abundance of all the visible growth going on around. I remember thinking 'Here is mind'. Then we had to get over a stile and suddenly I was confronted with a bramble bush which was absolutely laden with black glistening fruit. And the impact of that, linked with my former reasoning, gave me a great feeling of ecstasy. For a few moments I really did feel at one with the Universe or the Creative Power we recognize. I know it was a feeling of oneness with something outside my self, and also within. I must have been confronted with the source of all being, whatever one should call it. I have often told my friends about it, though it seems too sacred to talk about. The experience has never been forgotten. It was quite electric and quite unsought. (2848)

Interestingly, and in addition to the recognizable 'varieties' of religious experiences – such as mysticism and the presence of God – that were sent to the unit, a number of *other* sorts of experiences were soon submitted also. As with the more recognizably 'religious' experiences that were sent to him, these too continued to be received by Hardy throughout his lifetime and continue to be submitted to this day. There are currently, for example, a significant number of 'out-of-body' experiences within Hardy's collection. Many of these also date from the unit's earliest years, including the following:

> In 1948 I had an out-of-the-body experience spontaneously, in broad daylight, for no obvious reason, and being in perfect health. (At the time I did not know that such experiences were fairly frequent and well documented). The experience itself was unsensational – for a while I contemplated my body, which was lying on a divan, from under the ceiling; I felt splendidly liberated, light and only a little surprised, and it became amply clear that the 'I' was not the body on the divan but the consciousness which contemplated it. 'I' returned into my body with the greatest reluctance – I knew I had to return – and since then I have been quite unable to fear physical death. (505)

Also unafraid to die after her experience was the following lady, whose description of a near-death experience was submitted to the RERU in August 1971 – four years before the phrase 'near-death experience' was itself coined:

> The ultimate proof to me of life after death and the love of God came just after the birth of my daughter.
>
> It had been a long and difficult birth and I was very exhausted. As nurse helped me to sit up, I remember saying 'I do feel funny'. Everything whirled and blackness formed a tunnel, a long, long tunnel with an opening at the other end which glowed with a bright light.
>
> Down, down into the whirling blackness. It seemed a long time before I reached the opening and found myself floating gently in a soft warm mist, all golden as with sunlight, soft music and a feeling of complete happiness, and such peace that passes all understanding was mine; faces came out of the mist, smiled and faded away.
>
> I seemed to be fully conscious and knowing that I had 'died' yet I lived. God's plan of good death had no sting.
>
> Then came the remembrance of the baby – who would look after her if I stayed?
>
> My first reaction was to pain: my face stung as the doctor slapped first one side, then the other – hard.
>
> As I opened my eyes he greeted me with 'You naughty girl, you've given me the biggest fright of my life.' He looked startled when I answered, 'Don't begrudge me that: it was absolutely wonderful.'
>
> I still feel very grateful and humble for this experience, certainly have no fear of death, knowing it is as simple as walking from one room to another. (2733)

Some people responding to Hardy's appeals for accounts of experiences sent in descriptions of apparitions, telepathy, precognition, clairvoyance and other recognizably 'paranormal' experiences. Describing an encounter with her husband some time after his death, for example, one lady wrote to Hardy to describe how

> After his passing, I both saw and spoke to my husband and held his hand.
> This hand was strong and not at all ghost-like, nor was his appearance. I
> was alone at the time, so no medium there to act as a link.

Commenting on the overall meaning of her experience at the end of the account, the subject muses: 'Probably this is not a detail to prove God's existence, but to me, it indeed did' (1615).

One striking early account describes apparently supernatural knowledge of a geographically distant event that turned out to be dramatically and seemingly inexplicably true. In it, the subject writes:

> I was a young married woman with a 6 month old baby daughter. My
> husband and I got an evening off to see a film at K—— about 6 miles away.
> One of the hotel staff had volunteered to baby sit and we set off . . . We had
> not been long seated in the cinema when a terrible uneasiness overcame
> me. I could distinctly smell burning. I fidgeted a lot and my husband asked
> what was the matter. I told him I could smell burning. He said I'd probably
> dropped a bit of my cigarette. I stooped and had a look on the carpet but
> no sign of any glow. The smell persisted and eventually I told my husband
> I was leaving. He followed me reluctantly, muttering something derogatory
> about women. As we boarded the bus for home I prayed for it to go faster;
> at each stop I almost died. At last we were sprinting down the lane leading
> to the cottage. The smell of burning was now very definite to me though
> my husband could not smell a thing. We reached the door which I literally
> burst in. As I did so the dense smoke poured out and a chair by the fire
> burst into flames. I rushed through to the bedroom and got the baby out
> while my husband dragged out the unconscious girl. She had fallen asleep
> in the armchair and dropped her lighted cigarette into the chair which had
> smouldered for hours. Yes, God sent me home to save my baby. God was
> with me telling me to hurry home; of that I am convinced and also my
> husband. (1929)

Reading such an account it is, perhaps, easy to imagine Hardy recalling his own experiences of Mrs Wedgewood's ability to gain information at a distance. Dramatic as it is, however, it has a happy ending – for the writer at least. In fact, notable about the experiences Hardy began to collect are the overwhelmingly positive nature of the feelings they created in subjects together with the positive 'fruits' they usually produced in those subjects' lives. On occasion, however – and these accounts were to remain very much in the minority – experiences of a darker nature were sent:

> Suddenly I became aware of a sense of the uttermost evil, so much so that I became awake. I could feel this sense of evil enveloping me. I had the terrifying impression that this evil force or presence was bent upon taking possession of me. How does one describe evil? I only knew that I was enveloped by this revolting force, so vile and rotting I could almost taste the evil. I was in terror, so much so I could not call out or move. A part of my mind told me that I must at all costs act or I would be lost. I recall that I managed by a great effort to stretch out my right hand and with my index finger I traced the shape of the Cross in the air. Immediately on my doing this the evil enveloping me fell away completely, and I felt a wonderful sense of peace and safety. (667)

The spiritual nature of man

Having begun to collect such a range of fascinating material, what did Hardy and his handful of co-workers do with it? In 1979, ten years after the unit started, Hardy published *The Spiritual Nature of Man*, an analysis of the first 3,000 accounts received, and here he made clear just what had been done with the material sent to him. He wrote that there were certain things that *could not* be done with what was sent, largely because the subjects who wrote chose to do so and were therefore self-selected. They were in no way a random sample of the populace: women continued to outnumber men in the number of responses they sent, and the accounts could not therefore be used in any statistically rigorous ways in order to answer questions like 'Are men more likely to have religious experiences than women?' In order to answer a question like this it would be necessary to use much more sophisticated polling methods – as indeed was to happen later at Nottingham University under one of the unit's future directors. In addition, the vast majority of people who responded to the request for experiences were either British or American: thus the accounts gathered could in no way be seen as a cross-cultural collection.

Whilst a number of things were ruled out as a result of the 'skewed sample' of reports received by the unit, a number of other things clearly *were* possible. One early objective was to sort the accounts received into types, and *The Spiritual Nature of Man* was itself largely concerned with this. Despite his great interest in spiritual experiences by this time, it is notable that, writing this book at the end of the

1970s, Hardy remained very much a zoologist in his approach to his material. First, he writes, he had wished to separate 'those [experiences] describing a more general sense of spiritual awareness from] those which were of a more dramatic, ecstatic, mystical character'. Then, he adds, 'I had imagined that the various individual examples within each of these major divisions could be classed in a hierarchical system like biological specimens.' This, however, proved problematical, not least because it quickly became apparent that religious and spiritual experiences were *not* like biological specimens and tended to overlap and span two or more categories. Hardy was forced to admit in the end that much had to be left 'to the subjective judgement, or sympathetic imagination of the researcher'.

Despite this caveat, with its implication that a 'science of the spirit' was not to be so straightforward as he might have once thought, Hardy nonetheless managed within ten years of the unit's opening to produce a provisional classification of what had been sent to him. *The Spiritual Nature of Man* contains a large number of accounts divided under a number of categories. The breakdown of material is complex and sophisticated. Under 'Sensory or quasi-sensory experience: visual' for example, experiences are divided into 'Visions', 'Illuminations', 'A particular light', 'Feeling of unity with surroundings and/or with other people', 'Out of the body', 'Déjà vu' and 'Transformation of surroundings'. Likewise, under 'Supposed extra-sensory perception', experiences are divided into 'Telepathy', 'Precognition', 'Clair-voyance', 'Supposed contact with the dead' and 'Apparations'. There is also an attempt to list and to classify 'triggers' for experiences, including 'Natural beauty', 'Sacred places', 'Prayer, Meditation', 'Creative work', 'Depression , Despair', 'Crises in personal relations' and so on. No summary of this book's contents can hope to do justice both to the richness of the accounts presented or to the care with which they have been classified despite the difficulties encountered. Overall, the book retains much of its freshness and appeal a quarter of a century on and is well worth investigating.

A work in progress

By 1979, however, all was not well in the unit. The 1970s had been a decade of some expansion and *The Spiritual Nature of Man* charts the unit's progress well. Back in 1973, Hardy had published the results of his 1967 Caxton Hall telepathy experiments under the title *The*

Challenge of Chance, co-authored with Robert Harvie and Arthur Koestler. In 1976 he stepped down as director of the RERU, to be succeeded by Edward Robinson, a co-worker from the very earliest days. There were, however, frictions and tensions surrounding the future of the unit's research from this time. Edward Robinson saw the potential in the RERU's collection of accounts for the development of a number of studies within the field of religious education. There are indications that Hardy did not share this point of view. Financial difficulties compounded the troubles, but continued good publicity served to further the collecting of accounts. By 1984, Manchester College, concerned that little had been done by the unit to improve the premises so generously loaned to it, gave notice that the RERU would need to find another home.

The year 1985, however, brought happier news. In February Hardy learned that he had been awarded the prestigious Templeton Prize for Progress in Religion, the sum of £170,000 in the currency of his choice. The presentation of the award was to be made at Buckingham Palace on the afternoon of 14 May, but in the early hours of the 13th Hardy suffered a stroke. Ten days later he died.

Other directors would take over the unit's work. This ensured that both the collection of accounts together with ongoing research based upon and around them would continue. Both during and after Hardy's lifetime a wide variety of research projects were undertaken by the RERU and have continued up to the present day. These have included studies of the spiritual and religious experiences of childhood, national surveys of the frequency of reports of religious and spiritual experiences (and their various 'types'), a study of the relationship between religious experience and madness, analyses of the psychological well-being of persons reporting a range of spiritual experiences, a study of the influence of the environment on religious experience and a study of the accounts of experiences of spiritual evil in the archive.

Whilst it is not possible to summarize the results of these studies in any detail, it is interesting to note that research findings based on the accounts sent to the Unit have shown that persons submitting them tend to be well educated, articulate, happy, mentally balanced and concerned with social justice. In addition, they hail from a wide variety of religious (and non-religious) backgrounds. It seems that you do not need to be 'religious' to have – and to report – religious experiences. In addition, far from being pathological and therefore symptomatic of psychological disorder, it would appear that such experiences occur in healthy-minded individuals, sometimes indeed leaving them healthier in mind as a result of their occurrence.

However, whilst the list of research projects undertaken may seem impressive, it should be remembered that there are currently approaching 6,000 accounts of religious experiences on file. Only a fraction of these have been subjected to detailed analysis, and only a fraction of those that *have* been examined have been published. They represent but the tip of a huge iceberg.

The central focus of this book is 400 accounts of unusual light experienced over a large period of time. By now, most of the experiences stored in the collection are on computer database. It is a relatively simple operation to enter the word 'light' into the computer, which then lists every numbered account containing the 'trigger' word that has been entered. In the event, the original search produced over 700 accounts – too many to make the project manageable. By discarding clearly metaphorical uses of light – as in 'I saw the light' – and descriptions of unusual lights seen in dreams, the figure was reduced to a more manageable 400. Even reduced in this way, however, such a large number of unusual experiences of this type make the project one of the largest and most comprehensive studies of unusual light phenomena ever undertaken. Alister Hardy was typically prescient when he wrote that many of the experiences he devoted much of his life to collecting awaited analysis by researchers other than him and his colleagues. Today, over twenty years after his death, it is time to brush the dust from this vast number of unexamined and unpublished testimonies containing encounters with amazing and apparently supernatural lights. If the Religious Experience Research Centre *is* to be seen as one of the world's best-kept secrets, then, as we will shortly see, its incredible – and well-preserved – collection of intriguing and unusual light phenomena may turn out to be one of its richest treasures.

Cross-cultural considerations

This chapter has attempted to locate the study of lightforms in its historical and biographical context. Before moving on to examine the accounts of light in detail, however, it will be necessary to examine a further context crucial to the study. As we have already seen, one original aim of the project was to try and see if there was a 'common core' to the experiences of light being investigated. Would any commonalities emerge across reports? Would any significant number of accounts describe features that suggested a common source of the experiences being claimed? Might we even be able to deduce that the *same* experience was occurring to persons entirely *unknown* to each other?

The accounts in the RERC archive represent a narrow group of people: mostly from Britain and, to a somewhat lesser extent, the US. At the outset, therefore, it was deemed important to broaden the scope of the inquiry in order to consider unusual experiences of light reported from other cultures. This was at first problematical, for it was clearly neither practical nor possible to produce an appeal for experiences in the same way that Sir Alister Hardy did. For one thing, this would make an already vast project vaster still. And the collection he started is already over thirty years old, meaning that a substantial time period had allowed an impressive body of accounts to build up that would be difficult to match in a short time-scale.

Help in this regard came in the form of existing studies of experiences of unusual light, mainly anthropological, historical, theological and psychological in nature. Whilst there was nothing comparable in scope to the present project here, it did turn out to be the case that this literature was easily accessible and provided a jumping-off point for the current study by allowing a further range of potential questions to be asked. What would a survey of this literature reveal? Would it, too, show that mystical lights are found throughout the world's religions and spiritualities? Would it point to the particular types of persons most likely to experience these things? Would it point to any contexts that might make such experiences more likely? Most interesting of all: would it reveal the sorts of patterns, trends, commonalities and consistencies that this study was concerned to investigate? If it should turn out to show any genuinely cross-cultural patterns, then this would at the very least suggest what might need to be looked for carefully throughout the examination of the RERC accounts. In completing the analysis of the project's context, therefore, it was also hoped that such a cross-cultural survey might also help contribute to the project's agenda. To these important tasks we now turn.

2

Visions, awakenings and illuminations: unusual lights across cultures

Shamanic lights

Experiences of unusual light, frequently leading to spiritual, mystical or religious transformation, have been reported virtually throughout recorded history in a wide variety of different cultures, religions and spiritual traditions. They have been recorded and analysed by anthropologists, historians, theologians, psychologists and philosophers working in a wide variety of faiths, religions, spiritualities and cultures, both ancient and modern.

The renowned anthropologist Mircea Eliade has, for example, made a number of studies of unusual light phenomena as part of his research into shamanism and shamanic practices. Shamans are found throughout many of the world's traditions and tribal cultures. They are revered as medicine men: holy 'seers' who are endowed with special powers that allow them to visit heavenly realms, see into the future, locate lost persons and converse with gods and spirits. Eliade's fellow anthropologist Knud Rasmussen has described the experiences of a range of Eskimo shamans whose journeyings in search of the 'missing' souls of sick tribal members frequently take them into space and on visits around the earth or to the moon. What is particularly interesting to note here is how these special people receive their powers, for their 'initiations' frequently include powerful experiences of unusual light that leave them for ever changed. Eliade has drawn attention to many of these throughout his anthropological writings. He notes, for example, that these shamans receive their clairvoyant powers as a result of an experience of initiation known as *quamaneq* – meaning 'lightning' or 'illumination', and he cites Rasmussen as describing this as

> a mysterious light which the shaman suddenly feels in his body, inside his head, within the brain, an inexplicable searchlight, a luminous fire, which

enables him to see in the dark, both literally and metaphorically speaking, for he can now, even with closed eyes, see through darkness and perceive things and coming events which are hidden from others; thus [he can now look] into the future and into the secrets of others. (Eliade 1964: 60–1)

A good example of this type of initiatory experience was described to Rasmussen by Aua, an Iglulik Eskimo from the Hudson Bay coast, whose experience occurred after a long period of solitude, distress and instability. As Aua told the story to Rasmussen,

> I soon became very melancholy. I would sometimes fall to weeping, and feel unhappy without knowing why. Then, for no reason, all would suddenly be changed and I felt a great, inexplicable joy, a joy so powerful that I could not restrain it, but had to break into a song, a mighty song, with room only for one word: joy, joy! . . . And then in the midst of such a fit of mysterious and overwhelming delight I became a shaman, not knowing myself how it came about. But I was a shaman. I could see and hear in a totally different way. I had gained my *quamaneq*, my enlightenment, the shaman-light of brain and body, and this in such a manner that it was not only I who could see through the darkness of life, but the same light also shone out from me, imperceptible to human beings, but visible to all the spirits of the earth and sky and sea, and these now came to me and became my helping spirits. (Hollenback 1996: 35)

Eliade notes that Australian medicine men also experience initiations involving transformative lights. Here, he asserts, the light originates in quartz crystals inserted into the aspirant by supernatural powers during his temporary 'death' and that

> when he returns to life, he is able to see spirits, to read the thoughts of others, to fly up to Heaven, to make himself invisible, etc. Thanks to the rock crystals contained in his body, and particularly in his head, the medicine-man enjoys a different mode of existence from the rest of mortals. Baime's [the heavenly master of the initiation] throne is made of crystal, and Baime himself drops on to the earth fragments broken from his throne. In other words, the crystals are supposed to have fallen from the vault of heaven; they are in a sense 'solidified light'. (Eliade 1962: 25)

Kundalini 'awakenings'

It is striking how such experiences of transforming lights span both cultures and history. Quite distinct from shamanic cultures, Eliade notes that, in the Upanishads of India, encounters with 'being' – ultimate reality – take the form of 'pure light' and that 'man receives being by an experience of supernatural light' (Eliade 1962: 26). A variety of different yogic traditions teach that radical self-transformation as a result of various spiritual practices can be frequently accompanied by an eruption of powerful light. The practice of kundalini yoga gives a good example of this. Kundalini literally means 'coiled up' and yogic practices associated with this tradition have long taught that energy 'sleeping' at the base of the spine (like a sleeping, coiled-up snake) can be activated and made to move through seven *chakras* up the spine until it arrives at the head. Posture, breathing control and meditation are the means by which this is achieved. When the kundalini energy begins to reach and to open the highest *chakras*, unusual experiences of light accompany often dramatic transformations of consciousness, as in the following account narrated by the contemporary yogic practitioner Gopi Krishna:

> Suddenly, with a roar like that of a waterfall, I felt a stream of liquid light entering my brain through the spinal cord . . . Entirely unprepared for such a development, I was completely taken by surprise; but regaining self-control instantaneously, I remained sitting in the same posture, keeping my mind on the point of concentration. The illumination grew brighter and brighter, the roaring louder. I experienced a rocking sensation and then felt myself slipping outside of my body, entirely enveloped in a halo of light. It is impossible to describe the experience accurately. I felt the point of consciousness that was myself growing wider, spreading outward while the body, normally the immediate object of its perception, appeared to have receded into the distance until I became entirely unconscious of it. I was now all consciousness, without any outline, without any idea of a corporeal appendage, without any feeling or sensation coming from the senses, immersed in a sea of light simultaneously conscious and aware of every point, spread out, as it were, without any barrier or mental obstruction. I was no longer myself, or to be more accurate, no longer as I knew myself to be, a small point of awareness confined in a body, but instead was a vast circle of consciousness in which the body was but a point, bathed in light and in a state of exaltation and happiness impossible to describe. (Hollenback 1996: 36–7)

Such autobiographical descriptions of light associated with kundalini yoga are numerous. Compare, for example, Hiroshi Motoyama's description of his own kundalini 'awakening', below, with Gopi Krishna's:

> As the kundalini rose from my heart to the top of my head, it became shining white. It left my body through the top of my head and I rose with it into a much higher dimension . . . when I came to myself ten to twenty

minutes later, my mother told me that she had seen a golden light shining at the top of my head and at my heart . . . My psychological state also underwent some profound changes with this awakening. Notably, I developed an attitude of non-attachment to worldly things. (Ring 1984: 233)

In his book *Higher Consciousness*, Gopi Krishna lists the 'characteristic symptoms' associated with the practice of kundalini yoga as

> (1) sensation of light, which can be both internal and external. The subject feels as if a wondrous effulgence has illuminated his interior and maybe even objects in the outside world. The sensation is at times so realistic as to give the impression of an inner and outer conflagration; (2) an overwhelming sense of wonder and awe; (3) unshakable conviction about the reality of the experience; (4) a sense of infinitude and unbounded knowledge; (5) certainty of immortality; (6) intellectual illumination; (7) a vivid feeling of encounter with an inexpressible, all-knowing Intelligence of an omniscient Divine Being; (8) a flood of pure emotion, an overwhelming feeling of devotion, reverence, submission, love and adoration, cascading tears. (Krishna 1974: 28)

Lights in Buddhism

In a very different context, Buddhism includes a number of texts and teachings which seem to associate transformation and light. The Buddha himself is sometimes pictured as radiant. At the holy site of Amaraviti he is represented in the form of a column of fire. Eliade again notes how in one particular discourse he relates how 'I have become a flame and I have risen into the air to the height of seven palm trees'. *Shunyata*, an emptiness understood by some Buddhists as the ultimate goal of Buddhism, is described by one Buddhist as involving an apprehension of

> the great white light, and it was brilliant. It was what we call Shunyata, or total emptiness. In this emptiness – which is not a fearful thing, but a marvellous thing – there was peace, calm, a sense of being freed from the ego. I didn't achieve enlightenment, but I got a taste of what it might be like. (Berman 1996: 103)

Contemporary practitioners of meditation in the Zen Buddhist tradition frequently describe transformative experiences involving unusual light, as in the following account narrated by a retired mechanical engineer who had been reading and meditating for several days prior to his experience:

Then one day as I was walking very peacefully from the kitchen into the living room, the top of my head blew off. I felt as though a river of light and glorious emotion was racing down through me with the force of a fire hose. It knocked me down. I laid on the floor in total awe. For several minutes the brain did not think, the body did not move. I could only experience the amazing feeling and light flowing through me. It is impossible to exaggerate the intensity of the feeling. One experiencer said 'If you bring together every orgasm you ever had and every other feeling of love consummated and had them all happen to you at once – this will give you some idea.' For me, it changed entirely my understanding of what the body and mind are capable of; virtually of what the mind and body are. (Corcoran 1996: 130)

According to some Buddhist traditions, it is not simply in the midst of life that unusual lights can be experienced. The eighth-century Tibetan Buddhist text *The Tibetan Book of the Dead* includes teachings that reveal that at the point of death consciousness moves through various *bardo* states, each offering the possibility of enlightenment and containing numerous lights. During the passage through these *bardo* states consciousness may become expanded, and new powers such as the ability to see things far away or one's own body at a distance may develop. In the 'luminous *bardo* of dharmata' a variety of gods may appear surrounded by unusual light, pattern and sound. It is tempting in such teachings to find echoes of the shamanic initiations already described. Others, notably the Buddhist scholar Sogyal Rinpoche, find in them further echoes of modern near-death experiences (Rinpoche 1992: 284).

Jewish and Christian traditions

Nearer to home, both the Jewish and Christian religions contain a large number of texts and traditions including reports of unusual lights. Psalm 104:2 actually describes God as 'wrapped in the light like a cloak'. The prophet Ezekiel's vision amongst the Jewish exiles by the River Kebar includes a description of 'a figure like that of a man'. Ezekiel remarks, vividly:

I saw that from what appeared to be his waist up he looked like glowing metal, as if full of fire, and that from there down he looked like fire; and brilliant light surrounded him. Like the appearance of a rainbow in the clouds on a rainy day, so was the radiance around him. (Ezekiel 1: 27–8)

It is notable that such descriptions are not confined to biblical times. No survey of unusual lights in the Jewish–Christian tradition would be complete without discussion of two particular types of unusual phenomena found in Christianity today which frequently involve strange auras, beams and other odd lights: Marian apparitions and visions of Jesus.

Alleged sightings of the Blessed Virgin Mary have occurred regularly throughout Christian history and particularly in the last two centuries. These often begin when the subject who first reports the experience notices a strange light and begins to investigate. One of the most celebrated series of unusual events, including sightings of Mary, was to occur at Lourdes in 1858 when a young girl, Bernadette Soubirous, began to have a series of apparitions of the Blessed Virgin Mary that started when she saw a soft light in a grotto near some common land outside the town (Harris 1999: 3–9).

In Knock in the West of Ireland from 1879 various witnesses reported sightings of Mary together with other religious figures including St Joseph and St John. These began when the original visionary, Mary McLoughlin, noticed various strange figures in a field together with some kind of unusual 'altar' surrounded by light. Eventually a total of fourteen witnesses claimed to have seen unusual phenomena in the vicinity of Knock, and a special diocesan commission was set up to investigate. It heard of one sixty-year-old man who saw a globe of golden light on the night of 21 August 1879 that covered the gable of Knock church and made him think that some foolish neighbours had started a fire in the grounds. One description of Mary given during the spate of Knock sightings related how

> Our Lady's robe, strikingly white, was covered by a large white cloak that fastened at the throat and fell in ample folds to her ankles. On her head was a brilliant crown surmounted with glittering crosses and over the forehead where the crown fitted the brow was a beautiful rose. She held her hands extended apart and upward, in a position that none of the witnesses could have previously seen in any statue or picture. (Vallee 1970: 135–6)

Unusual lights were also a feature of a number of strange visions that began at Fatima in Portugal in May 1913. Descriptions of the events that subsequently took place included glowing lights, a 'bright flash', 'white light gliding above the tree tops' and 'a luminous globe spinning through the clouds'. Indeed, notable in the cases of the Knock and Fatima phenomena is the fact that they were observed by multiple witnesses (Vallee: 1970: 137). These are important cases for a variety of reasons, as future chapters of this book will make clear.

Visions of Jesus

Also encountered throughout Christian history have been visions of Jesus and, as with Marian apparitions, these have frequently included phenomena involving auras, lights and illuminations. Arguably, the first of these occurred during Jesus' own lifetime, on the Mount of Transfiguration. As St Matthew tells the story,

> Jesus took with him Peter, James and John the brother of James, and led them up a high mountain by themselves. There he was transfigured before them. His face shone like the sun, and his clothes became as white as the light. Just then there appeared before them Moses and Elijah, talking with Jesus.
>
> Peter said to Jesus, 'Lord, it is good for us to be here. If you wish, I will put up three shelters – one for you, one for Moses and one for Elijah.'
>
> While he was still speaking, a bright cloud enveloped them, and a voice from the cloud said 'This is my Son, whom I love; with him I am well pleased. Listen to him!' (Matthew 17:1–5)

Spanning the centuries from very shortly after his own lifetime up to the present day, encounters with a light identified as being Jesus have been a frequent cause of religious conversion. Conversion is often followed by baptism, and has been since the earliest years of Christianity. Notably, some of the early Church Fathers used the Greek word *photismos* ('illumination) for baptism rather than the usual word *baptizo* ('I dip'), and the New Testament Book of Hebrews gives the name *photistheneis* to those who have been baptized, thus describing them – either literally or figuratively – as being 'illumined' (Eliade 1962: 57–8).

It is, of course, Jesus who does the illuminating that so often leads to conversion in Christianity, and it is interesting to note how often this illumination takes a visible, tangible form. One very early example of this is the conversion of St Paul, as described in various places in the New Testament. The story is well known. Paul was a Pharisee, a member of a Jewish group active at the time of Jesus that adhered strictly to the Jewish law. As a Pharisee, Paul, known before his conversion as Saul, was actively involved during the early years after Jesus' death in the persecution of Christians. On one occasion he obtained permission to go to Damascus to send any persons suspected of practising Christianity to Jerusalem for punishment. As Luke takes up the story in the Book of Acts:

As he neared Damascus on his journey, suddenly a light from heaven flashed around him. He fell to the ground and heard a voice say to him, 'Saul, Saul, why do you persecute me?'

'Who are you, Lord?' Saul asked.

'I am Jesus, whom you are persecuting,' he replied. 'Now get up and go into the city, and you will be told what you must do.'

The men travelling with Saul stood there speechless; they heard the sound but did not see anyone. Saul got up from the ground, but when he opened his eyes he could see nothing. So they led him by the hand into Damascus. For three days he was blind, and did not eat or drink anything. (Acts 9:3–9)

A number of New Testament scholars dispute the accuracy of this story. Other academics, including psychologists, accept it in outline but favour a psychological rather than a spiritual interpretation of the events described. The well-known psychologist Carl Jung, for example, saw in Paul's blindness evidence of a 'psychogenetic' condition that was a result of his unwillingness to see the truth of Christianity and his 'fanatical resistance' to it (Thouless 1923: 190). Be that as it may, the fact is that Paul's conversion as a result of encountering Jesus in light has been replicated down the centuries and continues into the present time. Two examples of recent conversions to Christianity that occurred in circumstances similar to Paul's will serve to illustrate this point well. The first involves the well-known Hindu convert Sadhu Sundar Singh. Like Paul, before his conversion he was fanatically opposed to Christianity, writing:

When I was out in any town I got people to throw stones at Christian preachers. I would tear up the Bible and burn it when I had a chance. In the presence of my father I cut up the Bible and other Christian books and put kerosene oil upon them and burnt them.

However, the alternative, Hinduism, appears not to have satisfied him either:

I was faithful to my own religion, but I could not get any satisfaction or peace, though I performed all the ceremonies and rites of that religion. So I thought of leaving it all and committing suicide. Three days after I had burnt [a] Bible, I woke up about three o'clock in the morning, had my usual bath, and prayed, 'O God, if there is a God, wilt thou show me the right way or I will kill myself.' My intention was that, if I got no satisfaction, I would place my head upon the railway line when the 5 o' clock train passed by and kill myself. If I got no satisfaction in this life, I thought I would get it in the next. I was praying and praying but got no answer; and

I prayed for half-an-hour longer hoping to get peace. At 4.30 a.m I saw something of which I had no idea previously. In the room where I was praying I saw a great light. I thought the place was on fire. I looked round, but could find nothing. Then the thought came to me, 'Jesus Christ is not dead but living and it must be He Himself.' So I fell at His feet and got this wonderful Peace which I could not get anywhere else. This is the joy I was wishing to get. This was heaven itself. When I got up, the vision had all disappeared; but although the vision disappeared the Peace and Joy have remained with me ever since. I went off and told my Father that I had become a Christian. (Thouless 1923: 201–2)

What is interesting about this account is the depth of the crisis that existed in Sadhu Singh's life immediately before his conversion. Suicidal, the light appears and transforms him just thirty minutes before he had decided that he would kill himself. We will need to bear this fact carefully in mind as this study proceeds, for, as will become clear, times of crisis are particularly associated with the appearance of transforming lights.

A similar pattern occurs in the following testimony. Susan Atkins was one of the notorious 'Manson Family': followers of the charismatic hippie cult leader Charles Manson who were responsible for a series of brutal murders in California in the late 1960s. Finally caught and charged for her part in the crimes, she relates how, once in prison:

The thoughts tumbled over and over in my mind. Can society forgive one for such acts against humanity? Can it take this guilt off my shoulders? Can serving the rest of my life in prison undo what's been done? Can anything be done?

I looked at my future, my alternatives. Stay in prison. Escape. Commit suicide. As I looked, the wall in my mind was blank. But somehow I knew there was another alternative. I could choose the road many people had been pressing on me. I could follow Jesus. As plainly as daylight came the words, 'You have to decide. Behold, I stand at the door and knock.' Did I hear someone say that? I assume I spoke in my thoughts, but I'm not certain, 'What door?'

'You know what door and where it is, Susan. Just turn around and open it, and I will come in.' Suddenly, as though on a movie screen, there in my thoughts was a door. It had a handle. I took hold of it and pulled. It opened. The whitest, most brilliant light I had ever seen poured over me. In the center of the flood of brightness was an even brighter light. Vaguely, there was the form of a man. I knew it was Jesus. He spoke to me – literally, plainly, matter-of-factly spoke to me in my 9-by-11 prison cell: 'Susan, I am really coming into your heart to stay.' I was distinctly aware that I inhaled deeply, and then, just as fully, exhaled. There was no more guilt! It was gone. Completely gone! The bitterness, too, instantly gone! How could this be? For the first time in my memory I felt clean, fully clean, inside and out. In 26 years I had never been so happy. (Barton and Stanton 1994: 58–9)

As with Paul's experience, there is a considerable scholarly debate surrounding contemporary conversion visions of this sort. However, a significant number of scholars appear to take them at face value, or are at least willing to entertain the possibility that they are not all merely 'in the mind'. Recently, for example, Phillip Wiebe, Professor of Philosophy and Dean of Arts and Religious Studies at Trinity Western University in Canada, has undertaken a significant academic study of visions of Jesus, embracing historical, theological, philosophical, psychological and parapsychological approaches to the phenomenon. While an assessment of his conclusions, which are based in part around a large collection of present-day cases that he analyses in detail, is beyond the scope of this book, his study shows at least that some academics are not embarrassed to explore experiences that may appear to defy naturalistic and scientific explanation, including those involving unusual lights (Wiebe 1997).

Mysticism

Another type of cross-cultural and trans-historical tradition that frequently includes reports of unusual illuminations is mysticism. As with some of the other traditions explored in this chapter, the literature on the subject is vast, but a couple of examples will serve to show the frequent occurrence of experiences involving unusual lights within it. In her seminal study, *Mysticism*, Evelyn Underhill notes that many mystics 'experience a kind of radiance, a flooding of the personality with new light'. Far from being a symbolic attempt to describe a state of awakening – as in 'I saw the light' – Underhill asserts that an 'apparently symbolic name is really descriptive' and that 'A new sun rises above the horizon, and transfigures [the mystic's] twilit world'. As an example, she quotes St Teresa of Avila, who reported experiences of 'infused brightness' involving 'a light which knows no night [and where] nothing ever disturbs it' (Underhill 1993: 249).

Hildegard of Bingen's descriptions of her own mystical raptures are replete with accounts of experiences of unusual light. She writes, for example, of repeated episodes in which

The light which I see is not located, but yet is more brilliant than the sun, nor can I examine its height, length or breadth, and I name it 'the cloud of the living light'. And as sun, moon, and stars are reflected in water, so the writings, sayings, virtues and works of men shine in it before me . . .

Sometimes I behold within this light another light which I name 'the Living Light itself' . . . And when I look upon it every sadness and pain vanishes from my memory, so that I am again as a simple maid and not as an old woman. (Sacks 1985: 161)

Despite being dismissed by some modern commentators as nothing more than 'migraine aura', the effect of her experiences was to inspire her to a lifestyle both holy and simple, suggesting to others that more than merely neurological dysfunction was at work in her life.

Angelic experiences

Recent years have seen a spate of books dealing with two further types of spiritual experiences that frequently involve encounters with unusual lights: angelic experiences and near-death experiences. *Angelic* experiences have been collected and analysed by a number of researchers, including Glennyce Eckersley, Emma Heathcote-James and Cherie Sutherland. Hailing respectively from the United States, England and Australia, these authors' detailed studies include cases of encounters with angels reported by persons throughout the world, making the experience of seeing, feeling, hearing or even touching angels a genuinely global and cross-cultural phenomenon. What is interesting about many such angelic 'visitations' is the fact that they so often include unusual manifestations of *light*. Subjects report, for example, that the angels gave off unusually bright auras, appeared initially as light, 'wrapped' them in light, or appeared to brighten the environment with their presence. Glennyce Eckersley writes of 'John', whose experience during an episode of 'deep depression and physical decline' included an 'inner voice' that forced him to turn away from 'the dark abyss he feared'. Physically turning towards the apparent source of the voice, he was 'at once engulfed in the brightest light he had ever seen or could possibly imagine. The feelings accompanying this light were hard to articulate, but love was predominant. The darkness was gone and John could start on the road to a complete recovery' (Eckersley 1996: 96).

Cherie Sutherland, whose books have also included analyses of near-death experiences, recounts several detailed angelic encounters in her book *In the Company of Angels*. Many of these include unusual experiences in which the angel apparently appears as a comforting, shining presence, bringing light into situations often characterized by great darkness. The case of 'Diana' is a case in point. Lying on her bed crying and alone, she suddenly felt the touch of a hand on her arm. She continues:

> It startled me a bit but I just kept on crying. And then this voice said, 'What's the matter? Why are you crying? What is it? Tell me.'
> And I just said, 'I'm sorry. I'm really, really sorry.'
> And she said, 'What are you sorry for?'
> And I said, 'I'm sorry for my reaction to my mother when I was young.'
> She then said, 'Is that all? Anyone in your family would have reacted in the same way.'
> At that I opened my eyes to look at her. And standing there was this huge being in a brilliant white light. It was the most beautiful thing I've ever seen in my whole life. Words just can't express . . . (Sutherland 2000: 45)

Most detailed of all is an analysis based on more than 800 case studies of claimed encounters with angels conducted by Emma Heathcote-James as part of her doctoral research at the University of Birmingham in England. Her book, *Seeing Angels*, is once again notable for the number of cases it contains of encounters with unusual, often comforting, lights that are interpreted by subjects as having been angelic in nature. The following case is typical:

> Early one evening, at a time of year when it was already dusk, I left the office, in a peaceful little avenue off a long pedestrian walk, from the other side of which I was suddenly aware of a light, not tremendously bright but very strong, which seemed to rise above the buildings. The site of the light was also the centre of an enormous power. There were other people around; it was clear that they had noticed nothing of the sort, but I was unable to move until it had 'released' me. I had, and still have, no doubt that it was of a numinous nature, which left me considerably shaken. (As a former boxer and rugby player, I was and am not easily shaken.) I had not been thinking about anything even remotely of the sort before it happened. (Heathcote-James 2001: 220–1)

Another case that, as will become clear, bears a striking resemblance to many of the experiences that make up the current study, is reported by a woman who was working as a teacher when her experience occurred in the autumn of 1947:

> I was in lodgings with a friend . . . during the night when I was in bed, on I think about three or [so] occasions, I saw a glowing ball of light to my left

above my head near the ceiling. I sensed that it was something unusual and I remember pulling my head under the clothes and looking again to make sure it was still there. It could not have been a reflection because the window was at the left side of the bed and I was sure that it was something unusual, but I think I felt not afraid but unsure what to think. As far as I remember I have never seen glowing balls since then. (Heathcote-James 2001: 223)

As part of the conclusion to her study, Heathcote-James draws attention to the fact that such experiences often appear transformative and seem to be interpreted by subjects in accordance with their feelings and needs at the time they occurred. She writes:

Each and every experience that has been reported to me has some sort of effect and seems to be interpreted by the witness dependent on their individual needs. Experiences seem to have a corrective effect on the witness's life: for example, if the person was severely ill, the angelic presence either assisted their recovery in a physical way, or enabled them to accept their condition, or alleviated their suffering completely (as well as the suffering of their next of kin) in a spiritual way. If the person was afraid, then comfort was offered; if the person was in a life-threatening situation, the angelic intervention frequently saved their life. (Heathcote-James 2001: 243)

Also interesting is the fact that angelic experiences were reported to her by persons of many religious faiths and none. Despite being conducted almost solely in England, the study contains accounts described by Buddhists, Muslims, Jews, Protestants, Catholics, atheists and agnostics.

Near-death experiences

Even more numerous than the recent studies of angels have been the myriad studies of near-death experiences (NDEs) that have appeared in the thirty-odd years since the term 'near-death experience' was coined by Raymond Moody Jnr in his *Life after Life* (1975). These unusual and apparently consistent experiences, narrated by people at or near the point of bodily death when they occurred, frequently include out-of-body sensations, feelings of bliss and peace, 'journeys' towards lights via a passage through darkness, encounters with deceased relatives, a 'life review' and a transforming effect on subjects' lives. The number of books on this subject with the word 'light' in the title – such as *The Light Beyond* (Moody and Perry 1988), *The Truth in the Light* (Fenwick and Fenwick 1995), *Light and Death* (Sabom 1998), *Transformed by the Light* (Morse 1992), and *Lessons from the Light* (Ring and Valarino 1998) – testifies to the fact that for many subjects the 'encounter' with some sort of heavenly light represents the climax to their experience. Two examples will suffice to illustrate this. The first, reported by Moody in his 1975 study, occurred when the subject suffered a ruptured appendix. He describes how

> I became very weak, and I fell down. I began to feel a sort of drifting, a movement of my real being in and out of my body, and to hear beautiful music. I floated on down the hall and out the door onto the screened-in porch. There, it almost seemed that clouds, a pink mist really, began to gather around me, and then I floated right straight on through the screen, just as though it weren't there, and up into this pure crystal light, an illuminating white light. It was beautiful, and so bright, so radiant, but it didn't hurt my eyes. It's not any kind of light you can describe on earth. I didn't actually see a person in this light, and yet it has a special identity, it definitely does. It is a light of perfect understanding and perfect love. (Moody 1975: 104)

The following account, included in a study of over 300 NDEs produced by Peter and Elizabeth Fenwick, *The Truth in the Light*, describes an encounter with the light 'being' in similarly vivid terms and includes the common feelings of peace and joy that are so often associated with it:

> Then I saw a light that seemed to grow brighter and brighter until its brilliance had completely encircled me, as if my very soul had been transformed and enveloped in love.
>
> It was then that I had the sensation of being gathered up and held like a newborn child. Nestling in the warmth of this loving embrace, I knew that nothing could ever harm me again. Whether I was to live or die, I knew I should be given the strength to continue on. At the time I didn't know who I was or what kind of life lay ahead, but now I had the certainty that God would be leading the way. It was then that the Lord took me by the hand. (Fenwick and Fenwick 1995: 59)

As with angelic experiences, NDEs seem to occur across all cultures and to people of all religions and none. Even the atheist philosopher A. J. Ayer reported a powerful and vivid NDE toward the end of his life which, according to some sources, forced him to modify somewhat his views on death and the possibility of an afterlife. The fact that somebody like Ayer could have such an experience raises the interesting question of whether or not persons having NDEs or angelic experiences are merely seeing what they expect to see during their otherworldly 'encounters'. For it could be argued that his was most definitely an experience that was entirely *un*expected. Sceptics have argued that all religious and spiritual visions are merely delusional, or are 'projections' outward from the unconscious mind. Whilst these 'explanations' may sound attractive – and whilst they may serve to explain at least some experiences – they entirely fail to account for episodes that completely *surprise* subjects. In this vein, for example, consider how the following near-death experiencer encounters an entirely unexpected and somewhat surprising group of people 'within the light':

> At the time of my NDE I was a practising Roman Catholic. Had I died I would most certainly have expected that any visions I had would have related to my faith, and that if I were to see a being of light I would have related it to Jesus or Mary or an angel. As it was, when I suddenly found myself in this gentle glowing light and standing a little below the three beings above me, they appeared as young Indian men, and though they were dressed alike in high-necked silver-coloured tunics with silver turbans on their heads, I felt they were young Indian princes, or rajas. Two were facing each other and the third facing me. And from a jewel in the centre of each forehead or turban three 'laser' beams emitted, meeting in the centre.
>
> My whole lifestyle was changed as a result – much reading about various religions and philosophies. (Fenwick and Fenwick 1995: 132)

This case is interesting inasmuch as the experience conformed to no prior expectation on the part of the subject. Indeed, she states that her life was changed as a result of it – as if it somehow triggered a quest to find a truth hitherto unknown. As we will see as this study progresses, many persons encountering unusual lights in a variety of contexts also appear not to have been prepared for, or to have anticipated, what actually happened to them.

In common with angel researchers such as Emma Heathcote-James who have been concerned to look for consistent trends and descriptions across reports, many NDE researchers have been concerned to identify the common features in accounts of NDEs. Virtually all researchers would include an encounter with a 'being of light' as a feature of any 'model' or 'core' NDE. Furthermore, and once again in common with researchers such as Heathcote-James, many NDE researchers have argued that the 'being of light' has a fixed identity but is identified differently by individuals depending upon their cultural and religious backgrounds. Moody was the first to put forward this position back in his original 1975 study, and the view remains popular with other NDE researchers. It will be interesting to see as this study progresses whether the argument is supported or contradicted by a concentration on a large number of light experiences – including, as we shall see, a significant number of NDEs that actually *pre-date* Moody's original study.

Other experiences

In addition to the various 'types' of light experiences we have so far examined, there are a number of well-known cases that do not fall into any religious, spiritual or cultural categories. A number of individuals' encounters with unusual lights have, in fact, been responsible for their going on actually to *establish* religious and spiritual movements. Others have been led to build entirely new philosophies on the foundations laid by their experiences. Ellen White, for example, founder of the worldwide Seventh Day Adventist (SDA) Church, reported frequent episodes of unusual lights moving around her as she received the revelations from God upon which the SDA church rests. Pak Subuh, founder of the Brotherhood of Subud, had an encounter with an unusual light in 1925 that was to form part of a series of 'cleansing' experiences that prepared him to found the movement. According to one commentator, Subuh was with a number of companions 'when a ball of light more brilliant than the sun appeared above him and seemed to enter him, filling him with radiant light and vibrations'. The same commentator notes: 'It is recorded that others, too, from far away observed this extraordinary light and made enquiries the next day as to what it could have been' (Van Hien 1963: 29).

The researcher E. J. Dingwall notes that the eighteenth-century 'spirit bottler' Alexis Berbiguier began his ministry of exorcism as a result of a series of highly unusual experiences (including mysterious lights) that began after he had attended a séance conducted by a female medium named Mansotte (Dingwall 1947: 57). And the promoter of the idea of 'cosmic consciousness', R. M. Bucke, recorded in his own writings how he was led to his 'discovery' of this state of consciousness, higher and greater than that usually experienced, as a result of an encounter with both an inner and an outer light after a night out with friends:

I had spent the evening in a great city, with two friends, reading and discussing poetry and philosophy. We parted at midnight. I had a long drive in a hansom to my lodging. My mind, deeply under the influence of the ideas, images, and emotions called up by the reading and talk, was calm and peaceful. I was in a state of quiet, almost passive enjoyment, not actually thinking, but letting ideas, images, and emotions flow of themselves, as it were, through my mind. All at once, without warning of any kind, I found myself wrapped in a flame-coloured cloud. For an instant I thought of fire, an immense conflagration somewhere close by in that great city; the next, I knew that the fire was within myself. Directly afterward there came upon me a sense of exaltation, of immense joyousness accompanied or immediately followed by an intellectual illumination impossible to describe . . . The vision lasted a few seconds and was gone, but the memory of it and the sense of the reality of what it taught has remained during the quarter of a century which has since elapsed. I knew that what the vision showed was true. I had attained to a point of view from which I saw that it must be true. That view, that conviction, I may say that consciousness, has never, even during periods of the deepest depression, been lost. (Laski 1961: 434–5)

Excluded categories

One single chapter has obviously not been able to show the richness and diversity of experiences of mystical light across all cultures and throughout all of human history. It has, however, hinted at patterns and consistencies that span – and possibly underpin – the variety of experiences examined. Before we finish by listing some of these patterns and their possible implications, it will be necessary to describe briefly some experiences that this chapter has *not* covered, together with the reasons why.

Any survey of the literature on *apparitions*, for example, will reveal that many ghostly figures often appear either as glowing or as wrapped in light. Celia Green and Charles McCreery, in an exhaustive survey of ghosts and hauntings, include in their study the following account that typifies such experiences:

On New Year's Eve, 1852, I awoke about 12.40 a.m. and found my room so brilliantly illuminated that I imagined I had forgotten to put out my candle, and that something must have caught fire. I got up and, on looking round, saw at the foot of the bed a coffin resting on chairs, on each of which was a silver candlestick with a large wax taper alight; in the coffin was a figure of my father. I put out my hand and touched him, when it became quite dark. I felt for my matchbox and lighted a candle, looked at my watch and wrote down the time. The next morning I told my friend, with whom I was staying in Paris at the time, and on the morning of the 2nd of January we received a letter from Marseilles, saying that my father had died suddenly at 12.40 on New Year's Eve, and that he had expressed such a strong wish to see his youngest child (i.e myself) again just before his death. (Green and McCreery 1989: 47)

In more recent years, the study of after-death communications (ADCs) has grown, largely as a result of the pioneering work of Bill and Judy Guggenheim in the United States. Their work includes several descriptions given by persons who claim they have been visited by deceased friends and relatives. These accounts give several descriptions of unusual lights, and include the following:

I remember waking up, and almost instantaneously, this amazingly bright blue-white light was hovering near the ceiling. It was a large oval shape, about four feet tall and three feet wide.

As I was looking at it, I was told telepathically that it was my maternal grandfather, who had just passed on to the next world. I remember thinking this was really strange because I had no idea he had been ill. In fact, I didn't have any close association with this man. He was a little ornery and had a poor relationship with other members of the family.

The light lingered for a while, and after it left I looked at the clock and discovered it was 2:17 a.m. Then I went back to sleep.

The following morning my sister knocked on my front door. I knew why she had come and said, 'You came to tell me that Grandpa died, didn't you?' She looked puzzled and said, 'Mom called to tell us that he died of a heart attack at about 2:30 a.m.' I said, 'No, it was 2:17 a.m.', and I told her what had happened. (Guggenheim and Guggenheim 1997: 249)

In addition, the enormous literature on *unidentified flying objects* (UFOs) contains many descriptions of experiences of unusual light. Indeed, so frequent are such reports that the US Air Force's one-time official consultant on UFOs, J. Allen Hynek, produced a specific category dubbed 'nocturnal lights' within which to include and study them (Hynek 1972). Recent investigations of *orbs* – unusual fast-moving lights found at places of alleged paranormal activity – and *earthlights* – unusual lights seen at places of tectonic strain and often presaging earthquakes and other minor disturbances – have also added to the growing literature on unusual lights of various types. However, close investigation of this diverse literature, from apparitions to earthlights, shows that, with a few notable exceptions, these experiences are not interpreted as mystical, spiritual or religious and rarely produce the sorts of changes in subjects and observers that the other experiences examined in this chapter have been seen to do. For these reasons, despite being interesting in themselves, they have been generally excluded from the present analysis, with a couple of interesting exceptions, as the next chapter will show.

Conclusions and agendas

Even a brief overview such as this one, designed to place this study of lightforms in cultural and historical context, has revealed a remarkable array of experiences ancient and modern that contain a number of consistently-encountered themes. There is, as we have seen, a clear relationship between experiences of light and *transformation*. Eskimo shamans and their experiences of *quamaneq*, Australian medicine men filled with pieces of Baime's throne, practitioners of kundalini yoga awakening the serpent energy for its ascent through the *chakras*, Buddhists encountering *shunyata*, Saul becoming Paul on the road to Damascus, Sadhu Sundar Singh finding peace thirty minutes from death, Bernadette becoming St Bernadette in a grotto at Lourdes, hundreds of life-changing encounters with angels and near-death experiences reported worldwide from ancient to modern times: all suggest strongly that a modern investigation of the power of mystic lights deeply and radically to transform people's lives would reap rich rewards. Might we find, for example, in the RERC archives a similar array of accounts that follow the same pattern? Accounts where ordinary people going about their normal day-to-day lives undergo transforming spiritual experiences of light comparable to those of Eskimo shamans, kundalini practitioners, religious founders, and celebrated visionaries? If we could, it would at least reveal to us that shattering experiences of this kind are not the preserve of the spiritually favoured few, but are potentially available to each and every one of us.

Pushing the investigation further still, might we find in the RERC accounts other aspects of unusual light experiences that compare with those we have seen in this chapter? Might we find, for example, that occurrences of spiritually transforming light are frequently found at times of crisis? For that has been one of the findings of this chapter too. Recall: conversion visions frequently occur at such times, as do NDEs and angelic encounters. Might we, then, find in the RERC accounts a significant proportion of accounts that report experiences that *also* took place at just such times – times, perhaps, when the subjects needed them the most? If we *can* find a number of such accounts, then once again we are presented with the possibility that such help in times of distress is not reserved for those privileged enough to 'see' Jesus or angels, or for those unfortunate enough to experience temporary clinical death, but is instead potentially available to us all – whatever our crisis may be.

At the very least, our overview of a range of spiritually transforming light experiences has alerted us to know what to look out for, if the nearly 400 accounts of light in the archive posted there over the years by ordinary men and women are to match those reported through the years and across cultures. Indeed, if any significant proportion of the accounts we are about to examine match the patterns we have been discussing then we may even find ourselves able to discern a 'common core' at the very heart of humankind's spiritual and religious experiencing. This would, perhaps, be this book's greatest discovery of all. For after centuries of division by tradition, theology, creed and dogma, discerning such a core might even allow us to view something of the heart that beats within each and every religion and spirituality wherever and whenever it is found – a heart that is filled with light and that can appear to us and fill and surround us with that light too. If we are truly to speak of an experience of God, of the divine, of the transcendent, or of ultimate reality, perhaps that experience will best be found manifesting as light. That, at least, has been a conclusion strongly suggested throughout this chapter.

Part II follows: it is the *Lightforms* study proper. The accounts gathered from the RERC archives over many months are collected in the following chapters and presented according to their varying types and in their original form, with grammar and spelling untouched and unchanged. Clear distinctions can be made between the sorts of light experiences people report, and accounts have been divided in order to reflect the differences between testimonies. So, for example, separate chapters preserve and present a clear distinction between a reported experience of being wrapped in light and a reported experience of seeing a light with a clear size and location within a room. The various types of lightform will become clear as the study develops. Throughout, it should be borne in mind that the attention given to a particular category of experience does not necessarily reflect incidence of experience. There are few shared experiences, for example, but these have been deemed to have a particular importance of their own, as we shall now see.

Part II

3

Sharing the fire: unusual lights with multiple witnesses

Sharing the light

The 'problem of verification' is well known and much discussed whenever claims to spiritual and religious experiences are considered. Many of these sorts of experiences, it is argued, differ from 'ordinary' experiences in that they tend to be private, solitary episodes. The Virgin Mary, for example, usually appears to a single witness – even when others may be present, as was the case at Lourdes – and in solitary locations (Harris 1999: 4). Visions of Jesus generally follow this pattern too. Even dramatic conversions – many involving visual and auditory phenomena – seem to occur when the convert is alone: such as Alphonse Ratisbonne's celebrated conversion vision in the church of Sant' Andrea delle Fratte in Rome as reported by William James (James 1902: 226). Given the recognition of the solitariness of such experiences, it is frequently asserted that they are best explained by this-worldly, naturalistic interpretations rather than other-worldly, supernaturalistic ones: that the subject was hallucinating, perhaps, and in some unspecified way 'projecting' the experience outwards from mental space. By this reckoning, the value of alleged religious and spiritual episodes as 'proof' of supernatural, transcendent realities is weakened by the fact that one person's subjective impression of an apparently external presence or entity cannot be checked against the simultaneous experiences of others at the same location and at the same time.

It is also the case that many experiences widely dubbed 'paranormal' are open to exactly the same criticisms. By their nature, for example, near-death experiences may be expected to be private, solitary affairs. A prophetic dream, unless it is shared with others, is similarly private, as are so-called UFO 'abductions', which generally remain hidden even from 'abductees' themselves until subsequent hypnotic sessions 'unlock' them. Even apparitions and ghosts seem to prefer solitary observers; Celia Green and Charles McCreery, for example, were only able to devote one short chapter to 'collective' accounts in their seminal 1968 study for the Oxford Institute for Psychophysical Research (Green and McCreery 1989).

Having said all of this, there are, it is true, *limited* ways of sharing another's religious or paranormal experience. In a recent and widely discussed study, *Why God Won't Go Away*, Andrew Newberg, Eugene D'Aquili and Vince Rause have presented the results of experiments that have tried to allow observers to 'share' the experiences of meditators in deep, meditative states by using advanced brain-imaging equipment to map the parts of meditators' brains affected by such states. The results of these experiments are interesting, revealing that the 'input' to the posterior superior parietal lobe is blocked at such times. This is the very part of the brain responsible for differentiating the boundaries of the self from the rest of the world, and Newberg and D'Aquili surmise that it is involved in those deepest experiences of mystics in which the subject merges or fuses with everything else, effectively becoming 'one' with it. In fact, a central contention of *Why God Won't Go Away* is that part of the brain is 'wired' for religious experience, and the authors devote considerable attention to the implications arising from this (Newberg et al. 2001). Meanwhile, at Laurentian University in Canada, the neuroscientist Michael Persinger continues to carry out similar brain-mapping experiments, even claiming to have produced a device which, by stimulating selected parts of the brain, can actually induce certain types of religious and paranormal experience at will, as we shall see in more detail in chapter 11 (Cotton, 1995). As things currently stand, the future seems promising as regards our understanding of the brain's role in creating and/or mediating religious, paranormal and other 'varieties' of transcendent experience.

Even in the absence of such startling research, however, there is still a large enough body of testimony to shared experiences within such contexts that allows investigators considerable scope for inquiry. Whilst, for example, collective religious visions are much rarer than private, solitary visions, they are by no means unreported. On the contrary, on repeated occasions numerous witnesses have experienced Marian apparitions, together with accompanying phenomena which frequently include unusual displays of light. At Medjugorge in the former Yugoslavia, for example, the Virgin Mary has on occasion appeared to up to six young visionaries simultaneously, and sometimes many more persons have been witnesses to the extraordinary phenomena that until recently accompanied her appearances, as the following testimony dramatically shows:

> About 50 neighbours went along . . . and we all began praying. All at once seven or eight of us began shouting, 'Look at that light.' It came from the sky, as if the sky had opened up about ten metres, and it came towards us. It stopped over the hole in the ground (he pointed to where the people had been digging up the earth). There was a wooden cross in the hole and the light seemed to stream from it. It was as if a balloon of light had burst and there were thousands of tiny stars everywhere. We were just bathed in light. . .We were all crying. As long as I live I shall never forget that night. (Craig 1988: 90)

The association of unusual light phenomena with apparitions of the Virgin and sometimes witnessed by large numbers of people is not confined to Medjugorge. The widely reported 'dance of the sun', occurring at Fatima in 1917, was witnessed by approximately 150 people, of whom one, a taxi driver, reported:

> I was with a large group of people outside the church, and suddenly I noticed the sun doing strange things . . . it began to swing to and fro . . . Finally a ray of light separated itself from the sun and travelled like the rays of a rainbow towards the place where the Virgin had first appeared. It then rested on the church tower, on which a clear image of the Virgin appeared. (Craig 1988: 91–2)

Given the opportunities for corroboration of detail that such experiences offer, it is not surprising that researchers in recent years have spent considerable time looking for shared accounts across a range of religious and paranormal experiences that can be checked and, if possible, verified. By their very nature, many UFO reports offer real possibilities of investigation and verification, not least because such phenomena are often aerial and hence – potentially – visible to considerable numbers of witnesses. In this context, consider the following account of a celebrated UFO landing at Rendlesham Forest in Suffolk in December 1980 which bears interesting comparison with the extract, above, describing the light phenomena at Medjugorge. The report begins with a radio exchange, clearly indicating that more than one witness observed at least the beginning of the episode:

> Someone reported over the air: 'Here it comes. Here it comes. Here it comes.' Over the far end of the field, from the direction of the North Sea

I noticed a small red light. The light came closer each second. At first I thought it was an aircraft, but it came at us too fast and silently . . . The red light cleared the pines bordering the field and quickly made a downward arc until it was directly over the illuminated fog. Only about 20 feet above the ground, the object was now stationary and roughly the size of a basketball . . . As my mind tried to register what I was looking at the ball of light exploded in a blinding flash. Shards of light and particles fell into the woods. I couldn't move; I tried to cover my eyes, but was too late. (Warren and Robbins 1997: 45)

Dramatic as such shared experiences may sound, it is worth noting that in recent years other religious and/or paranormal experiences have been found to be shared, some that would appear as very unlikely candidates for shared experience indeed. The field of 'near-death studies', for example, has very recently acknowledged and presented evidence of the existence of shared near-death experiences known variously as 'empathic NDEs', 'death coincidents', 'conjoint near-death experiences' and 'mutual NDEs'. Raymond Moody, for example, who did much to stimulate the modern interest in NDEs with his best-selling 1975 study *Life after Life* has in very recent years presented a small number of such cases, including that of 'Joan':

While sleeping beside her terminally ill husband, Joan dreamed that they were strolling down a pathway, through a meadow, and into a dark tunnel. Inside, a soft yet brilliant light surrounded them and illuminated their way. She was feeling love and peace as never before when her husband said, 'Joanie, you must go back now.' At first she ignored him and continued to stroll, but when he tugged at her elbow, she spun around. To her amazement, he appeared healthy, athletic, and without glasses – much as he had in his youth. 'You must go back,' he repeated. 'It isn't your time. I'll be back for you when it is.' Joan sensed that they were at a point of no return and turned to leave, but just then a noise outside their window startled her awake. Opening her eyes, she saw that her dear husband had continued his journey into death. (Moody 2001: 163)

The recent spate of interest in shared experiences of an unusual nature is by no means confined to the field of NDE research. As might be anticipated, the huge popular interest in angels in recent years has thrown up a significant number of conjoint *angelic* encounters. Emma Heathcote-James, for example, in her recent study of angel visitations includes several, of which the following is representative:

My grandmother . . . and her younger sister were in Eastbourne to visit my great-grandmother who was very ill and not expected to live very long.

Walking away from the house one afternoon – and having found her very much at peace, though quite obviously very poorly – they were discussing the situation and, no doubt, preparing for the inevitable, when they both stopped in their tracks and caught hold of one another, saying 'did you see that?' They both – independently – claimed to have seen two shining winged people, who [they] were convinced must have been angels, gently escorting a human away. It was over in a second, but my grandma and aunty never forgot this experience, as they heard on their way home that their mum had died – at the precise moment they saw the angels . . . (Heathcote-James 2001: 177–8)

There are certainly elements of the above account that compare with other, possibly 'stylized' accounts reported globally and cross-culturally. In particular, the theme of perceiving some sort of apparition – recognizably human or angelic – at the point of another's death bears close comparison with 'crisis apparition' experiences reported virtually universally and already the subject of detailed academic investigation by the Society for Psychical Research and other bodies.

Shared lights in folklore

Reflection on the possibility that testimonies to unusual experiences of light, including shared experiences, may be a consistent, cross-cultural and trans-historical phenomenon leads neatly to a consideration of the consistent appearance of unusual light phenomena within superstitions and folklore separated, sometimes widely, by time, space and culture. The study of superstition and folkloristics is vast, yet it may be useful to consider just one consistently encountered light-related superstition here: that of the corpse candle. This is variously known also as the hobby lantern, jenny-burnt-tail, kit-in-the-candlestick and the *cannwyll corff*. The variety of names by which this unusual light is known even in a country as small as Britain indicates that it is widespread. Throughout most regions it is thought to be a harbinger of death: hence the association of its candle-like properties with the notion of a corpse soon to follow in the name 'corpse candle'. As with the other 'varieties' of unusual lights we have so far examined, however, this strange light has its fair share of multiple witnesses, as this testimony collected by paranormal researcher Paul Devereux makes clear:

It looked like a bright candle flame, without the candle; and it kept on coming nearer and nearer to us . . . It passed by us, on the other side of the hedge, just where the footpath came up from the valley. It went on, hopped along a few inches from the ground, and then vanished in the distance. (Devereux 2001: 165)

Devereux adds, interestingly, that such lights are reported globally, although different interpretations are sometimes put on their appearance. In Brazil, for example, such a light is known as a *Mae de Ouro*, which means Mother of Gold. Here, far from being a harbinger of death, the light is seen as a good sign and as leading the way to a site of buried treasure. Devereux adds other cross-cultural parallels to the corpse candle in *Haunted Land*, including the so-called Hessdalen lights of Norway, the *chota-admis* lanterns of Darjeeling and the 'Bodhisattva Lights' of the holy Chinese mountain of Wu Tai Shan. In each case, it seems at least plausible that whilst the light may be a manifestation of the same 'core' phenomenon (whatever that may be), the interpretation which is ascribed to it may be a function of the beliefs of the culture in which it is found. In Darjeeling, for example, the *chota-admis* are little men and the lights are their lanterns. In Chinese Buddhism the lights are sometimes seen as expressions of the *Dharma*. Meanwhile UFO researchers have descended on Hessdalen regularly over a number of years in the hope that precise photographing and measurement of the size and activities of the lights there may give clues to the still elusive mystery of unidentified flying objects (Devereux and Brookesmith 1998: 138–59).

Questions

All of the above examples, diverse though they may appear, are connected by the fact that what is reported in each case is some sort of unusual experience of light that appears to defy conventional rational explanation. Although the oldest case, that of the 'dancing sun' at Fatima, is a little under a hundred years old, it is worth underlining the obvious point that unusual lights have been reported in earlier ages also. The corpse candle is part of a tradition of lights tracing the routes of impending funerals going back many hundreds of years. In a very different context, it will be recalled that in at least one account we possess, that of Acts 22: 5–11, the 'heavenly' light on the road to Damascus is described as being seen not just by Paul but by his awestruck companions too. Given the – for some – surprising weight of evidence in favour of such a rich historical and cross-cultural, not to mention contemporary, tradition of shared encounters with unusual lights, it became clear early on that any study concerned to uncover and evaluate accounts of light in the RERC archive would need to take detailed account of it.

Indeed, from the outset it was clear that the occurrence of a significant number of such shared accounts in the RERC archive would be potentially revealing in itself. It would also be interesting to see if such shared experiences contributed significantly to any quest to find a 'common core' to religious experiences involving lights. In addition, it might be possible, if such accounts *did* turn out to exist, to determine what percentage of the total number of accounts containing unusual lights were shared.

Other questions quickly presented themselves as well. What contexts, for example, might such shared encounters occur *in*? Would they be significantly different from single-person encounters? Or would they be consistent with the other categories of experience the archive contained? Then there was the question of the *effects* of the experiences on their subjects. What might the overall emotional responses of witnesses be to the events they experienced? Would the experiences lead to positive or negative 'fruits'? Were there any accounts in which multiple witnesses had reported the same events, thoughts, feelings and fruits, perhaps independently of each other? And finally: what of the 'categories' of shared experiences themselves? Did the archive contain any accounts comparable to those reported in the existing literature? Were there, for example, any shared Marian apparitions, shared UFO sightings or shared angelic encounters? Perhaps more interestingly still, did the archive contain any significant categories of shared experience totally *unlike* anything in the literature? Would it yield new categories of shared experiences of unusual lights that might push our appreciation and understanding of the phenomenon in new – and perhaps unexpected – directions? Overall, and given the potential for understanding such encounters with light offered by shared accounts, it was hoped that their unusual nature and broad contemporary appeal might yield some of the study's most useful and significant conclusions. For these reasons, we begin our analysis of the RERC's light-experiences with an examination of shared experiences.

Analysis

At first sight, the number of cases of shared experiences appeared disappointingly low: only ten cases out of the total number examined. However, the content of these cases was such that the particular time and attention devoted to them was richly repaid.

Of the ten cases, one featured a Marian apparition experienced by two soldiers on patrol in the Falls Road area of Belfast, Northern Ireland, in October 1969. As the respondent tells the story:

> Until October 1969 I could take or leave religion. I believed there was some sort of a God, and that was that, I had an inborn hatred of the Pope and everything he stood for.
>
> Then, while I was serving with the Queen's regiment in Belfast, a strange thing happened to me.
>
> One cold, damp night I was patrolling the grounds of a Catholic school just off the Falls road, and cursing the people who lived in that area under my breath as I went on my way.
>
> About an hour passed and I had a feeling that I was not alone. I must say, I was surprised that the feeling did not frighten me, as it was about 2.45 in the morning and quite dark. Suddenly I felt quite warm and at peace not only with myself, but with everyone. From across the road the black shape of a Catholic Church seemed to draw my attention. When I finally turned, I saw in the sky a white light; as I looked, the light gradually took the shape of the Virgin Mary. My friend came into the courtyard at this moment and he saw exactly the same as I did. She was standing, her arms out stretched towards us. It nearly made my friend die of fright, but it had the opposite effect on me, although our lady didn't speak, all those misgivings I once had, melted away. Soon after this, I converted to the Catholic faith, and have never looked back.
>
> I *know* that God, in his personal love for me, sent this manifestation of our blessed lady to save me from hell. (3008)

A number of features merit particular comment here. The apparition has a dramatically contrasting effect on both experients: seemingly creating warmth and peace in the narrator, whilst frightening his friend (a fellow soldier on patrol, perhaps). The fruits of the experience are particularly striking, leading to the conversion of the writer to Catholicism (and an apparently dramatic change of heart towards those he once despised). Indeed, this feature is notable for another reason. It is often commented on in the relevant literature that visions correspond to prior expectation, leading to the conclusion that, somehow, experients' cultural and linguistic repertoires of beliefs, concepts and values somehow cause the experiences they then have, shaping them to conform to those expectations. Don Cupitt expresses this position well, if flippantly, when he remarks within the context of a discussion of Marian apparitions:

> Mary's various personal appearances on Earth . . . must be carefully pre-planned from the heavenly end. She must be kitted out for each occasion with the right skin-color, costume, dialect, message to deliver, and so on; and there must be no mistakes. Think how traumatic it would be if she were to speak the wrong dialect, or to garble her message! Fortunately, one has never heard of a theophany, or of any other 'ophany of a denizen of a supernatural world, in which the one who appeared wore the wrong clothes or fluffed her lines. It just doesn't happen, does it? (Cupitt 1998: 38)

The implication here and elsewhere in his discussion of such visionary 'encounters' is that prior beliefs – primarily language-driven – give rise to and shape the types of experiences visionaries have. It is absolutely not the case that they are seeing visitants from other realms as they are 'in themselves', and not even the case that they are 'clothing' somehow 'authentic' visions with post-experiential interpretation, but rather, that language 'comes first' and hence creates the conditions and possibility of their existing at all. As he writes of another type of unusual encounter, 'Only after human beings have begun to think of building spaceships does human religious experience begin to include apparitions of flying saucers.' Cupitt's position, shared to varying degrees by fellow philosophical theologians George Lindbeck and Steven Katz, is that, somehow (usually in unspecified ways), language creates experience (Katz 1978; Lindbeck 1984). Yet a moment's reflection on the above account shows how problematical such a position is. For what is Cupitt to make of that mass of experiences in which experients see what they do not expect to see or, as in the above account, undergo experiences that they were previously resistant or even *hostile* to? If expectation does create experience, what of situations in which experience contradicts expectation? Of course, Cupitt may reply that, despite the deliberate disavowals, experients such as the Falls Road soldier are seeing what they expected to see *really*, perhaps even unconsciously. Whilst recognizing the validity of this position, it should be borne in mind that it weakens the force of the argument, for it means in practice that there is nothing to stop us modifying and moulding any set of expectations in any way whatsoever we like in order to conform them to any experience that we are trying to explain. We shall have much more to say about this debate in the chapters that follow.

Close encounters of the strangest kind

Two of the ten shared accounts involved unusual UFO-type encounters. Of these, one took place whilst the subject and two friends were camping approximately 90 miles from Nairobi, in Kenya, at an unspecified date. As the respondent's testimony describes:

> At about 7 p.m we had set up our camp at the foot of a hill in the Matthews range, in the foothills of Mount Kenya. It had just got dark and we were just sitting down to enjoy a drink, when suddenly a bright ball of light emerged from the top of the hill and moved quite quickly in an arc across the sky. I said, 'Did you see that?' to my companions. The husband had seen it because he had been facing in the same direction as I had, but the wife had not, since her back was to it. Aeroplanes do sometimes [fly] overhead, but I thought this moved too quickly and was only a single light, whereas planes at night usually have several. I thought it might have been a military flare or something like that but subsequent enquiries showed there had been no army exercises in the area at the time. So we just called it an U.F.O. – that is, unidentified by us. (4469)

Unusual as this account is, it is as nothing compared to the second, much longer account in the archive involving a shared encounter with a UFO-type lightform. This account, submitted to the RERC in March 1987, describes an experience that took place in August 1968 when the respondent was on holiday with his girlfriend and another couple at a rented cottage in Irish Hills, Michigan. They arrived late at night and the first few days were apparently uneventful. The respondent then describes how he was in his car with his girlfriend, at night, drinking beer, when

> Suddenly she got very tense and nervous and said there's something out there! About this time the other couple had come along and asked what was wrong and she told them the same thing. My friend and I said we would go up the road and see if we could see anything. My girlfriend became very upset and insisted that we both stay with them in the car. There were absolutely no noises of any kind from insects or other wildlife whatsoever which was most unusual as it was a rather warm summer night.
>
> As he and I approached the road to the cottage area I noticed a pulsating light down the road [at] a distance that was in the shape of a surfboard and appeared to be hovering about a foot off the ground. Knowing that I was not drunk or hallucinating and not wanting to sound crazy, I said nothing but was greatly relieved when he asked me if I saw that light; and being relieved, said, yoo.
>
> As I stated the light seemed to pulsate, first dimming and then growing brighter. My friend who was a good deal more braver than I started walking

towards the light in spite of my suggestion that we return to the girls and the car.

As we approached or rather tried to approach the light it would recede from us and only return when we would backtrack our footsteps. Several attempts were made to approach and each time the light would recede.

At this point, the pair of friends were distracted by a second strange phenomenon: 'a sound coming from the brush on the side of the road to our left' apparently approaching the road and then moving away, *back* into the brush. Clearly, the writer's courage was indeed considerably less than that of his friend, who then decided to go into the brush with a knife and torch to investigate the sound more closely. Finally, however, not wanting his friend to be left alone 'facing God knows what', he changed his mind and followed him, only to find the foliage too thick and impenetrable. Back on the road again, they began to return to the car, 'when the noise again started only this time much closer to us'. The writer continues:

> As we again paused to listen to the sound, suddenly from a bush directly in front of us there came a single loud expulsion of air as if it were someones dying breath. I was petrified and the knife literally fell from my hand and I couldn't move. I don't know how long I stood there but vaguely remember . . . my friend pulling my arm and leading me back to the car.
>
> Upon our return to the car both girls themselves were in a state of terror and stated that they felt as if they were being watched and heard heavy breathing. It was at this point that the experience was just too much for me and I broke down and started crying due to the terror I had felt. (4812)

Interestingly, the account continues by describing subsequent attempts made by the writer to determine the exact nature of the phenomena that had frightened him so. The possibility that the 'surfboard'-shaped light might be swamp gas was quickly discarded on the grounds that nothing resembling a swamp 'or for that matter any wet area' could be found in the vicinity. Later still, after the holiday had ended, the writer discovered that another party in the state of Wisconsin had experienced something similar on another occasion, although this piece of potentially corroborative detail is weakened somewhat when the overall size of the state is considered: quite apart from the fact that the writer's experience took place in the state of Michigan.

None the less, his experience seems to have had a spiritual effect on him at least somewhat akin to that of the Falls Road soldier whose account has been examined above. For the Michigan respondent, the overall 'fruits' of the event included a turning to Hatha Yoga and a deepened interest in spiritual matters, and he adds to his account of his experience that it 'has had a profound impact on my point of view and life philosophy as well.' He ends by wondering, ruefully, 'what would have happened if we had let the light come to us.'

Both the Kenyan and Michigan UFO-related cases contain significant parallels with a number of cases that can be found in the now-massive body of UFO literature. The Kenyan case bears interesting comparisons both with other cases reported from Africa and with the work of Paul Devereux and Michael Persinger who have long maintained that unusual lights may emerge *from the ground*, often at places of tectonic strain and frequently just before, during or after episodes involving earthquakes and/or smaller earth tremors (Devereux 1982). While the Kenyan case appears to have aroused in the author little more than a mild curiosity, it is worth noting that, like the Michigan case, it was felt worthy of subsequent checking by the parties involved, who appear to have satisfied themselves that it was unrelated to any military exercises taking place in the area at the time.

Shadows without lights

Also unparalleled elsewhere was another shared account located in the archive in which the subject and his companion found themselves casting shadows on the ground as if a strong light was present and shining on them from behind but where no light could be discerned. The respondent, writing in 1971, refers to an event that took place 'some 12 years ago' when 'a friend and myself spent a few days at Easter at a remote Lakeland Inn. I was about 54, & he about 52.' The subject adds that his wife, at the time of the experience, was ill and in a London nursing home. On Easter Sunday the landlord of the inn invited the two friends to the morning church service and afterwards they began to discuss 'the Service and its religious aspect' before drawing very different conclusions. Clearly, while the friend was inclined towards a 'scientific' reading of the Bible, the subject was 'a believer in the C. of E.' Later, deciding on a walk before bedtime, the two friends set off:

> It was a beautiful night, with no moon & only the stars & the outline of the mountains to be seen, & not a sound to be heard.
>
> After a quarter of a mile along the lonely lane our two shadows appeared in front of us & continuing for a further ten minutes got brighter & sharper

as if a bright light was behind us, but there was no light & no moon, & eventually the vision faded.

I don't mind saying that I was troubled & possibly frightened as if I was in the presence of something beyond understanding & even my learned friend was shaken.

Reflecting on the meaning of the experience in his 1971 letter, the writer adds: 'I think at the time, I thought of the Bible story of the Burning Bush, & was it Moses? was also frightened.' He recalls that, after the return from the trip 'I told my wife the story & quite simply she said "It was only God reminding you that He *is* there."' He adds: 'Shortly after, she died' (2519).

This strange account of an invisible light casting strong shadows which was interpreted in religious ways by the subject and his wife is rather unusual in that it troubles and frightens the respondent and even shakes the 'learned friend'. Unlike the Falls Road Marian apparition – and, as we shall see, unlike most of the remainder of the shared light encounters which we will consider – the experience appears to result in disquiet and distress rather than peace and comfort. The implication at the end of the account is that the light may have been conforming to the writer's wife's interpretation of it: coming to remind the subject of God's presence, in anticipation of his wife's passing and his own, subsequent widowhood. We do not know, because he does not tell us, whether the experience was of any comfort to the writer in the years following the episode. As we will now see, however, the appearance of calming, peaceful, loving light in the midst of illness, grief, anxiety and distress appears to be a consistent feature of a number of shared experiences of it, bringing us closer to a fundamental feature of encounters with unusual lights that may point towards their possessing some kind of a common core, identity or source.

'Crisis lights'

Five accounts out of the ten shared experiences of light appeared at times of clear crisis and usually in association with a serious, life-threatening illness. In some instances, the light appeared actually to presage a death, paralleling in certain respects the corpse-candle tradition already discussed. If it makes any sense to talk of the light possessing or arising from a common core (or perhaps performing some sort of consistent, core *function*), then its appearance and sometimes comforting presence in times of human distress and duress must be considered as a primary aspect of this potential core.

This at present tentative conclusion is certainly suggested by some clear and intriguing consistencies exhibited by the following shared accounts. Consider this one, for example, written in August 1971 about an experience that occurred many years previously:

> It was during 1914–18 war, I was 15 years old & my sister age 17 years had died with TB. Just two or three days before this happen[ed] she was in [the] same room [as me and my mother]. I was sleeping with my dear mother & I saw a most beautiful light coming from [the] corner of [the] ceiling just like we see when Our dear Lord's in pictures. I said Mum & she answer[ed] me by saying did you see it, so we both witness[ed] it.
>
> In those days we had no Electric lighting, the street lamp was gas mantles what had to be lighted by men & also no cars, but it was most beautiful & I will never forget it. (2866)

The writer of this account is clearly not an educated lady, but the attempts made (and discarded) to find alternative 'conventional' explanations of an apparently heavenly light show that the writer had clearly considered these: no electric lights, no cars and apparently no explanation to be had from the existence of gas street lighting will do to explain the light seen. The lack of a conventional explanation for what was experienced is also present in the following account, quoted here in full:

> In 1937, while still teaching, I nursed my father for five months. He died of cancer in 1966. When I learned that my aunt (mother's sister) who was one of our family, aged 84 years, was a cancer victim, I was appalled at the thought of having to nurse her. Now retired, I was able to devote myself entirely to my nursing duties which this time lasted for three months.
>
> One night I settled my [aunt] patient for the night and sat down in my chair near her bed, with my back to the window.
>
> Why, I do not know, but my eyes seemed drawn to the corner of the room. There, at the top of the wall shone a small light which slowly grew in size and brilliance. I could not withdraw my gaze but I had no sense of fear. I determined to be quite practical and made myself look out of the window, thinking that an outside light might be reflected in the bedroom but there was no outside light. I sat down again and kept my eyes on the light. I have never, before or after, felt such a sense of peace and comfort. I felt a powerful presence in the bedroom and I knew that I would be given Divine strength to carry on with my duty to the end. I felt an exhilaration, a peace and well being and I knew that I had been given a manifestation of God's care for me, unworthy though I was. I went to sleep, calm and re-assured, knowing that the burden was no longer mine.

There was an unexpected sequel to my experience.

On the following night, when I had again attended my patient, I noticed that she did not, as usual, close her eyes. I followed her gaze and was surprised to realise that she was staring up above at the very place where the light had shone for me. I asked my Aunt what she was looking at. She replied: Nothing.

I said: Come on. Tell me. What do you see up there? She replied: I'm not going to tell you. It's a secret.

My aunt died a few days later. I am convinced that we were both, however unworthy, privileged to be granted this manifestation of Divine help in our hour of need.

I can assure you that none of the above account is due to imagination. I am a very practical person. (2026)

This extremely interesting testimony is noteworthy for a number of reasons. As was the case with the previous account, it is clear that the light appears at a point of great anxiety and in the midst of a situation where a life is nearing its end. To this extent, in fact, it bears close comparison with a number of comparable accounts collected by William Barrett of visions reported by the dying and reproduced in his 1927 classic *Deathbed Visions* and also with a smaller number of shared accounts of such visions reproduced by Karlis Osis and Erlendur Haraldsson in their more recent study *At the Hour of Death* (Barrett 1986; Osis and Haraldsson 1997). In addition, the light in the account clearly brings with it – at least for the carer – a great sense of peace, bestowing feelings of comfort, exhilaration, well-being, calmness, reassurance and strength to endure in the midst of a situation of clear distress: another characteristic of deathbed visions generally, and reminiscent of the previous respondent's description of the light as 'most beautiful'.

Further, whilst not witnessed simultaneously by aunt and niece, there is a strong implication that the same light was being gazed at by both of them on two separate but related occasions in this account: at least, the shared location of what was seen implies that this was so – although it is interesting that the carer did not see the light on the second occasion when, we may assume, the aunt did. Finally, it is of note that, as with the previous account, the writer went to some lengths to discount 'conventional' explanations of where the light may have come from before concluding that it must have had some sort of divine origin. At one point she actually relates how she looked away from the light and out of the window in order to look for an outside source. In addition, as an appendage to her original handwritten account, she adds a diagram of the room designed to show how the location of the light could not have been outside and hence shining through the window. As with the previous account, this piece of corroborative detail, whilst not absolutely conclusive, is at the very least impressive.

Another comparable account, equally impressive in detail, can be added to those already examined. It was sent to the centre in August 1971 and concerns an experience that took place in 1932. In the account, the writer, the writer's 'premature, frail' baby son, and her mother went together to a bedroom they were to share after mother and baby had arrived in Penarth, the mother's home town, where the experience took place. As the writer states,

> We put the baby in a bassinette in the corner, on my side of the double bed. There was one tall window only, well away from the cot, which was in a corner, and it was a back bedroom (house built in 1910).
>
> About 2 a.m (it was a still night) I awoke suddenly and was conscious at once of a BLUE light in the room. I turned my head and saw suspended over the baby's cot a large blue star which remained there, distinct in outline, for quite five minutes and then faded away.
>
> In some astonishment, (but I recollect, no fright), I lay in silence for about an hour. Suddenly, the light appeared again, and once more, the star. This time, a soft voice said quietly, 'Dolly?' – it was my mother. I replied 'yes'. 'Do you see what I am seeing?' The answer was 'yes', and she further astonished me by remarking that she had been aware of it an hour previously but had been afraid to see if I was awake, or had noticed it, in case she was suffering perhaps from 'delusions'. To this day, I do not know why either of us saw this phenomenon. The star was right over the cot. (2287)

As with the previous two accounts it is clear that the light appears in a context of anxiety, for we may reasonably assume that the frail, premature son was giving cause for concern. There is a difference, however, concerning the events that were to follow the episode in that the son *survived*: going on, as the writer states, to gain a degree at Cardiff university and himself to father a child. The 'normality' of his life, however, only appears to have reinforced her view that the light was inexplicable, for she ends her account by remarking: 'This experience is in no way explainable, as my son has done (so far) nothing remarkable to help mankind or distinguished himself in any way.'

Another apparent difference between this and the previous two accounts is that the light appears to have had no calming influence on either the writer or her mother: the only emotions recounted are astonishment and a lack of fear. It is also interesting to note that the light appeared not once but twice and was seen by both witnesses on both occasions. As with the previous two accounts, however, the writer entertains and discards 'conventional' explanations for the light. As she states, there was only one window in the room, it was well away from the cot, and the bedroom was at the back of the house where presumably no outside street lights were shining. The colour of the light also deserves brief comment here. As is clear, on both occasions it is described as *blue*. Whilst we have not so far seen any other descriptions of the light as having this colour within the category of shared experience, analysis of the other categories of light experiences in the archive will shortly make clear that blue lights are rather consistently encountered.

A further incidence of an apparently shared experience of light at a point of extreme crisis is provided by the following account which took place at an undisclosed date and location. In it, the writer reports how

> My father had had a severe heart attack and I laid him down in bed, semiconscious. Then put out the light and let him sleep. Suddenly he turned his head and looked over to a corner of the room. There was a bright light shining, which, on looking at my father, was reflected in his eyes. 'I have seen the Glory of God and I am not to die yet' he said. He lived and walked about for another year. I am 69 and can see that light in my memory as if it were yesterday. Never have I seen a light which could compare with it. (2031)

In addition to its appearance at a point of crisis involving life-threatening danger, it is clear that this experience, like the other 'crisis lights' examined, possesses an unusual nature. The writer makes no mention of looking for a 'conventional' source but strongly implies that it was no ordinary light by making reference to its incomparable quality. The father survived his encounter with it by a year, suggesting the intriguing possibility that this might actually be a 'shared NDE', both father and daughter seeing the light that, whilst frequently reported by NDErs, does not necessarily presage the immediate death of them. No calming feelings are reported by the subject, but the father's exclamation strongly suggests that the encounter was both positive and meaningful and even, perhaps, communicated something to him.

What has been emerging with particular force over the course of this analysis is the existence of a particular category of light experience that occurs at times of clear crisis. As has already been suggested, the occurrence of unusual lights, defying 'conventional' explanations, and manifesting at times of extreme crisis might even be said to hint at a common core or function that such lights possess. What has been additionally interesting and emerging in this chapter has been the fact that so many encounters with unusual lights, whether in contexts of crisis or not, are, in fact, *shared*. Shared deathbed visions are rare in the literature. Osis and Haraldsson mention only two or three, Barrett none at all, and neither source includes shared visions of *light*. To this extent, the present study has already drawn attention to a highly interesting category of shared religious experience that has been hitherto rare in the literature. It is to be hoped that more accounts may now be forthcoming, not least because of the possibilities of corroboration that these experiences afford.

Two more cases of shared experiences of unusual lights remain for analysis. The first involves the by now typical context in which a life is apparently in danger, but is unusual in that the sick person was not apparently present where the light was seen. The case occurred at Mansfield, Nottinghamshire in the early hours of 18 October 1962 at 1.30 a.m. The subject's brother had called the evening prior to the experience, and this visit had deeply concerned her. He had, she writes,

> looked very, very ill & how he had managed to come at all I just do not know. Outside it was deep in snow with gale force winds. He asked me to do something for him which was almost impossible. He would take no refusal & as he was so ill I promised I would do all I could. That evening I could not settle & before going to bed [I] prayed for help.

This prior situation of deep anxiety and concern was then followed by a dramatic experience:

> At 1.30 a.m. I was still awake & looked across to the mantle shelf to verify the time as my husband had to be up at 5 a.m. for work. Instead of seeing the clock I saw a round white light but as the clock was luminous [I] thought it strange not to see the figures. I got out of bed & went towards the light & it vanished. I got back into bed & lay pondering. The room was in total darkness. I lay hoping it would come back & suddenly a tall white candle of light sprang up wavering at the top, I was so terrified that I slid out of bed & hid my face. When I got into bed again I woke my husband. He put out his hand to touch it & I said 'Don't'. We lay there almost petrified. I said to my husband, 'Don't go to sleep. It may go.' & suddenly

It sank down & out, then I said 'Let's wait & see if it comes back' and immediately It did so. Altogether it must have been with us about 1 hour & 20 mins.

The writer appears to have connected the presence of the unusual candle of light with her brother's illness because she immediately follows this description with the comment that 'The next day I had three offers of help for my brother, who recovered his health.' Altogether this is a most unusual and remarkably detailed account. The fact that the light disappears and reappears has been encountered before, as has the positive outcome of the episode, and it clearly resembles the other shared crisis light accounts in that the light appears in a context of extreme duress. But here the similarities end. The wavering shape of the light, compared with a candle's flame, has no parallel elsewhere. The emotional response is also unusual: rather than produce feelings of peace and calm, the light terrifies both witnesses. Finally it is of note that the *duration* of the experience is quite remarkable. Indeed, few of the experiences examined in the course of this entire study approach anything like the eighty minutes that this episode apparently occupied. The fear of both witnesses during this time can only be imagined, and we recall the writer's later recollection that 'We lay there almost petrified' (2362).

A final account in this category also reveals similarities and differences with cases so far examined. As with the case in which the niece saw a light in a corner of the room where her aunt later gazed before dying, the case implies a shared experience but does not explicitly state it. The subject's account begins with the death of her son in November 1964. At this point, she writes, her four-year-old daughter began to have conversations in bed with an unseen presence. When asked who or what she had been talking to, the daughter claimed that it was Jesus. The account continues:

Then one morning after she had been having a very lengthy conversation the night before, I casually asked her who she had been talking to. She said it was a pretty lady. I asked her to describe the lady and she did. She gave me a detailed description of the Virgin Mary. At this time my daughter was not yet five and had not had any religious instruction. After that her conversations stopped and I thought nothing more about it.

Then in Nov. '66 my mother died. A few weeks after her death I went into my daughter's room and there was a dim light over her bed. It disappeared as I entered the room and I put it down to tired eyes. But that light was there again many times, until I moved my daughter into another room with her younger sister.

This account is included in the 'shared' category because there is a clear implication that the presences the daughter talked to were in some sense identical with the dim light the mother saw. The proximity of the light to the daughter's bed suggests this, but it is clear that at no point did mother and daughter 'view' the light simultaneously. In other respects, however, it bears close comparison with the other cases already examined in this category. There is at least an implication that the deaths of the writer's son and mother were associated with the light's arrival. The recurrence or return of the light on more than one occasion is also by now a familiar feature. Also noteworthy is the positive, benign effect of the light, particularly on the daughter, for at the end of her account, the writer adds:

> My daughter is now eleven and is a perfectly normal child, except that she has never been really ill in her life. She has had the normal child ailments like measles and chicken-pox, but even they didn't get her down like they do other children. As far as I or my husband can remember she has not even had a cold. (2537)

Does the writer mean to suggest here that the daughter's remarkable health is in some sense the result of the earlier presences and/or light? Again, this is at least implied, and the detail is particularly poignant in view of the tragic circumstances that signalled the beginning of this curious series of conversations and sightings.

Conclusions

The accounts in the RERC archive containing shared experiences of unusual light, whilst few in number, are fascinating in detail and quality, and analysis of them has yielded some interesting findings. It has become clear, for example, that the shared light accounts in the archive bear clear resemblances to shared light accounts elsewhere, but that in a couple of cases there are accounts with unique features. What to make, for example, of the curious tale of two shadows with no light to cast them or the curious breathing in the spooky Michigan UFO case? As far as I am aware, these features are without parallel in the extant relevant literature.

Secondly – and of extreme importance to anybody interested in seeking a common core within the various types of spiritual and religious experience – these shared cases contain consistent, common features. The fact that fully 50 per cent of the shared experiences of light occurred at a time of crisis is the most obvious finding in this regard. In fact, over 50 per cent of the number of experiences of light in the entire archive occurred at a time of crisis, as the next few chapters will show. Other consistent features that the shared experiences of light have contained have been the positive, uplifting feelings they bring to at least some witnesses and the positive 'fruits' they leave in their lives. We may recall, for example, the lady nursing her aunt who spoke of remarkable exhilaration, peace and well-being at a time of deep anxiety, and of the Belfast soldier's deepened interest in spiritual matters subsequent to his Falls Road encounter with the Blessed Virgin Mary.

To be sure, there have been some exceptions to this emerging pattern. The shared accounts, for example, contain a significant number of expressions suggesting that negative, frightening emotions accompanied at least *some* experiences. The Michigan UFO case is terrifying virtually throughout. The nocturnal Mansfield candle-shaped light also clearly petrified the respondent and her husband. And in the case of the shadows in the absence-of-light case, the dominant emotions engendered seem to have been negative. Having said this, it should be kept in mind that despite negative feelings being reported in three cases, in the majority of shared accounts the emotions recounted remained overwhelmingly positive in tone. It remains to be seen whether future chapters exploring other 'types' of unusual light experiences will discover a patterning similar to that which this chapter has begun to uncover.

4

A light when alone: solitary experiences of unusual light

Definitions

Eighty-six accounts fell under the heading of solitary experience of unusual light, making it the largest single category. As will become clear, the accounts in this chapter contain some consistent themes and details which reveal a 'type' of unusual light that appears to a *single* witness, apparently 'superimposed' on that witness's environment. In addition, this 'superimposed' light appears to have a *specific location* in relation to the solitary witness; a location that can be described precisely.

Although, as we will see, there are some variations on these central themes, there are clear consistencies also. Some examples may help to make this clearer. The first is described by a forty-year-old respondent as occurring when she was a fifteen-year-old evacuee living in Berkshire during the Second World War. She had taken a job in a private household, and her account describes how

> The mistress of the house had the task of telling me my brother had been killed in Italy. This was naturally a terrible shock.
>
> That same evening I went to bed as usual in a bungalow attached to the main building. It was a dark night & the employers had gone out to a party so the main house was in darkness. I mention this for a reason which will become clear later on.
>
> Feeling utterly depressed &, as I am not 'religious', except for the usual Sunday School & occasional Matins (C of E) – also feeling *lost* I pondered over the great mysteries. Why are we born? Where are we going? What's life all about? Etc.
>
> Suddenly there was a misty ball of light over towards the door of my room, I will repeat, this door opened on to the garden & in any case my employers were all out for the evening. My mind seemed to 'change gear'. I use car terminology to suggest a change of normal activity difficult if not

impossible to describe. It was as if a voice spoke in my head 'Don't worry any more about X he is quite well and happy.' On 'hearing' this I suddenly felt quite relaxed after the great emotional storm of the day. I have never since then worried about the after-life & have been content to leave it in God's hands. During my years of agnosticism I have often recalled and tried to explain the foregoing experience to myself in terms of 'hysteria', 'overwrought imagination' etc. But today at age 40 I am convinced it was real, true, & not to be explained away. That it was a message to me for comfort and inspiration. (982)

There are a number of features of this account that will deserve more detailed attention later in this book. For now, however, it is enough to note how specifically the witness *locates* the light: it is not a vague, diffuse or general illumination; rather, it appears 'over towards the door' that opened on to the garden. A second account from a different respondent that pinpoints the light's location in a similarly specific way describes how

A very dear friend had died suddenly without warning – I was wakened during the night, my room pulsating with life & filled with a rosy light, this was very deep in far left corner; I was thrilled & puzzled. The next day I learned of the death. This pulsating life continued for about another week in another room where I sat down very late at night working at my books & the friend had always fiercely disapproved of this – I stopped & so did the pulsating. (682)

Identifying the light

Another experience is noteworthy for two reasons; first, in its implication that once again the light had a specific location (at the centre of the room and not at its perimeter) and secondly because of the subject's surprise at how the figure within the light actually *looked*. We have already noted and will have much more to say as this study progresses regarding the question of whether people's expectations determine and create what they experience. For now, we simply note the remark made by the subject towards the end of his account that suggests that the figure he saw may have *corrected* a prior impression as to how it might be expected to look. The experience occurred at a time of crisis when the subject was at a loss to decide how he might cope with his mentally deteriorating wife. He writes:

In August of 1949, I recall I had had a particularly trying day at work and on arrival home I could do absolutely nothing to please. I well remember my prayer of that night – 'Oh Lord, take her from me; take her from this life.'

At this period I found it difficult to sleep following many continuous nights of broken sleep answering her many calls and it had become a habit to prop myself up in bed while waiting for her to go to sleep. It may be argued that what followed was a fantasy dreamed while in a half-sleep, the wish-fulfilment of an exhausted and tired mind, a sub-conscious desire for solace or, maybe, sympathy.

However, in the early hours of the following morning (it was very dark) it seemed that the room gradually filled with light in much the same manner as the slow progression from darkness to light in a Cinema. This is difficult to describe. It was not light in the accepted sense – rather a diffused glow which left the perimeter of the room in deeper darkness. I was intrigued rather than frightened and filled with a peculiar sense of quiet and magnified perception. The glow of light slowly assumed the shape of a man. Quite tall, he was dressed in a loose white robe, had thick, dark, shoulder length hair in the style of an Ethiopian, a small dark beard (no moustache), a prominent but symmetrical nose and the most sad and compassionate brown eyes I have ever seen. He just looked at me over his left shoulder, smiled, and said 'I – am the resurrection and the life.' During this brief dream, hallucination, call it what you will, one thought persisted in my mind. 'He's dark skinned. Of course he would be dark.'

The suggestion here that the experience may have been a dream is puzzling, as the subject's own later reflections on the episode seem to rule this out completely. The fruits it left suggest something more than a 'mere' dream also:

Dream? Hallucination? I saw the Lord Jesus. I remember that I was sitting up in bed, wide awake, wondering at the fact that I had never previously considered that he would be dark. I lay down. Although my problems were still with me I was filled with wonderment, a sense of ease and relief, and of guilt. Guilt, in that I had prayed for my happiness in this life – not her happiness or our happiness – just mine alone. That feeling remained for a long time. (2494)

Another particularly vivid description of the light's apparent identity in addition to its location is given by the following respondent, whose experience occurred at a time of deep spiritual distress:

From about 16 years I attended an evangelical Bible Class – Crusaders – & consciously or unconsciously resisted the appeal to be 'corrected', but I began to read the Bible & to pray regularly. Some months later my sister got married & for the first time I had a bedroom to myself.

One night I suddenly woke up & saw a blazing light between the cupboard & the wardrobe – I could see nothing but the light, yet I knew

Jesus was in the midst of it. I scrambled from bed, fell on my knees & sobbed my heart out, asking forgiveness for my stubbornness & sin, & yielding my life to Him – I was in fact 'converted'. Looking back, I can remember many 'links in the chain' by which God gradually drew me {to} Himself – but I suppose I was too obstinate & pigheaded, too sure of my own self sufficiency, and so, like St. Paul, I had to have a blinding light before I would believe – though unlike him I did not then become a 'saint'. (1775)

Yet another identification of the light as Jesus is given in the following, long, account, notable also for the situation of deep crisis which it describes:

I married and had a son and after nearly 21 years of marriage which I liken to a good wine which improves with keeping, I was suddenly told that my husband had cancer of the stomach and nothing could be done for him. I nursed him day and night for 3 months and was given the strength to do this and keep the knowledge from him. During this time we both received the Sacrament at home and my husband received the laying on of hands each week. My husband died when I was in my middle forties, exactly 3 years ago tomorrow. I got myself a job after a few months, working to the point of exhaustion for a Consultant Physician in a large Hospital. Meanwhile I had been left with a son at the very rebellious age of 17. He had just started a new job, 18 months after his father's death and was driving home in terrible conditions, when his car went into a skid on a corner – which could happen to anyone – and he crashed. I received the 'phone call alone, to say he was injured. His leg had been smashed and he was in Hospital for 5 months. I felt that it was not possible to endure any more and then, as I lay in bed one night, not praying or even thinking of anything, a light was turned on at the foot of my bed and there was Our Lord and as he looked at me so He raised His arms and blessed me and then He was gone. I can remember everything about Him vividly, His clothes, His face and the movement of His arms as they were raised to bless me, but the thing that strikes me so vividly is the remembrance of the feeling of my mind actually being emptied in preparation for this experience. I feel so grateful and full of humility. My faith has, since then, increased daily. (2241)

That the light seen was clearly of an identifiably spiritual or religious nature is also implied by the following unusual experience that occurred when the subject had just entered a prayer hall. 'As I entered the hall', she writes,

I was suddenly filled with a most wonderful joy & found myself smiling, as one does on suddenly meeting a friend: about 6 ft. in front of me was a large oval of light but {with} nothing in the middle of it, like an empty photograph frame. I found myself thinking, 'If only I had been a minute earlier I would have seen Him.'

Whilst it is clear that the light is sometimes identifiable as a religious presence or figure, this is by no means always the case, as the following experiences will make clear. The first describes a moving encounter with a lost loved one:

I lost my husband just on 24 years ago and on this particular Sunday . . . I had been thinking about him all day. You see it was the anniversary of his death. Well I was watching a programme (BBC2) called the Messiah which was being [televised] from Ely Cathedral. I was sitting in the dark and there was only the light from the Television when all of a sudden there appeared a very bright light in the corner of the room and it was my husband all in white . . . I was so overjoyed I called out his name but the vision slowly vanished. I felt as if I wanted to rush out and tell someone as I do live on my own. I may add this was no illusion but real, [and] a great experience for me. (2182)

Another experience describes an unusual light with an identifiable *voice*:

I had been suffering very great grief since my brother suddenly died about two years ago. We had lived together since my husband's death.

One day, just after breakfast I stood quietly before starting housework etc when I heard a faint sound & looking up I saw a very bright light just like the sun in my room & the sound of my Mother's Voice (who passed away some years ago).

I knew her voice at once (not like our voice); and I seemed to know she was telling me to look after my sister who is very deaf & has difficulty in seeing things properly which makes her unhappy. (1964)

The following most unusual account describes in vivid detail the overwhelmingly positive feelings which are emerging as typical of light experiences. But, whilst these might sometimes be expected to form part of experiences in which religious figures or deceased loved ones are encountered, what is unusual in this account is the clothing in which an apparently unidentified figure surrounded by light appears. The subject, twenty-eight years old at the time of his experience, describes how

I had been reading a chapter of a book, smoked half a cigarette and turning off the bedside lamp fell into a deep sleep. In the early hours of the morning I was having a very vivid dream which on reaching a climax I awoke with the sensation of an explosion in the head. On awakening I was inclining my head to the right side, the room was pitch black, I lay for some seconds in this position thinking over the dream. When turning my head to my left I was suddenly aware of a figure standing by the side of me. He was dressed in Royal Navy uniform, and would be about my own age at the time. The figure was as solid as any mortal except for the fact he was surrounded by brilliant light, like the sun only it did not dazzle the eyes. Great waves of peace were emanating from this figure as he smiled down upon me, indescribable, I have never felt the like since . . . [After what] seemed an endless time the wonderful light surrounding the figure began to slowly change to the most magnificent colours, finally going to a deep purple, ever deeper the figure merging with the colour and finally all merging into the night, once again leaving the room in pitch darkness . . . I remained sitting for perhaps half an hour thinking how marvellous it all was, then I lay down and slept till morning light. (1035)

A light associated with an *unseen* presence was encountered by the following respondent. Once again, note the situation of deep unhappiness into which the light appears:

I was going through a period of extreme unhappiness which made me question the conventional C. of E. beliefs in which I was brought up. I was unable to sleep one night & it was going through my head that religion had failed me completely when I became aware of brilliant light & a presence on my right side, a feeling of overwhelming peace & love & a voice saying 'I am there.'

Afterwards I slept & when I woke I had the feeling that nothing would ever be the same again & that my doubts had gone for ever.

Times of crisis

The following experiences also appear to have occurred at times of trauma and crisis, adding to a growing suspicion that there is a link between such distressing times and the manifestation of unusual lights. An experience submitted to the RERC in July 1971 makes this link particularly clear:

Ten years ago my husband was in hospital, dying of cancer, I was sitting alone in the lounge, in despair.

I had the feeling that I was no longer alone, & saw a figure of light standing quite near me. That is the best way I can describe what I saw, as It appeared as a form, about 5ft tall, & I know that it radiated comfort to me; all my worries faded away, & I was elevated to Heaven, & carried right out of this world. No miracle saved my husband, but I am convinced that this was an angel of goodness; sent to comfort me. (2212)

Another experience of light that appears to have had a definite location appeared to a woman who was deeply worried after reuniting with her husband after a separation lasting seven years. She writes:

> My husband and I had been separated for seven years, and had decided to reunite (for the sake of my son, then aged twelve). The three of us spent this night on the [boat] and I occupied the lower bunk in the cabin. I was very worried as to whether I had made a wise decision and was wishing for corroboration from 'God or someone'.
>
> In the middle of the night I woke to see a light growing in the cabin. It grew in intensity until it seemed six feet or more tall, with rays shooting out in all directions. I put up my hand to try to pull the blankets off my husband in the upper bunk [to wake him] so that he could see it too. I was not frightened, just full of wonder. I was overcome by a feeling of reverence, and felt obliged to get out of bed and kneel on the floor and bow my head before the brilliant presence. A voice seemed to say, 'You have made the right decision. A daughter will complete your happiness.'
>
> The light began to lessen, and I thought 'Dare I look up? I must catch a glimpse of him before he goes'. I saw the shooting rays change from white to all pastels – pink, blue etc, but I could see no form. The light slowly dimmed until the cabin was in darkness again. I woke my husband and told him about it, and he wishes he had seen it too.

The writer ends by adding that, sure enough, 'a daughter was born to complete our happiness' and insists: 'This vision was not a dream. I could feel the blankets as I got out of bed, and the hard floor under my knees as I knelt' (1142).

Difficult to dismiss as a mere dream is the following experience, related by a man who at the time it occurred was 'in bed alone, therefore sitting up, [and] the light of the room was then on'. Obviously in a state of some distress he turned the light out whilst still sitting up. He writes:

> I then thought of various matters and these caused me to lightly lachrimate . . . then suddenly there shone at the right hand side of the mantelshelf a clear bright light, silver-white and from it came a voice which said, 'These are your friends.'
>
> I then felt as though this had removed the sadness of the moment prior completely, and I simply and easily lay down and slept. (2201)

It is clear that times of crisis appear conducive to the occurrence of unusual lights – at least those of the present category. Before moving on to examine some other characteristics, however, one final crisis-related light remains to be examined. This one is unusual, however, in that the light seems to have appeared *before* the onset of a series of traumatic events. The subject writes:

> In 1952, moving into an old house, I had a golden glow just above and to the right of my head, for which there seemed no natural explanation. As I moved, in my work, it moved with me. There followed the ten most terrible years of my life. The death of my dear mother, illness, accidents, marital & family troubles, &, eventually, loss of most of my sight.

She adds, by way of explanation, 'I used to wonder whether it was [a] warning or a guardian angel come to help me with my trials' (1571).

'Outdoor' lights

Up to this point it has been notable that the light described in this category has, as it were, 'chosen' to appear indoors. A variation on this theme, however, is implied by the following accounts in which the light's location is clearly described as being *outdoors*. In the first, an agnostic 'yearning for the Truth' reports how

> I was working in the field one morning . . . with {a} horse in {a} crop of sugar beet, then suddenly the horse stopped and a wonderful light shone around the leaves of beet and between the horse & myself a lovely pair of feet appeared near the bottom of the gown, and a most beautiful voice said 3 times, 'I shall come again' from then I knew. There is a real God in whom we can trust. (3856)

Another account, also occurring outdoors, includes the description, by now familiar, of anxiety as a prelude to a most uplifting experience. The subject writes how, 'anxiously wondering in my mind about a trouble connected with my daughter', she was out in the garden 'wondering and pondering' when

> suddenly a wonderful Light appeared before me . . . I can't describe the brilliance of it – but here again was the complete assurance that all would be well, and I felt a feeling of ecstasy, & again great happiness – twice I have had this wonderful Light – it shines against anything even a light blue sky, or dark trees, or in a room. (2454)

What is notable about this account is the very real sense it conveys of a single light, experienced on other occasions, appearing in a specific location to a respondent familiar with its brightness and the assurance that it brings into a situation of anxiety and crisis. The following experience, whilst apparently overpowering and dramatic, clearly seems to have produced similarly positive feelings in the subject:

I awoke, and looking out of my window, saw what I took to be a luminous star, which gradually came nearer, and appeared as a soft, slightly blurred, white light. I was seized with a violent trembling but had no fear. I knew that what I felt was great awe. This was followed by a sense of overwhelming love coming to me, and going out from me, then of great compassion from this outer Presence. After that I had a sense of overpowering peace, and indescribable happiness. I remember saying to myself, 'This is no dream, I am awake, and experiencing it with my whole self.' I remain convinced of this.

Up to this point we have repeatedly encountered the positive nature of the light, its appearance at times of crisis, and its *singularity*; we have yet to examine any accounts in which more than one light is encountered. In keeping, however, with the above observation that this category of experience permits of some variations on its central theme, that of the specific location of an unusual light reported by a single witness, consider the following account in which *more than one* light is reported:

I was born in Nov 1884, & had 7 brothers & sisters, most of them went abroad. My husband was killed outside Jerusalem, the day before Allenby marched in. I was left with a baby-boy. We had to go back home & lived with my Mother, & I looked after her until the day of her death. I was sitting looking after her one night, the nurse was resting. Suddenly I saw strange lights over her head, it was early morning, then I heard the death rattle, & ran for the Nurse. She was an R.C & did not laugh at me. (1746)

'Multiple' lights

Four further accounts in this category describe the specific location of *multiple* lights, and three of these are amongst the most unusual experiences we have examined up to now. In the first, a freshly bereaved man begins by describing a series of voices that started twenty-five days after his wife died. Twice a male voice spoke, followed shortly by his wife's voice, saying 'Take me to see him now.' Just over a month later, the lights first appeared:

Early in February 1964, strange lights began to appear in all parts of the room where I happened to be. Beautiful pale blue, slowly fading-in, and staying for a few seconds, then slowly fading out. They were at their best in a darkened room while I was by myself and thinking of her. Sometimes they came singly, very bright and large, sometimes numerous and smaller. In about the middle of February, just before settling down for the night, the lights were extra numerous, fifteen or twenty, but more numerous than previously. While contemplating them and wondering as to their significance, a different light appeared, more like a flame of light, about as large as my hands, golden flame-colour, high up in the room, approximately ten feet away. This startled me and brought an exclamation to my lips, unfortunately so, as the flame-light immediately vanished and has never returned. The other lights are now a daily experience. Over the five years from my bereavement no day has passed but that they appear. They come at all times of the day and night, in any and every part of the flat where I happen to be. They come when I am thinking of the ordinary business of life or doing the most mundane of things – a perpetual reminder of whatever it is they signify.

As an addendum to this curious sequence of events, and drawing attention to the oddness of the voices he heard before the appearance of the first lights, the writer adds, almost matter-of-factly: 'Incidentally, I am acutely deaf, and cannot hear ordinary conversation. There was no difficulty in hearing the voices' (31).

A second most unusual experience of a number of lights being experienced together is reported by a man who, at the time of his experience, had been praying regularly as part of an ongoing attempt to increase his spiritual condition. 'Every day for about a week', he writes, 'I had been trying to attune my mind with this object in view, praying regularly and trying to refine my personality generally.' He continues:

> Then one night while I was lying in bed *fully awake* it happened. Suddenly I saw several globes of very bright light floating past at the other end of the room. These were about the size of full moons. They came through the wall as if it didn't exist, floating slowly on through the opposite wall as if it offered no hindrance. I was very startled – and I must admit very afraid that one or more of them would float towards me – for I knew with absolute certainty that they were living, conscious entities, existing on another plane, and apparently not a material one. (2058)

The unusual nature of the third case of multiple lights that we will consider here consists in the feelings that their appearance create in the witness. To this point we have encountered mainly positive emotions produced, apparently, by the light's appearance: good feelings seemingly enhanced by the fact that so many episodes appear to occur in the midst of life's storms. The above account of multiple lights makes no reference to any feelings associated with them. The following account, however, makes clear the frightening feelings created by the subject's experience:

We were staying with some American friends for the first time in N. Dakota & on the first night we retired to bed at about 11.45 pm. I was on the verge of sleep when I was aware of some one or thing standing at the foot of my bed.

It was as though I was looking through a blue filmy curtain at a tall figure somewhere around 6.5 feet tall. I was so terrified that the hair on the back of my neck & head seemed to be standing on end & I was incapable of uttering a sound or waking my husband. After what seemed an age the figure started to fade & in its place the wall behind it was covered in small flashing coloured lights. This was not a nightmare but a very frightening experience & whatever it was, it felt extremely evil. We stayed a further night which was uneventful. We are very fond of our American friends but I have never plucked up courage to return to this house though I believe they have since moved. We made some enquiries re[garding] the previous location history & have been told that the area was once a Red Indian reservation and burial ground. (4546)

Despite this frightening experience, in this category of light experience and throughout all of the others, as we shall see, the encounters are almost always positive in feeling-tone, making this fearful episode unusual although not unique. The following description of an experience of multiple lights that occurred at the end of a subject's 'mood of depression' whilst he was fighting in the First World War contains the by now familiar feelings of uplift and exaltation. Walking along a river tow path, the writer talks of a feeling in which he became gradually convinced that 'Something was going to happen'. He continues:

Then it happened. The experience lasted, I would say, about thirty seconds and seemed to come out of the sky in which were resounding majestic harmonies. The thought, that is the music of the spheres [,] was immediately followed by a glimpse of luminous bodies – meteors or stars – circulating in predestined courses emitting both light and music. I stood still on the tow-path and wondered if I was going to fall down. I dropped onto one knee and thought, How wonderful to die at this moment. I put a hand over my forehead as if to contain the tumult and fend off something. Wonder, awe and gratitude mounted to a climax and remained poised for a few seconds like a German star shell. Then began the foreknown descent. The revolving flares in the sky were extinguished; the orchestration faded into silence, the river and its guarding poplars lost their magic. And the moon, which was still shining in exactly the same place overhead, regained its impersonal detachment. I got on to my feet and the thought came, Get back to your room and get into bed. You can think about all this tomorrow. (35)

Lights that move

The movement of the lights in this account is interesting, as it was in account 2058, examined above. Up to now we have noted that unusual lights sometimes appear to flicker, flash or fade in and out, but by and large there has been little indication of movement. With this in mind, however, consider the following two accounts in which clear movement of the light is reported. In the first of these, we are presented with the by now familiar context of distress:

> I was sitting in my kitchen crying, and asking for help from god, I was praying with my eyes closed, when all of a sudden i saw a light, that started to come closer and closer, it knocked me backwards off my stool, I turned over on my hands and knees and opened my eyes, but found I had no eyesight, I crawled and pulled my self up by the sink unit, I opened my eyes and still had no eyesight, I was just about to scream for help, when i heard a voice telling me not to panic, that my prayers had been heard, and that this light had defeated armies and knocked people off horses in the past.
>
> I was then told to find my stool and say my prayers and my eyesight would be returned, of which it was.
>
> I was told my life would be altered and it has. (4044)

In the second account involving movement we are presented with yet another familiar motif: like a number of the experiences so far examined within this category, the experience appears to have left lasting, positive 'fruits':

> In 1964 I had the experience of visually seeing a ball of light of undescribable brilliance, spinning and travelling at immense speed towards me from a remote distance far beyond the confinement of the walls of the room. My first feeling was of fear and yet I had an overwhelming sense of it belonging to me and when it 'hit' and engulfed me I had a feeling of unity, of warmth and peace. I thought little more of it at the time other than an unusual happening as with other odd occurrences of and about the same time. However, the memory has never diminished as one would perhaps expect after ten years; indeed it has become firmly embodied in my paintings and writings as an expression of illumination and more. Three years later, after a series of illnesses, I retired from commerce and have devoted my life to painting quietly and I hope progressively. My life has changed from an active to a more contemplative one, partly from 'choice' and partly because of a number of coronary attacks which, at the crucial times have produced rather unusual experiences, some of which I have illustrated. (3083)

It is clear, here, that a typically uplifting and positive encounter with light – 'I had a feeling of unity, of warmth and peace' – produces a number of similarly uplifting and positive changes in the subject. Quite apart from being unforgettable, it also appears to have influenced his writing and painting whilst contributing to his more 'contemplative' lifestyle. Indeed, an encounter with light leading to positive 'fruits', often spiritual in nature, was reported in several other experiences in the current category, some as yet unexamined. Consider, for example, the following account, containing an experience once again arising out of a situation of distress:

> [In] Oct. 1958, when I was 41 years old, I had the following experience: Having gone to bed, I was unable to sleep. I had had a very upsetting disappointment that day – I found myself silently 'talking to God': 'whenever I think I know it all, my God you show me that I know nothing at all'. – Then I saw a huge light, like the Sun, approaching me & I felt my whole being opening to it. I felt it enter my heart & fill it with an overpowering love.–
>
> I wondered whether I would still feel the same when I woke up next morning & then fell peacefully asleep –
>
> I awoke the next morning & was immediately aware of this love & joy still completely filling me. I had to tell my family of it, although I knew they would think me 'odd'. I told them I was 'reborn', although I had never before heard that expression used as regards to Christians. (1829)

Another experience reveals a clear link made by the subject between her warm and loving light encounter and the resolution of an anxious situation caused by the imminent posting overseas of her husband during wartime:

> We had had a very happy home with our three children, and I was feeling absolutely bereft and did not know what to do next.
>
> One night when sleeping alone in our house – I became aware that I was awake and that there was a marvellous warm loving light shining over me, and I seemed to be raised about 2 feet from the level of the bed being lifted towards the light. Then a voice said to me 'And underneath are the everlasting arms'.
>
> I cannot tell you what an indescribable feeling of comfort and joy flowed through me at the feeling of being tenderly and strongly lifted towards this wonderful warm, loving, light which was like a large oval of light right over me. I know I was awake as I could see the familiar things in my bedroom at the same time.
>
> The next day I felt quite different and able to face whatever was in store for us, and the thought of it has been a wonderful source of comfort and

strength throughout the years, especially in times of sorrow and trouble of which I have had a good deal. (2445)

The locating of the experiences examined so far into one general category has not been completely without difficulties. Despite the unifying thread running through them it is clear that there are variations in detail concerning things like the number of lights seen and the movement (or lack of movement) they exhibit. Nevertheless – and this will become clearer as we proceed – all of the experiences so far examined contain consistent features that set them apart from other categories of light experiences yet to be examined.

Even at this early stage, however, a pattern has begun to emerge quite apart from the 'superimposition' of light upon the landscape that has marked out this category as a distinct 'type' of lightform. We have noted, for example, the high proportion of experiences that seem to occur at times of anxiety and/or physical, spiritual or mental *crisis*. We have seen that in a significant number of cases the light produces overwhelmingly *positive feelings* in subjects. And we have noted carefully the *positive nature of the fruits* produced in the lives of experients by their experiences. These consistently-encountered features provide, at least, a number of motifs that we may look out for in future chapters as we examine the other categories and classifications of unusual lights that make up this study.

Drawing conclusions

As a conclusion to this chapter it will be useful to sum up its findings by presenting some final accounts that typify this 'category' of unusual light experience, accounts which contain the features of the emerging pattern of crisis/positive feelings/positive fruits that we have continued to uncover. The following account, for example, describes an encounter with a light that has a specific location and which appears in a situation of anxiety apparently in order to bring calmness, happiness and a changed future:

> The incident I wish to bring to your notice happened on 19th May '70. (1 day after my dear Husband died.) After his death I left the house and stayed with my daughter, overnight. My husband distinctly called my name after I woke. During the morning I returned alone to my empty home and immediately upon entering the hall there appeared a very bright light over my right shoulder. Somehow, without being at all alarmed, I immediately and instinctively knew that it was the spirit of my dear Husband, who had

come to reassure me that there is something beyond death, and I felt very calm and happy.

Since that time I have always felt that he is near me and helps me over difficulties, with guardian Angels around me, also. I cannot understand it all but I do feel since I lost my Husband that God is near, whereas before I was not so certain. (2293)

The next experience, which occurred, according to the writer, 'after a long period of trial and distress', also contains the features of our emerging pattern. She writes:

It was a warm and quiet summers evening. Still light and unable to sleep I lay on my back when suddenly my eyes as it were compelled by some sudden intuition were wrenched open and my gaze born upwards observed hovering above me a shape tremendously luminous bearing around the edges a flare of gold. Filled with awe (I was transfixed) I watched this hovering shape (shapeless, like a field of energy) from which issued a roar or vibrant sound and a most awesome force beyond description. I felt myself drawn up and at the same time borne down upon as if I would become it and by it be possessed and at the same time I intuitively sensed this shape in some way to be myself. So mighty and beautifull was this visitant and so awsome the power it generated that feeling I might die I cried out and it vanished. These manifestations of our mysterious destiny take courage to witness being of a nature, as yet unknown to us. But from my heart in the days that followed rose a great and joyous 'hosanna' for I felt I had seen some light in the wilderness and there is hope that man may find the wisdom yet to develop this other and furthest shores of his destiny. (1143)

The sound and identification of the luminous figure as 'in some way ... myself' reminds us also that there are clear variations as well as consistencies in the accounts we are examining and that classification cannot be done as precisely as we might seek to classify different species of, say, plants or birds. The following, final account also reminds us of how moving it is to read of the appearance of comfort and hope in the midst of agony and despair:

My husband died on a Green Line coach at 10.20 p.m. and the police informed me at 1.30 a.m.

We were a very loving husband and wife, and altho' I am resilient by nature, I was emotionally shattered.

When the police left I wanted to be on my own to wrestle with the situation,

My heart started to pound and I thought I must surely die.

I endured the agony until about 4.30 a.m. and was lying on a divan in my breakfast room.

To my amazement and wonder, the window at the foot of the divan was flooded with a wondrous gold light – the colour of 22ct. gold. I was so astounded that my heart gained control and I fell into a dreamless sleep until 7.30 a.m. when I was able to face the shock.

One cannot talk of this experience to all and sundry, but I did tell my nephew who is an Anglican Priest.

He told me that many people have seen this light, and I feel blessed that I was comforted from the great unknown. (2010)

5

Enfolded and infused: unusual lights that embrace and fill

Filled or wrapped?

A significant number of the experiences examined as part of this project, seventy-seven, contained descriptions by subjects of episodes in which they were *either filled with light (often from within) or wrapped in light (usually from without)*. The original intention was to deal with each 'type' of experience separately. However, as will become clear, it was often in practice impossible to place some accounts in either one or the other category. Consider, for example, the following episode:

> One night before my wife and I finally separated, in Feb 1957, I was very depressed. I didn't want to separate. I felt I still loved my wife. She had found another man unbeknown to me. She insisted we had to separate. We were living in downtown Toronto. She and I had been arguing in the living room. I was feeling really bad. I went into the kitchen and went into a drawer for a butch{ers} knife. I was thinking of killing myself. All of a sudden something very strange started happening to me & [I] seemed to come alight from the inside and felt a warm glow all over me and around me. It seemed to me that I was being visited by what you might call The Holy Spirit. I was not drinking. I felt good all over. Entirely different than when I walked in the kitchen. I didn't ask for help or pray before this experience happened. It just happened. But I believe some power knew what I was about to do and gave me help to prevent it . . . I don't suppose I will feel that experience again on this earth. I don't think I'll need to, or need it. It was the most wonderful feeling. I felt like I came alight like an electric light bulb. I felt warm and good all over and as if I were aglow. (1507)

On the one hand this subject appears to make clear that his experience was of a light that filled him from within. We recall his description that he 'seemed to come alight from the inside'. On the other hand, however, his description also suggests that light enfolded him or wrapped itself *around* him; particularly where he talks of 'a warm glow all over me and around me'. A second account also makes clear the fuzzy boundaries between these two types of experience: 'filled' and 'wrapped'. In it, describing a recurrent experience that typically takes place in 'the small hours of the morning', the subject describes 'thoughts [that] come to me which fill me with what I can only describe as immense light, warmth & power, and through either my forehead or diaphragm I am charged with an immense universal battery' (1434). Though short, the experience is revealing inasmuch as, on the one hand, the subject talks of thoughts *filling* him with 'immense light' which appear, on the other, to originate *outside* him: at least, this is implied by his linking of the experience to being 'charged' by some kind of apparently external 'universal battery'.

A third account also reveals why it was deemed necessary to conflate these two types of experience into one category. In it, the subject describes pausing from her normal jobs as a housewife in order 'to see whether my mind was free from all thought about something which had caused me a great deal of unhappiness and pain'. Then, she writes,

> My mind was perfectly controlled, and I was just about to give myself a pat on the back and a well-done old girl – when! my vision was completely blacked out and light seemed all about my head – not the daylight – but a light in my mind and around – I could as it were feel the walls of my head crumbling down. I cannot explain the degree of light; there is nothing to compare it with. I seemed to become this light and conciousness of my personal self seemed to be held very faintly and of no consequence – how this light was left behind or how I came out of it I do not know, but there was another light – different – a nothing or void – which I gazed at, or was aware of. There seemed to be nothing in this second light – no body – no sound – empty – and yet I knew it wasn't empty. As quickly as I had merged into light so I once more was returned to my duties. (613)

A number of features of this account deserve attention. Its sheer *oddness* is one of them. Also notable is the description of two lights. Leaving the first light behind, the writer describes 'another' light, 'different' from the first: empty yet paradoxically not empty. The blurring of category boundaries is also very apparent here: on the one hand light is experienced by the subject 'all about my head'. Yet very shortly afterwards it is contrastingly described as 'a light in my mind' as well as 'around'. Filled or wrapped? Again the distinction is unclear and once again the answer appears to be *both*. We will encounter more such 'fuzzy boundary' cases in the current classification as we proceed.

Subjects 'filled' with light

Some accounts in this category were clear in their relatively unambiguous descriptions of experiences in which subjects were filled with light. Two brief descriptions will provide some good initial examples. In the first, the subject describes 'doing nothing in particular' when 'I felt some thing start to grow inside me ... it grew untill it completely filled me, it was – a bright light – a presence, I was filled with a feeling that again I can't describe. This lasted about ten mins, then slowly disappeared' (3963).

In the second, we encounter the by now well-known context of crisis as a prelude to a most uplifting experience:

> Ill-health (mastectomy operation, not cancer though), darkness, anxiety, guilt feelings, religion a trial rather than a help or comfort. One ray of light: I visited my mother to find her in bed and obviously anxious. Out of the blue I guessed the cause (slight haemorrhage which she thought was cancer). Suddenly I felt filled with a wonderful light and I felt my face streaming with light. My mother said afterwards that she would never forget my face. This wonderful experience was short lived. (1160)

This second experience is unusual amongst the accounts we have so far examined inasmuch as the light that filled the subject was visible to others – or, at any rate, its effect was. Another unusual experience is reported by a puzzled ex-student whose light episode accompanied the discovery of a solution to a pressing theological problem. We will have more to say later in this book about the possibility that experiences of actual light may accompany mental or spiritual experiences of what is metaphorically described as 'seeing the light'. For now, we simply note the experience as it stands, in which an actual, physical flash of inner light seemingly accompanies a mental illumination leading to a theological breakthrough:

> This occurred after my return [from a French Studies course in Paris] – much contact with students/lecturers on French Catholic Theology. I had puzzled for a long time over the apparent need in Christian theology for there to be a death of Jesus – a central tenet. To my (Jewish) way of thinking, life was the important element & death a normal stage for everyone. At a bus-stop – I can pinpoint the exact stop – I had a sudden answer to my thoughts – experienced as a flash of lightning inside my head – quite physical. [It was – cf. the incident of the sacrifice of Isaac O.T transmuted into animal sacrifice. Later NT reversion to human sacrifice. I later discussed this with a major Jewish theologian, a disciple of Jung, now at Jerusalem Univ.] (3868)

Once again, we note that the light is plainly described as occurring inside the individual and given an exact location: 'inside my head'. Equally plainly described is another, longer, experience of light infilling that occurred shortly after the death of the subject's premature 6½-month-old baby:

> When I was 30 I married (my twin was married at 23), a year later I had a son on Feb 11ᵗʰ 1943 I had a second son he was small premature & quiet, at 6½ month's old he died, a non-conformist minister attended his funeral, a week later this minister said to me 'Sometimes the Saviour lifts in to the fold the little Lamb's so the Mother will follow' there, & then I confessed Christ as my Saviour but with no emotion just an act of faith one week later I lay in bed with my eldest son nearly four year's old, I was dreaming in my sleep I was kneeling in a Church then suddenly I was wide awake my son stirred in his sleep & placed both arm's around my neck, as he did so, an unearthly light seemed to come from my inmost being at a point & spread out like a triangle, the light was brilliant but did not dazzle it was clear, I had a feeling of Peace not felt on this earth, & in thought speech I heard a voice it said several things but the only one I heard was the last & it said 'You are on the right path' & the light faded, at first I felt afraid but that soon went. (2792)

Yet again, we note the time of the occurrence of the above account as one of crisis, and in the following account, yet again, we note the by now familiar good fruits that result from a light experience. In this particular case a meditating curate was 'suffused with what I can only describe as an internal explosion of light'. He adds:

> It lasted the merest fraction of a second or so, but in that time one was given what I can only describe as a Dame Julian of Norwich view of all existence . . . [a] . . . transfiguration with the knowledge that 'all manner of things would be well.' It was an experience during which one's comprehension seemed to achieve a kind of cosmic dimension. My subsequent reaction was to be healthily restored. Life around me was somehow lighter in both meanings of the word. Particularly I found this world to be very gross – large – clumsy – almost unbelievably so. (4548)

Turning-points

Striking in both its graphic description of the nature of the inner light and vivid in its description of the fruits that followed as a result of the subject's experience of it is the following account, unusual in that it happened when he was a young boy. Recalling the experience in graphic detail some sixty-seven years later, the subject writes:

In about 1905, when I was about 8, something happened that is difficult to describe in words. Analogies help, but none are exactly IT.

If one imagines one has an etheric or life body permeating the physical and imagines a light switched on to fill this body with a glow, leaving the physical unaffected except for a faint tingling, that would be an indication but not complete or precise. The atmosphere, the walls, the whole of existence had a new significance and importance, some dignity and nobility had been added or else some commonness and mediocrity had been washed out.

The mental shift also was striking. I knew with a different kind of knowing that everything was absolutely and unfailingly ALLRIGHT, valid, authentic, and I was an intrinsic part of this ALLRIGHTNESS and that whatever happened I was unique as everything else was unique, aware of another kind of existence of immutable security and importance . . .

Now nearly 70 years later, it is a memory of a memory, and I am using my present vocabulary to describe what happened to a boy of 8.

It has never recurred, alas, but has never lost its significance. Until now I have never mentioned it to anyone, it is too important for casual chat. (2929)

It is tempting to speculate as to what precisely the relationship of this light's appearance to the fruits that follow it actually is. We have already repeatedly noted the appearance of lights at times of crisis and the fruits that so often follow – with this and with previous types of experiences so far examined. Can we now go further in our search for consistency in the accounts we are examining? Could it, in fact, be the case that the reported lights somehow *ease* or resolve individuals' crises and *produce* the good fruits that so often ensue? In other words, *could it be that these lights that subjects encounter somehow represent – or in some sense create –turning-points that resolve their personal crises and transform their lives, redirecting them in new, more positive and often spiritually enriched ways?* Consider, for example, the following, brief, extract from an account that describes a subject's series of ongoing experiences: 'I think it first started two years ago I was pleading with God/my late father to help me over a problem. My head became filled with light and I became very relaxed from then on I found a way to help myself' (4339). Here, in a very simple form, we have the sequence suggested above. There is a crisis followed by a light experience leading to (or perhaps producing) a turning-point in the subject's situation. The short account ends with a very strong suggestion that the episode was also in some sense the cause for or trigger of a permanent transformation of his life.

This same sequence of 'crisis–light–turning-point–resolution' is also found elsewhere in this category. The following account gives a good example. In it, the writer begins by describing her husband's death on holiday in France. Then she describes how

> One evening I wanted to write a letter but was unable to because I was in such a state of grief & misery. I did not know what to do with myself. I had palpitations, breathlessness. I could not stop crying and I was trembling & so restless I had to walk about the room. It must sound extraordinary but I wrung my hands and said allowed {aloud}: 'I can't go on, what am I to do, I can't bear it.'
>
> Suddenly, I realised I wasn't alone and that now I must pray. I said: 'Oh Lord please help me. I can't go on like this & I don't know what to do.' I stood with my eyes shut. Gradually I was filled with a warm glow inside which increased until I felt I was held in a miraculous light. Time meant nothing, though I do not think it lasted more than 1/2 to one minute then slowly it left me & when I opened my eyes I was quite calm and composed. I was able to write the letter. Then the telephone rang & I remember answering it. I was going to read over the letter but suddenly decided to go to bed. I had a wonderful nights sleep, & the next morning I read through the letter & it was exactly what I wanted to say.
>
> I am not a particularly emotional person. I have never had any experience of that kind before & would never have thought I was the kind of person to have such a thing happen to me. I have spoken of this to a few people – I am always deeply affected & cannot stop the tears. Indeed writing this the affect is the same, and moves me deeply.
>
> Although I still grieve this experience had made me aware that however hard & seriously unbearable at times life appears to be there is still a very real purpose in it.
>
> I should like to add I have a most loving daughter, a brother & many friends who have helped and supported me – so I would have to go on in anycase – but that was a turning-point. (3808)

The same sequence is reported in the following account, once again triggered by a bereavement:

> My father died fairly suddenly. He had not been ill, but we all knew his heart was weak. In the midst of these doubts the news was brought to me during the evening, quite unexpectedly. My first reaction was for my mother and myself – tears for our loss – but whilst I was trying to take in the fact of his death, that is, in the very first few minutes – I was 'visited' (I can only use this word to describe the feeling) by such a feeling of peace, a sort of light (like an illumination from within) – a feeling of joy and warmth, such as I have never ever before experienced even in the most profound moments of happiness.

I am still confused and full of doubt and searching for some faith, I suppose, as much as ever, but since that one experience, which still stands out clearly in my mind, I feel that in fact there is something to search for and there have been moments when I have approached again this feeling – moments in the middle of periods of anxiety and doubt, when I have wakened in the night and felt a strange sort of peace, though nothing so vivid as the experience I have described. (14)

Neither of these accounts requires much further comment. The commonly reported sequence of events we have gradually discerned over the course of this analysis is present in each, and our recent linking of the light's occurrence with a turning-point in the lives of the subjects is also very clear. Indeed, as we have seen, the lady whose bereavement in France was the cause of her experience actually uses the phrase 'turning-point' at the very end of her account.

Subjects 'wrapped' in light

When we turn to consider the second 'sub-section' of this category of experience – episodes where the subject reports being 'wrapped' or 'enveloped' in light – the same pattern is once again clear. A number of further, fascinating, accounts will serve to illustrate this well, and will also draw attention to the differences between these 'wrapping' accounts and those of 'filling' that we have already defined and examined. In the first of these, whilst the 'crisis' only appears to consist of a general sense of anxiety at events, the sequence is none the less vividly described:

My mother had died, 5 years before this experience. I was at the time worried about my 19 year old unmarried daughter, who was expecting a baby. I am not a spiritualist – but attend spasmodically C. of E. church – & before that not specially religious – I was getting a meal in dusk in my kitchen & not specially thinking of anything at the time, except the general worried feeling of the time when suddenly I felt as if I was wrapped in warmth & love & arms around me from the back – and a light came down all one side of me & I saw no-one – but I felt what I took to be my mother – (don't know how I knew it was her but sure it was) telling me not to worry & that everything would turn out quite alright. After that (it's 8 years ago) everything fell into place – the young couple were married (after difficult to obtain his parents' consent) & they had a nice baby boy, and have lived 'happily ever after' – both families very pleased the way things have turned out, & now a 2nd boy too. (1949)

Note here the direct reference to 'wrapping'. Although it is not clear whether the subject was wrapped in *light* in the same way as she experienced being wrapped in warmth, love and arms, nonetheless it is clear that light does in some sense surround her, or at least part of her: we recall her assertion that 'a light came down all one side of me'.

A dramatic description of being enfolded in light is also contained in an account written by an ex-soldier whose experience took place in France in 1939. Again, note how the experience of being 'enveloped in a blaze of light' appears to constitute a turning-point in the life of the subject:

> I was back again in the Forces, this time on liaison duties, billeted at the time on an elderly French widow, whose house, not far from the Belgian frontier, was also near the farm at which I had been billeted some 25 years before when serving as a trooper in the Yeomanry. It was during the period of the phoney war, but it was a very anxious time for me & it was so strange being back again in uniform near where I had been wounded in 1915. I had been unable to sleep one night & had been reading some favourite passages from the New Testament & Psalms in a special pocket edition, a copy of which George VI had sent (I think) for Christmas to every serving officer.
>
> Suddenly I became aware of being enveloped in a blaze of light, the intensity of which it is not possible for me to describe adequately in words. It only lasted a minute or two. But, at the same time, a feeling of overwhelming well-being came over me and of complete relaxation.

He adds, simply, 'The anxiety had vanished.'

The same description of an enveloping light is given by a Church of Scotland minister whose experience took place at a time of apparently profound spiritual need. Once again it is dramatically described and the light seems to appear, as it were, right on cue:

> At Corrie, Isle of Arran, September 1941. In utter disillusionment with self and church, I came to 'the end of my tether'. In a state of intense inner wretchedness, of such intensity, that my mind seemed on the point of breaking, I got up at 4 a.m. and began wandering aimlessly in the wooded hillside. This went on for some time until, unexpectedly, the words of the one hundredth and thirtieth psalm sounded clearly in my mind – 'And plenteous redemption is ever found in Him; and, from all his iniquities, He Israel shall redeem.' With those words a light seemed to envelop me, and there flowed into my desolate heart such a flood of Love and compassion that I was overwhelmed and overpowered by the weight of it. I was stricken by such wonder and amazement that I burst into tears of joy; it seemed to flow through my whole being with a cleansing and healing

virtue. From that moment I knew that Love was the nature of reality. I was fit and well. The experience is as real today as it was then. (226)

The following account, which occurred during a time of prayer, leads the subject to a similar breakthrough into a realization of the nature of ultimate reality. This time, however, the crucial discovery leads not to love but, rather, to a state of being described in terms more reminiscent of W.T. Stace's definition of extrovertive mysticism:

> My experience happened some years ago, and I have been searching for an answer. It happened during a period of prayer that I found myself going through a tense physical struggle, somewhat similar to childbirth. I became suddenly aware of light rays about me.
>
> It frightened me, thinking that I had entered a forbidden realm by mistake. But what happened to me was most wonderful. I actually felt that I was in tune with the entire Universe. I became involved with a feeling of unity toward all mankind. That feeling to a certain extent has stayed with me.
>
> It was a startling experience and I honestly felt that I had made a new discovery. (673)

Another account leads to yet another realization of ultimate reality; this time regarding what will happen at the end of life. In it, the subject describes how, whilst eating dinner alone, she

> was immediately confronted with a vista which opened before me. It was all warmth, all harmony, all sweetness, but most of all it was a tender brilliant light which was all around me: almost, but not quite, I was entering into it and it was absorbing me and I thought that in another instant I should be utterly and finally overwhelmed by it (and by finally, I mean that I felt there would be no return once this had happened) but this engulfment was withheld just as it seemed about to happen. Like a door shutting in my face, it was gone. I believe it was the door which will open for us at the end of our journey on this earth, and I know it will be much more wonderful than these words can explain. (1418)

A rather interesting variation on the typical sequence that we have been discussing is contained in the following brief account, in that the experience of light actually presages – perhaps even foretells – a major life upheaval:

> Having moved from the district it was two years since I had been in St. James for the Christmas morning service, as we left and entered the open doorway my entire being seemed to be in a ball of golden light. No one else seemed to have experienced it but myself. It stayed with me and while

having lunch a telegram [arrived to say that] my Father had died on Christmas eve. (1113)

One of the most interesting accounts to fall in this current category, however, contains a curious mixture of details with which we are very familiar, together with details that are highly unusual. We begin with the subject in a state of desperation:

> I had reached a point in my life where an all-important decision had to be made. I was away from home at the time and my mother was dead, so I had no one at all to discuss it with. I was staying at the village where my mother had lived as a child and her ashes had been scattered in the graveyard there. So, in desparation I set out for the cemetry to have a quiet hour or so to think things out.
>
> When, at last, I made my decision as to what I must do I realized that darkness had fallen during my meditation. The instant I realized that my decision had been made I saw that, in the darkness, I was bathed in light. Suddenly the light left me. It had been like a spotlight, but it changed into an arrow-head shape and sped away from me. It disappeared into a clump of bushes at a great speed. The graveyard was not really familiar to me and until then I had not known that there were bushes at all. I saw them by the light of the arrow-head.
>
> The subject adds: 'My decision was made' (1606).

A number of features of this interesting account press for comment. On the one hand, it contains our now predictable sequence of events. However, this being acknowledged, it is not at all clear whether the light actually *creates* or *causes* the turning-point or whether it somehow *accompanies* it. Indeed, a careful rereading of the testimony suggests that the final making of the crucial decision is the turning-point in the narrative. By contrast, the subject only becomes aware of the light when the decision is made. I have hinted already that in some cases of unusual light episodes a light accompanies – rather than creates – a crucial breakthrough or transformation in the lives of some subjects, and this is yet another emerging feature in the study to which we must return in a later chapter.

We note also the unusual behaviour of the light in this case. When the subject first becomes aware of it she is 'bathed' in it. But it quickly changes, leaving her at high speed and disappearing into bushes. Later, musing on the meaning and significance of the experience, the subject adds the interesting fact that 'The light did not go to where her [i.e her mother's] ashes had been scattered'. We also note her brief attempt at veridical 'proof' of the unusual nature and existence of the light where she talks of it illuminating bushes that she had not known were there. The arrowhead shape is also strange and, as far as I am aware, unique in the literature. It is certainly unique in this study.

There is also no hint in this account of any feelings – good or bad – associated with the experience: other than the suggestion that it was in some sense positive as it led to an important decision that clearly needed to be made. This being said, however, it will have already become clear that the accounts we are currently examining share another crucial feature with those already examined in previous categories: that is, they are overwhelmingly *positive* in feeling-tone. We recall, for example, the Church of Scotland minister's description of 'Love and compassion' and his 'tears of joy' (226). We recall too, the ex-soldier's account of his 'overwhelming well-being' and his 'complete relaxation'.

Love and light

Many other accounts in this category revealed similarly positive, often overwhelming feelings associated with the experiences described. The following testimony is particularly rich in its description of positive emotions apparently brought about by being both surrounded *and* filled by light:

> A friend, knowing I was in emotional distress, had asked me to pray 'for a fortnight' at least, as a 'trial' of prayer. At the end of the fortnight, as it happened, I was at a concert with a friend, given by the Hallé Orchestra. They were playing the Choral Symphony (Beethoven) and as I did not know the music well, I retreated into my own thoughts – which were pretty depressing. I prayed to be taken out of the 'black pit of my own mind and selfishness' and suddenly, in answer, there was a rush of LIGHT, which surrounded me, lifted into LIGHT and at the same time seemed to melt my physical being so that LIGHT welled up also from within me, or rather, burst out of me, to meet the LIGHT that was without. With this LIGHT came BLISS, happiness a million times stronger than anything I had ever experienced on earth: and on earth I had been, at times, completely happy. At the same time I felt a cool breeze playing on me, and within me a whirling sensation and a feeling that I was somehow above myself – my body – but not completely, only a foot or so. (1916)

The following account contains an equally dramatic description of powerful and positive emotions seemingly created by the subject's being surrounded by light. She begins the account with the typical description of crisis and despair:

Some fifteen years ago my husband had a very serious fall and was not expected to live. I had a baby at the time and could not imagine life without my husband. I had prayed very hard and upon leaving my room was surrounded with a feeling of loving arms and an inner voice saying do not worry everything will be fine. A few months later this was actually the case and Tom did regain his complete help. This experience aroused something in me and I started on a search for God and a true way to live. We had many more problems over our next nineteen years together but I always could count on this particular inner peace to soothe my fears.

One night, quite suddenly I was surrounded with a glowing light and an ecstatic feeling of love combined with the most glorious happiness I have ever experienced in my life. It was such an inpouring of love and happiness that I thought if it doesn't stop soon I shall surely burst. It is most difficult, if not impossible to put into words as it was not something which earthly words can describe. During this experience I remember trying to think of someone I did not particularly care for but this feeling of love would not be individualized. It was as though there were no individuals and all was one. The outcome of this vision was an earnest desire to follow as closely in Christ's footsteps as possible, while being the best wife and mother I could be. (2181)

Whilst more understated in its description of the comfort brought into a situation of trial, the following account nevertheless reinforces this study's growing recognition that experiences of light are overwhelmingly positive in nature:

I had been told that my mother had cancer and in bed one night I prayed very earnestly that she might be spared any suffering. While in prayer I became conscious of a light enveloping me for some seconds which brought a warmth and feeling of peace. I had no doubt that my prayer had been answered and, in fact, my mother died a few weeks later without suffering any pain. (2099)

In similar vein the following account is clearly positive, uplifting and lasting – although unusual in that the subject appears not to have been under any stress at he time:

At the age of 22–23, I remember standing in my room at Cambridge when suddenly I felt 'dizzy', overwhelmed by a sensation of 'light'. It felt as if flame was around me. It seemed as if I was transported on to another plane of consciousness, shot through with an almost unbearable Joy. I don't know how long this experience lasted, may be a few minutes or even only a few seconds: it did not belong to a time-space world. The sensation of joy & inexplicable happiness lasted two or three days gradually fading. It happened at a time in my life when I was enjoying things enormously in a normal way. (2476)

One further, extremely well-written account returns us to the regular pattern that has been emerging throughout:

> I was very disturbed about my marriage – my husband proved increasingly difficult and neurotic. I was extremely distressed. Finally one evening when some quarrel had occurred (I no longer remember the cause) I turned to go into a room to be alone and in my thoughts raged against God, saying to Him in my mind, 'Why have you done this to me, why should this happen to me when I have tried so hard!' and I realized with a shock that I was blaming God and felt terrible because it has always been my belief that faith in God was a special grace given to some people – a kind of gift, and momentarily I felt that gift had been withdrawn. In the dark I fell to my knees and said in the depth of my being, 'Oh God, please never leave me!' At once I was enveloped in a most wonderful seemingly pulsating golden light, more penetrating than the sun and yet without glare – and with that light came a feeling as though someone had put arms of love around me so that I was filled with the most amazing sensation of being loved and filled with light – it is difficult to describe but I guess one would say that it was ecstasy. This happened in a matter of seconds and I quickly said to myself, 'I must be mad – the strain of my life has been too much and I've gone mad' – instantly the light went out and was gone. (2267)

Note here the blurring of the boundaries between 'filling' and 'wrapping' that has made placing experiences in this category problematical. Also noteworthy is the lack of any mention in this account of the experience producing any lasting fruits. However, it will have become very clear by now that the analysis of experiences in this category has revealed many lasting effects caused by being wrapped or enveloped in light. We recall again, for example, the Church of Scotland minister's experience on the Isle of Arran and the permanent changes wrought in him by the discoveries to which it led him (226). We recall as well the simple description given by a man whose head so 'filled with light' that his experience led to his finding 'a way to help myself' (4339).

Fruits for life

A number of further testimony-extracts should serve to put the good fruits created by many of the experiences in this category beyond doubt. One respondent, for example, whose experience was of 'being surrounded by a wonderful Golden Light . . . full of golden Spirit, Love, Beauty, Peace, Joy [and] Strength', writes that it left her 'feeling very humble and full of peace and love for others' (2307). Another respondent writes of feeling 'crushed by the intensity of the love' that his experience brought. He adds:

> [W]hen this light left, I was crying. I cried for quite a while with complete joy. My mind said – 'God is! God is! – and God loves me as I am'. As I recall, the light was unusual in appearance because of its rich goldenness. There is no way in my command of the language to share with you the magnitude of that love, nor my own feelings of humble joy. (2764)

Another respondent, reporting another dual experience of filling and wrapping by the light, reports how

> My husband died as the result of an accident at the age of 42 after an extremely happy marriage of 8 years. I was left with 2 small daughters & a son, 9 months old. I was completely shattered & unable to imagine how I could carry on.
>
> I must add that I had not been brought up with much faith, & was I suppose what is called a free thinker, & yet could not face the thought of life being entirely pointless & without meaning, which his dying seemed to me to be.
>
> I can truly say I was at the bottom of a black pit, knowing that no earthly props were going to help me.
>
> One night I was kneeling by my son's cot in great anguish, when suddenly I seemed to be surrounded by, & filled with light & warmth & incredible peace. I don't know how long it lasted, but I lay down on my bed, & slept as I hadn't slept for weeks. In the morning, the feeling of peace was still there.
>
> Over the following months, I knew that only God (& my fellow beings through Him) were sustaining me. (3390)

The 'breakthroughs' in belief in the reality of God's existence that these experiences seem to have led to are mirrored in the following account also. Here, a spiritual seeker, having left the Church, reports that after a brief period of elation she felt that 'life seemed to have no purpose'. Still seeking and 'struggling along' she began to read a religious book, when

> [I]t seemed that a white light shone around and a voice spoke (a voice of authority is the best I can describe it) and it said *There is a God* and my doubts seemed to vanish at once – and I've never doubted since – naturally I've thought and wondered how, and why, God's spirit works and in what ways etc. – but I feel He *is* there . . . (2894)

A beautiful account, *partly* shared and containing dramatic and immediate effects and submitted to the RERC by a State Registered

Nurse, concerns an experience in which she was caring for an elderly gentleman with a terminal illness. She writes:

> One afternoon in Feb 1972 I was sitting by his bedside holding my patients hand, his face was moving continually with great pain (all day he had suffered extreme pain – I had given him every treatment at my disposal also many old fashioned nursing procedure{s} in my effort to ease him & I was feeling very useless & helpless) as I watched him a great pity first seemed to well up within me which gradually became a love so powerful, quite different from any other feeling I had ever know[n], it flowed all around my patient & it seem[ed] to even form a gentle light about us, almost involuntarily I spoke, 'Dear God please help this man' within seconds my patient turned his head to me, smiled & said 'the pain has gone' again the words 'Thank you God' were drawn from me, then the light returned to normal I leaned over to say to my patient (for he was very deaf) 'just say 'Thank God' & he replied 'I do! I do!'. (3525)

Very different fruits are reported in the following account by a lady whose experience took place in 1933 in the midst of a period of longing for a child after a miscarriage. It is reproduced in detail here, and is noteworthy for containing a rather unusual postscript. Three months after the miscarriage, she writes, 'my feelings were near despair as I was walking down the country road to do shopping in the village.' Then:

> Suddenly I was enveloped (I can only call it that) and lifted high above the high bank and tall hedge on top, as though by unseen and unfelt hands, enveloped in a wonderful living brilliant light. I saw a small deserted quarry or cutting below, but everything, plants, bushes, even the stones on the far side were exuding a pulsating life and bathed in an unearthly bright golden light. It seemed an eternity I was held aloft with the most wonderful glow of peace and awareness of the wonder of God.
>
> Then I found myself standing on the road and looked to see if anyone had seen me, it was so vivid, no-one was in sight. I walked on, to the shops, but with an unutterable feeling of peace within me. My longing for another child just disappeared.

Next comes the postscript:

> A few days afterwards, as the bank and hedge were too high to look over, I found by going up a side path I could look down, and it was as I had seen it, only the scene was just normal. We were newcomers to the area, and I had never wondered what was behind the high bank and hedge. (3865)

A number of the features of this striking account deserve further, brief, comment. The fruits are both short- and long-term. First there is the peace that comes with the light, replacing the despair and distress. Longer-term, however, the experience appears to have borne fruit too, removing the longing for another child. There is another sort of fruit involved as well, in that the subject later attempts to verify whether the observation of the hitherto unseen quarry/cutting made during the experience was accurate. Incredibly, it was. Finally, this experience appears to cut across numerous classificatory 'boundaries', as has been the case with some of the others already examined. Is it to be defined as an out-of-body experience, for example, or as an unusual lightform in which a subject was enveloped in light? Overall, we are dealing here with another experience of light that is both rich in description and puzzling in content.

A familiar sequence

Two final accounts will bring our presentation of this category of light experience to a close. As will be clear, they both conform well to the sequence that has been emerging throughout this study as being very commonly encountered in unusual experiences of light: from crisis to fruits. The narration of the feelings that accompany each light experience is additionally rich in the familiar, positive, descriptors – in both accounts. The fruits are in one sense lasting and certainly profound, but not apparently permanent in the second case, as will become clear.

The first account describes an experience that occurred to a twenty-eight-year-old male in 1952. His description of the mounting crisis that led up to it is particularly vivid and worth reproducing in full. The subject writes:

> In 1952, being then 28, I was teaching in a temporary appointment, being recently out of finals as an art student and awaiting admission to a teacher training college. I did not relish this at all, and in fact the 'experience' followed a long period of inner unrest during which nothing seemed worthwhile, often intense, but only vaguely defined, and usually overlaid by the jumble of day-to-day occupations.
>
> A particular moment came when, overwhelmed by what seemed the utter futility of things, I utterly broke down and, in blind desperation (sitting alone by the margin of some field) spoke into space something like, 'Oh, God! You come and see to my life, I can't run it alone'. I did not, of course, expect any response.

However, a response – if response is the right word – appears not to have been long in coming, for in the very next paragraph the subject continues:

> Following this I sat quietly, feeling exhausted, for some minutes. I was then aware of a curious 'light' which seemed to grow up within me, and which became stronger and more defined as the minutes passed. I cannot now say how long it took to develop, but the 'ecstasy' lasted over roughly three weeks. The main sensation was of being loved, a flood of sweetness of great strength, without any element of sentimentality or anything but itself. The description is quite inadequate. I also felt a unification of myself with the external world: I did not lose my own identity, yet all things and I somehow entered into each other, all things seemed to 'speak' to me . . . Something was communicated to me, not in words or images, but in another form of knowing. Towards the end of the period I was aware that the 'light' was being withdrawn.

Despite this 'withdrawing' of the light, the experience, in common with many others we have considered up to this point, appears to have left lasting and profound 'after-effects' and these are spelled out graphically in the testimony's most detailed paragraph:

> Although the freshness of the vision has faded, it is clear that my life is quite different as a result. Only positive things are of any significance to me, negative thoughts and actions (whether 'true' or not) give pain, whether relating to myself or not. This is somehow bound up with the unification of myself with the world, 'I' am a different 'I', partly again overlaid with selfish desires, yet with 'self' still extended in some way to include external things, in whose well-being or otherwise I actually participate. Before the experience I had read the New Testament, or heard it read rather, and received no lasting impression: after the experience I recognized it as a reflection of my new self, the way in which I now thought, and of Christ's enlightenment (Matt 3.16) as being of the same essential nature (perhaps of different degree) as my own. The real point is that this is not a matter of adopting a set of intellectual precepts, but of becoming simply a different person in essential nature, of being 'born again', as if a deep well had opened within the depths of the self, and within this depth and in the external world a 'something' is encountered with which a personal relationship is established, and this is based not upon thought, although the intellect is satisfied, but upon emotion or love, as a child reacts to a parent. (793)

The next and final account also follows the now familiar pattern Only the location is unusual: a crowded departure lounge at a busy London airport. The respondent begins her account with a brief autobiographical description of herself as 'not "religious" in any orthodox sense of the word.' She professes a significant degree of bewilderment as to 'why [the experience] happened when, and where, it did'. And she declares at the outset that the fruits were striking and profound, declaring that 'my whole being was shifted into another state of consciousness for several months after the incident'. Her description of the experience itself is vivid and detailed. She begins with her state of mind at the point at which the episode begins with her father seeing her off to Canada in the departure lounge at Heathrow:

> Events leading up to this complete break with all previous ties had been difficult and emotionally very harrowing – it involved the breaking of a deep bond with a particular person, and I had been going through the last weeks of farewells and arrangements like an automaton. Some inner conviction or intuition that I was doing the 'right thing' had sustained me and kept me going throughout the months since I had made my decision to go and start life anew but I felt, and looked, a sorry figure. My emotions were completely flattened, my nervous energy totally depleted, there was a heavy, sick knot in my stomach, I hadn't been able to eat solid food for days and I was barely able to stand up straight as the nervous tension in my mind and body made me feel physically ill and weak.

It is at this point in a narrative clearly rich in descriptive power that the writer introduces her own experience of being 'drenched' in light. But despite her obvious ability to write vividly and well, notice once again how she presents us with yet another account in which the boundaries between 'filling' and 'wrapping' are blurred:

> I was forcing out banalities to my father about the flight, my new job, last minute messages and feeling more and more robotic when in an instant my life changed! It was wonderful. The only way that I can describe it was that I was suddenly drenched, or bathed, in light. It surrounded me in a blindingly beautiful moment which seemed to last forever; with glorious golden-white radiance it suffused my whole being, body and mind, and I felt totally whole, complete and calm inside the vibrancy. I cannot say even now whether the light came from outside of me or from some inner core, I only know that I was surrounded by, and, at that moment, was completely made of light and that I was one with myself and everything in the world. It was wonderful.

This clearly unexpected experience bears fruit immediately, to the extent that it is apparent to the subject's father that *something* has happened to his daughter:

How can I tell how long it lasted? It could have been a milli-second or minutes but it sharpened my consciousness totally, everything I saw and touched was more beautifully defined – the radiance stayed within me – I grew up tall and turned outwards with composure, confidence and radiant serenity – the words I use sound fulsome and sentimental perhaps but they adequately and truthfully describe how it was.

My father *saw* the change in me – he couldn't know how or what had happened and I knew that this 'light' was for my awareness only. He said, 'Hazel, you've changed. You are altered. You look different.' I said, 'I know, I'm ready to go now.

The experience clearly had more than a short-term effect:

I wish I could really describe the effect it made upon me – it was too profound to be called 'happiness', but I radiated *something* for months afterwards. There was a quiet conviction inside of me that I could cope with anything which life could throw up at me – that sad or momentous events would be handled in the right way at the right time with no worrying anticipation of what 'might' happen which had been my normal way of thinking.

People called me the 'English girl with the smile', and male and female, young and old, gravitated towards me and sought my company in a way which I had never before experienced. I enjoyed everything I did and saw with an increased awareness and although the heightened level of consciousness I had experienced at Heathrow did not continue at least I knew what things were really like.

Up to this point, apart from the somewhat unusual location, the experience typifies many that have gone before. However, it continues on a somewhat sad, almost wistful note:

Against my better judgement I was persuaded to return to England and I think my sickly automaton took over again – but whatever it was which took place at the airport that day showed me that there is something outside of the everyday range of human emotions and that an ecstatically 'happy' feeling or occurrence within the normal range of feelings is nothing – simply nothing – compared to that sublime moment and the ensuing months that I, and the others who shared it from me unknowingly, experienced.

The account ends, simply: 'Oh I do hope that it happens to me even once more' (3967).

There is a temptation to look for psychological clues to the cause and meaning of this experience by combing the narrative for them. And several clues there are. Could it be, for example, that the breaking of ties that the emigration entailed was subconsciously what the subject yearned for and needed? That she found sudden joy, freedom and maturity in the breaking away that released floods of pent-up feelings? We recall her description of the short-term fruits that flew with her to – and apparently stayed with her in – Canada: 'I grew up tall and turned outwards with composure, confidence and radiant serenity.' In fact, this interpretation is somewhat reinforced when we consider what marked the end of the experience and the dying of the fruits: the subject's return to England and, perhaps, the renewing of the old ties that had once bound so tightly. But this, of course, is little more than speculation. And it does not in the least explain the experience of light which, as with the other accounts so far examined, looms large in the narrative as one of its most significant and arresting features. Future chapters will need to take up again and reconsider afresh any possible psychological explanation that might account for *this*.

6

Transformations and auras: strange illuminations of landscapes and people

Unusual 'brightenings'

Thirty-five accounts fell within the category of unusual 'brightenings', although perhaps 'dual category' might be a more accurate description, for, as will become clear, both landscapes *and* human beings may, on occasion, become brighter, as if lit from within by a hidden source of light. The following account gives a good example of a description of a *landscape suddenly and mysteriously rendered lighter and where no apparently natural source for the illumination could be discerned*, the central 'theme' of this category of lightform:

> I was in the garden of my parents' home in Sussex and aged nineteen at the time. I was standing near the trunk of an oak tree looking down at a bank and the fresh green leaves of wild violets and other small plants on the ground. I was experiencing thoughts of joy and love towards all the small and great manifestations of nature around me in that quiet place. As I watched, there was quite quickly a silent change. I looked with astonishment at the leaves and blades of grass. They had taken on what appeared to be an internal light of their own. They shone with a quiet radiance, and so did everything within my field of vision. I stood dead still, not daring to move. I felt tremendously uplifted and thankful as I watched this extraordinary living light which seemed also to have gentle sounds associated with it. It was as if all my senses had suddenly become more acute and as if I could hear the leaves growing. I noticed that all the colours were enhanced and brighter, and more alive than normal. The impression received was that I was looking at something real and fundamental and not just imagined by me. I do not know whether it lasted for seconds or minutes before, equally without warning, everything quietly returned to the relative dullness of its material exterior. (3144)

As with the previous category of experience, this category contains a number of clear variations on its central theme(s). One concerns the colour of the illumination reported. In the above account, whilst the writer alludes to the enhancement of the colours of nature, there is no indication that the illumination had a particular hue or tone. In the following account, however, an occasional illumination of the subject's environment appears to have distinct coloration, as the final sentence of his testimony makes clear:

> As far back as I can remember there has been a sweet, cool presence in and around me – someone called it a Dazzling Darkness. This varies in intensity. It is in everything and is always there. On the rare occasions when it *has* receded I've felt frightened and alone. It is in me, it knows about me and I belong to it, but it is not a Person, so that praying in words seems crude. I prefer to 'inhale it' at prayer time, or at quiet moments in the day. I find this presence strongly in old churches, some old houses, in wild countryside, music, and in a few people. About 3 times it has intensified into what I suppose could be the mystical experience – a pinkish golden light which was in everything, was love, and made everything look beautiful, even Council Houses and a Corporation bus. (489)

In the following account, a wide range of colours appear to have accompanied the experience:

> I have had a few slight and perhaps doubtful psychic experiences but one was significant and very wonderful. During the war we were stationed at Laggan House, Ballantrae, Scotland. In August (?1942) I had been in a darkish hut checking store inventories. I left the hut and walked down a drive with a double line of trees down each side. Halfway down the drive I became aware of the great beauty of the late afternoon scene. To my left was a fairly wide valley and then a hill. To my surprise the valley seemed quite quickly to fill with a great light, living iridescent rainbow coloured light. The phenomena was huge, towering in an oval form up into the sky. Its centre was living dense coloured gold, the colours got fainter to the edges, the whole was ringed with a cloud of silver white light . . . The 'vision' provoked some very warm responsive feeling in me. It lasted some minutes then faded. It in no way disturbed me. It seemed quite natural. (1120)

Another account describes a remarkable combination of sound, colour and light:

> The whole world was irradiated with light and love. Natural things seemed superimposed on a pulsating network of light filaments: stones and shells hummed with sound: inanimate objects were pregnant with life and meaning, while every living thing seemed to be part of a great kinship, synthesis and oneness. Music particularly was a rapturous combination of sound, light and colour: every landscape and in-scape merged. (1904)

Another account describes a spectrum-wide range of colours, and ends, interestingly, with a brief theological speculation as to their possible biblical parallels:

> One summer afternoon I was sitting on a lawn in a shady London back garden. There were some small trees there and a low brick wall. I was quite relaxed and my mind vacant when suddenly I saw the whole transformed into the pure colours of the spectrum in a glorious illumination. I think this was instantaneous. It seems to me that this is the explanation of Moses' burning bush and the transfiguration of Christ. (1341)

Illuminations of people

We have already noted the dual nature of this category of lightform. The above examples are all descriptions of an unusual illumination of a subject's landscape. The examples that follow contain descriptions of illuminations of *people*. In the first, the writer describes what she sees as a 'divine shine'. Interestingly, as with the above account, this account also attempts to relate the experiences described to biblical analogues:

> [M]uch more frequently I saw the divine as 'shine' in people. I was familiar with it in certain individuals and I looked at visitors to see whether it was there or not. It resembled the glow of people in love more than it resembled anything else. To me it was just as plain and obvious as blue eyes or brown – I assumed everyone saw it. There were repeated references in the Bible to individuals whose faces 'shone', and as I grew up and saw art galleries, I supposed that it was what painters depicted as a halo. The people to whom I have been closest – my mother, my husband, and my sons – always seemed to know what I was talking about if I mentioned it. Its really only in old age that I have begun to realize that many people never see it.

Her comparison of what she sees with the faces of people in love suggests that this subject may be writing metaphorically when she describes her experiences. The following paragraph of her letter, however, appears to make it very clear that an actual light is what she sees when she sees the shine:

> People in whom I have seen 'the shine' had it intermittently, not continuously. I think they have all been people given to prayer. It was most obvious once in my mother, some months before she died at 80, when I came upon her when she had been in prayer and her face was shining like a girl in love. It blazed. And in Delhi I saw, on the far side of a great hall, someone crossing the room who looked as if light were streaming from

him – like a comet. It turned out to be a well-known Englishman, an Anglican Bishop, whom I did not even know by sight. I asked who it was. Naturally the shine has nothing to do with intellectual or other eminence: it was very visible in an old peasant I knew in Tanganyika who had been a slave and was barely literate. (3918)

Similarly literal in its description of a person seemingly surrounded by light is the following account:

I cannot now remember the exact year but it was in early summer and it was cloudy and we all took our seats in the front room of the house. Sister Gemmel spoke to us about her work among the methylated spirit drinkers that she cared for down on the Stepney ramp. Gradually as she spoke I became aware of the fact that she was bathed in light. It was as if the sun had come out and a shaft of light was falling on her. It was only when we emerged outside that I realized it was still cloudy. For the first and only time the 4 ladies in the car were silent with wonder on the journey home. I always regret that I did not share my experience with the 3 passengers in my car – perhaps they had seen it too. (4126)

Two further accounts contain descriptions of a very general illumination that encompasses both persons *and* the landscape. The first appears to have been both vivid and memorable:

[W]hen I was about 15 or 16 at boarding school I remember a sudden flood of light and love which shone out of everything and everyone – There was no particular reason, and it did not lead to any action, but it was so intense for the time which it lasted that I can still see and feel it after 45 years. (3674)

A second, longer account includes a description of lights around people using the well-known imagery of 'auras' before opening out to describe in detail some heightened states of awareness that include transformations in the 'quality' of the landscape. 'After beginning meditation,' the subject writes,

I began to see lights around heads and bodies of people I believe these are referred to as auras. The increased sensitivity of vision grew and the lighted areas around the heads became coloured and now at times they are multicoloured in a rainbow like effect. (I do not wear glasses and suffer from no eye disease or ailment.) At times walking the outer world takes on an exquisite quality where even old walls and common things have an infinite beauty to them. At one time just after meditating sitting at the kitchen table all things I viewed became to my eyes possessed of an infinite quality, so that each object was so incredibly fascinating I could hardly take my eyes off of anything. (1189)

More light and love

It is notable that all of the experiences considered so far in this category have, like many of those within the previous categories, been overwhelmingly positive in nature and rich in positive descriptions of good feelings created in subjects by their experiences, particularly where those experiences have been of a general illumination of the landscape. Respondents have talked of feeling 'tremendously uplifted and thankful', of 'love' as the essence of the light, of 'light and love' and of 'warm responsive' emotions. Indeed, no account within this category was found to be negative in feeling-tone or affect, and the following extract captures vividly the profound sense of uplift created in the subject by her experience:

> [W]hen I was about twenty an extraordinary thing happened. Instantly one day everything changed before my eyes, all I saw was marvellously and miraculously beautiful, more beautiful and lightful than I can describe as it was of another order of things altogether. I remember I stood there murmuring 'Oh God! Oh God!' Then it faded, leaving a wonderful feeling of joy that lasted for several days. (810)

Another experience that reveals similarly positive feelings throughout is also noteworthy in that the illumination begins in a church, 'accompanies' the subject outside, remains with him there, and produces joy and euphoria that stays with him afterwards. The subject, who does not give his age at the time of his experience, writes:

> It was probably during the summer of 1945 when as a soldier I visted the church of St Gudule in Brussels, Belgium. I had been praying silently, and was alone as far as I know, and perhaps fell into a kind of reverie. Then I became aware of a radiant light which appeared to fill the whole building, and I was conscious of most heavenly music. I thought to myself that the whole thing was imagination and made sure, and knew that I was awake. All unlooked for I was in transports of joy and had a great sense of love for all creatures.
>
> After awhile I got up and looked to see if I could find anyone about. (I had been in, I think, the Lady chapel.) I subsequently found the verger and asked him if the organ had been playing and if there had been a choir singing. He said very definitely that there had not been.
>
> On coming out of the church I found that this beautiful 'light' was still with me, and everyone and everything was so lovely to look at. I can only say that this Light of Love was everywhere, and I loved everyone and every creature. This extraordinary state lasted, as far as I remember, about two days. I had never expected such euphoria and heavenly elation. (3121)

Crises, fruits and feelings

The typically positive nature of emotions created in subjects by their experiences is now familiar. What, then, of *other* consistent features of experiences encountered thus far? What, for example, of the *fruits* of these illumination experiences? Are these positive also, as they were before? And what of the context of *crisis* so frequently encountered in experiences examined up to now? Was this found to be present in 'illumination' cases also?

Interestingly and intriguingly, it appears that these questions can be answered in the affirmative. We have already heard from a subject who reported 'a wonderful feeling of joy which lasted several days' and from a subject whose experience was so vivid that he could 'still see and feel it after 45 years'. The Second World War soldier whose experience was presented above reported, we recall, an 'extraordinary state' lasting for two days after his experience. Another respondent describes the aftermath of an experience in which 'everything around me was bathed in clear white light' in the following terms:

> When I recovered my bearings, there I was sitting as before, but somehow everything had changed. I was suffused with an awareness of the entire oneness of the universe, I felt sure that I had available to me, opened up to me, all the knowledge and wisdom and understanding anyone could ever need, all was divine harmony, and I had in some way 'come home' to myself. (1235)

Another account makes very clear both the vividness of an overwhelming experience of an illuminated landscape *and* the lasting fruits it left. The subject, whose experience occurred when he was a young man living in Glasgow, writes:

> I have never yet been able to know what to make of a wonderful experience I had as a youth. I was out walking one night in the busy streets of Glasgow when, with slow majesty, at a corner where the pedestrians were hurrying by and the city traffic was hurtling on its way, the air was filled with heavenly music; and an all-encompassing light, that moved in waves of luminous colour, outshone the brightness of the lighted streets. I stood still, filled with a strange peace and joy, and the music beat on in its majesty and the traffic and the pedestrians moved through the light. They passed on their way, but the music and the light remained, pulsating, harmonious, more real than the traffic of the streets. Then I, too, lingeringly moved on, looking back at times till I found myself in the everyday world again with a strange access of gladness and of love.

This subject's further, final comment regarding the ultimate result of the experience is particularly striking. Whilst not seeking a repeat of the experience, he none the less acknowledges the life-changing impact it has had upon him:

> I have found two references to similar experiences in literature and one was mentioned to me by a friend on his death-bed, but in the course of my long life I have never had a repetition of the experience; nor have I desired it. It entered so deeply into my being that my mind has rested in it all my days. (208)

Another subject, whose experience took place when he was with his classmates during a daily 'compulsory silence of ten minutes', writes that after his experience he 'settled down in bed but was fully aware that an aftermath remained and continued for several weeks. It was a sense of warmth and glow, of utter contentment mixed with an expectancy and hope that the experience might be repeated' (147).

Yet another respondent, writing of a frequent experience in which 'all around me literally glows with Light, colors become absolutely vibrant, and such a tremendous feeling of Divine Love washes over me', adds that, as a result,

> My life has been greatly changed. Animals come to me, people have written me and stopped me on lecture platforms and asked where the radiating Light around me comes from. The only answer I can give is God. God is love and if we become filled with true love for all things around us, we must radiate that love in our auras. (3062)

Finally another subject writes of a change in theological orientation as a result of times of 'quiet waiting on God' that sometimes led to 'the trees and flowers [seeming] to come alive with a sort of glow of light'. 'Brought up a liberal evangelical', he writes,

> I began to read catholic books on prayer such as Arthur Chandlers First hand Religion, and Ludovic de Besses Science of Prayer. I became more attracted to Anglo-Catholicism in Oxford because it was able to resolve my increasing sense of guilt sacramentally and also gave more definite guidance of methods of prayer. (2117)

A most unusual case in which the fruits of a subject's illumination experience appear to have been visible to others was reported by a man who was forced to undergo a painful operation during wartime so that he would be able to apply for a hoped-for commission in the RAF. In addition to containing a detailed description of the aftermath of an illumination experience, this account is notable in that the context for the episode appears to have been one of crisis and anxiety occasioned by 'considerable' post-operative pain that, in true stiff-upper-lip RAF fashion, the subject refers to as leaving him 'in rather low spirits'. 'Fairly early in the morning about two or three days after the operation', he writes,

I was lying in bed, alone in the room, looking out of the window which was to the right of my bed. As my room was on the first floor my view was restricted to the sky and the tops of some trees; it was a sunny morning.

After a little while I got the impression that the light towards the left hand side of the window was unnaturally bright as if there was some powerful source of light nearby but out of my line of vision.

As I looked I began to realize that what I was seeing was something beyond any experience I had ever had and while I lay there I felt I was shedding all pain and worries and I was overcome by a sense of profound peace and happiness; nothing seemed to matter any more.

Shortly after this experience, which only lasted a few minutes, my doctor and the nurse came in to pay me their usual morning visit and I noticed that the doctor gave me a very curious look; he seemed surprised and somewhat taken aback and instead of the usual 'Well, how are you today?' he said nothing to start with. After examining me and having the usual chatter with the nurse, he made some remark to her to the effect I was certainly looking much better, to which she agreed, at the same time giving me an odd look, as if she was surprised at what she saw.

As a postscript to his experience, the subject writes by way of clarification:

I do not wish to give the impression that I had undergone any physical change. I made a perfectly normal recovery from the operation and I only mention the doctor's and nurse's visit as they evidently saw something in my expression, which was not there before the incident took place. (1406)

Familiar sequences

The previous account was notable in that it contained each specific feature that we saw as being common across a wide range of accounts of light in the previous category examined. Whilst perhaps deliberately understated, a context of anxiety is the setting for the experience: post-operative pain combined with uncertainty regarding a hoped-for RAF posting. At this time of need a light manifests, apparently bringing with it feelings of peace and happiness: arguably the very feelings most needed by the subject at the time of his discomfort and anxiety. And this manifestation, in turn, leaves the subject better than he was before it occurred: we recall his assertion, above, that the doctor and nurse 'saw something in my expression' not visible previously. Bearing this sequence of events in mind, consider another account that took place shortly after an acquaintance of the writer had died:

> I was standing in my kitchen looking out of the window & thinking about the account of his funeral which had appeared in our local paper that morning. Quite suddenly everything, the kitchen, the garden & the sky seemed to be filled with a bright light & within me was a glowing warmth & with it came the certainty that it was from God. I cannot recall how long it lasted – I think one hour or just over. I walked round the house & although the light was normal I still felt the warm glow inside of me & I knew that for that space of time I was set apart from ordinary things. (2365)

We do not know the extent of the subject's grief here, making it impossible to determine for sure whether a context of anxiety provides the setting for the experience. However, it is once again clear that the experience is positive, creating a 'glowing warmth' within the subject together with a conviction that it comes from God. The by now familiar good fruits are indicated too: although the light returns to normal, the warm glow and a sense of 'set-apartness' clearly remain.

The following account also contains a sequence of events starting with a subject in a situation of deep crisis and ending when she finds a 'way out' of it as a result of an experience of a mysteriously illuminated landscape. She writes:

> It happened about ten years ago in Devonshire. At the time I had been to a Retreat in an Anglican Convent – not that I was very 'religious' in a formal sense, but I had been through a bad time, with a miserable tangled love-affair which had really cancelled itself out, leaving me feeling utterly disintegrated and guilty almost to the point of insanity, I couldn't go on like that any longer, and my mother persuaded me, as I felt too dubious of the outcome to go to a psychiatrist, even if I could have afforded it, to go to this retreat and see if I could sort myself out in the peacefulness of the atmosphere.
>
> For some days I felt absolutely insulated in my own misery, and unable to take part properly in what was going on. When the Sister in charge of the Retreat saw that I did not take Communion she tried to find out what the trouble was and persuaded me to go to Confession. This I did, and afterwards took Communion and then went for a long walk by myself along the country lanes. Suddenly the whole scene seemed lit up, irradiated, transformed in some way, the colours and shapes of trees & flowers, and especially, I remember, a field of corn, heightened and intensified, I felt a kind of liberation, for the first time in months I felt myself relaxed and

smiling at the beauty of everything, and later able to smile also & to communicate with people; the future which had seemed blank and unimaginable seemed to open out as if one had found a pleasant road round the corner instead of ending up in a cul-de-sac. Though it took me some time to get really back to normal, and though later on there were other bad patches, this does seem to have been what they call a 'turning-point'. Looking back on it, it really seems like an authentic experience, not one semi-deliberately worked up by the imagination. (1640)

A further, vivid account repeats this by now familiar 'crisis–light–turning-point–fruits' sequence in equally striking detail. As part of the background to his experience, the writer begins by describing six years of frustration as an actor which had created within him feelings of dissatisfaction and which had led him to question his motives for wanting to be an actor at all. Finally having left the theatre, having moved back to his parents' home and having taken up work in a cycle factory, he writes,

> I was in an extreme state of tension after coming off a shift and had gone to bed about midnight. I was unable to sleep and lay awake thinking about the factory, which I felt was destroying me, and the theatre which I missed but knew would destroy me in another way.
>
> Eventually I got up at about 4 A.M. and made some tea. I sat in the living room and more or less prayed that I could survive this depressing period and make the right decisions. After sitting for some time I went out onto the balcony just outside the living room window (this being a 5th floor flat in a modern block). Dawn was just beginning as I looked out across the industrial landscape. As I watched the light creep into all the dark corners, an overwhelming sense of peace swept over me. Then, like a subliminal picture on a screen the whole reason for life and everything in life flicked through my mind. It had been to[o] quick to grasp but I had seen it, it was a reality.
>
> Obviously a good dawn is always beautiful and I have seen many on the coasts of Scotland and Devon but this wasn't just the dawn. I felt the whole Universe embrace me. I was no longer a man separated from the natural world. I was a part of the whole. The very bricks and metal around me glowed with life and I felt as though I was glowing with it. All through this experience my mind kept repeating – 'As darkness is the absence of light so evil is the absence of good.' This was no mystical voice, it was my mind's reaction to what was happening. It was almost as though there were two selves, one being bathed in a beautiful experience and the other calmly assessing its meaning. After a short while the landscape returned to normal and I was left with a tremendous feeling of serenity. The factory was no longer a problem, it could be faced as long as necessary. (3614)

It is clearly not necessary to draw any detailed attention here to the conformity of this sequence of events to the emerging pattern of experiencing we are discovering and discussing: the account speaks very well for itself. And the writer makes clear here and elsewhere in his letter to Sir Alister that the light he saw was plainly not natural. We recall his contention: 'this wasn't just the dawn'. Indeed, he appears well placed to describe this experience, for he goes on to describe a second, similar one, with obvious points of comparison that occurred some six months later and with which this chapter closes:

I had gone to Nottingham for a weekend and on the Saturday night had attended a party, got drunk, made a fool of myself and embarrassed the girl I had taken.

On the Sunday morning I was suffering a terrible hangover and guilt. I went to see the girl to apologise, the meeting was over-polite and a failure. As I sat on a bus at the terminus I tried to assess how the situation had come about. I gradually saw that I had been playing a part and had been unable to keep it up at the party. I had been trying to be what she wanted me to be and the strain had proved too great.

Something in this thought process seemed to click the world into place far above and beyond this tiny incident. Once again a miracle seemed to occur, my pounding head stilled and a soothing peace came across me. Though this was 11 A.M. I saw everything as I had seen it on that dawn – the same glow, the same brilliance about everything. The people sitting on the bus were beautiful and without any actual contact I was part of them and filled with an enormous love for them. As the bus moved along colours were almost luminous, the drabbest of buildings shone with light and were alive. I felt as though God were leading me through the world by the hand, showing me that love and benevolence are living forces, not only in people but in every brick, stone and blade of grass. To my amazement this state lasted the whole of that day and the next. When I felt it ebbing it was as though a hand was gradually letting go so that I might stand on my own strength. The glow went but the love and regard for life remained and I felt literally as though I had been given a re-birth. (3614)

7

Shining in the darkness: lights seen during near-death experiences

The RERC study

By definition, any unusual light seen at or near the point of death might reasonably be said to occur at a point of crisis, arguably the deepest, gravest crisis any human being can ever face. I have already alluded to the fact that the RERC archive contains a significant number of accounts in which persons experiencing life-threatening crises at or near the point of death have reported unusual experiences containing a number of consistent features. During research for a separate study, I made extensive use of the RERC archive in a quest to discover experiences containing these features, and the resulting analysis, which I dubbed the RERC study, has already been published elsewhere (Fox 2003: 243–329). Indeed, many of these features – including a brief episode of 'floating' above the body, movement through an episode of darkness, feelings of peace, and 'fruits' arising from such experiences that include vastly altered views of death – are such that they invite obvious comparisons with so-called near-death experiences (NDEs), for many such NDEs, as collected and explored by researchers such as Raymond Moody, Kenneth Ring, Bruce Greyson, Peter Fenwick and Pim van Lommel, have also been shown to contain a variety of the same or similar characteristics. In addition to these, a vivid description of a 'being of light' is often reported by persons either dying or who have actually been resuscitated from clinical death. The following testimony-extract is typical of many descriptions of this 'being':

> I got up and walked into the hall to go get a drink, and it was at that point, as they found out later, that my appendix ruptured. I became very weak, and I fell down. I began to feel a sort of drifting, a movement of my real being in and out of my body, and to hear beautiful music. I floated on down

the hall and out the door onto the screened-in porch. There, it almost seemed that clouds, a pink mist really, began to gather around me, and then I floated up straight on through the screen, just as though it weren't there, and up into this pure crystal light, an illuminating white light. It was beautiful, and so bright, so radiant, but it didn't hurt my eyes. It's not any kind of light you can describe on earth. I didn't actually see a person in this light, and yet it has a special identity, it definitely does. It is a light of perfect understanding and perfect love. (Moody 1975: 62)

During research for the present project in the RERC archive, a number of NDE-like experiences containing descriptions of unusual lights were uncovered which I had not found at the time of my earlier study. On analysing these, it was clear that they contributed significantly to the previous study's findings as well as – potentially – to the study of NDEs overall. It was equally clear that they contributed to the present project also. For these reasons they are presented and analysed at this point, once again in the context of our ongoing attempt to discern commonality within and across reports of unusual light in the RERC archive. Whilst not enough experiences were unearthed to merit dubbing the current analysis the RERC study II, none the less they may usefully be seen as an appendix to the original study that allows us to extend its conclusions yet further – particularly as regards the mysterious 'being of light' already examined there.

Atypical experiences

Somewhat atypical of the several experiences that were unearthed is the following, submitted by a female who was sixty-eight at the time she sent it to the archive. It is atypical in the sense that, as we shall see, most experiences in this category appear to take place in some other or altered state of consciousness in what might be described as a 'visionary' or 'heavenly' realm. By contrast, the following account of a subject's encounter with an unusual light at a time of severe illness locates it very specifically as having appeared in *this* world:

Ten years ago I had a major operation and had been warned that I would feel ill for a few days after. During the second night after the operation I was muttering to myself 'I feel so ill – I feel so ill.' On opening my eyes I saw the ward doctor, night sister and nurses standing at the foot of my bed. I asked the doctor the time and was told it was 2.30 a.m. I then said 'I'm going to die, aren't I?' but was assured by him that he had worked too hard to let me die now. This didn't convince me, feeling so desperately ill, then

I glanced at the corner of the ward and saw the most beautiful brilliant light I have ever seen – it was suspended from the ceiling about 6 feet long, about 3 feet wide. I couldn't take my eyes from the sight – never have I seen anything so beautiful. Such a bright soft light and somehow so comforting. I couldn't define any particular shape – no figure – yet I am absolutely certain that I was dying at that time and that it was God who had shown Himself to me. When the surgeon visited me later that morning he was astounded to find such a great improvement after such a big operation. He always referred to me as his prize patient, but it's my belief that God himself came and helped me through that dangerous time.

When I was better I tried to discover how the light was caused but could find nothing whatever. It was a visitation, of that I am convinced. (2666)

This account reminds us of a number of features of other accounts already examined. We note, for example, the (failed) attempt made subsequent to the experience to interpret it in terms of a natural light source. It is also another reminder that neat categorization of each individual account is problematical; not least because, as we have seen, so many experiences fall across boundaries and may be located under more than one heading. This experience, for example, could easily have been located under the heading of lights 'superimposed' on an individual's ordinary background – save for the very real presence of a potentially life-threatening crisis that suggested its inclusion, instead, here. Indeed, students wishing to understand it in terms of its closeness to 'traditional' accounts of near-death experiences might not wish to view it as such an experience at all, preferring instead to see it as a 'deathbed vision' of the type explored in the writings of William Barrett and, more recently, of Karlis Osis and Erlendur Haraldsson. It is certainly consistent with other categories of lightform already explored in *this* study inasmuch as it creates clearly positive emotions in the subject and leaves her with clearly positive fruits. The feelings it produces are described as 'so comforting' – and this in the midst of post-operative illness and obvious medical concern. The fruits appear plain for others to see, with the doctor 'astounded' at the patient's subsequent recovery. And did the episode create a *turning-point* in this process? There is indeed a very strong suspicion that it did.

Another somewhat atypical experience that also bears close comparison to the older 'deathbed vision' type of episode collected by Barrett, Osis and Haraldsson is contained in the following account. It differs from the lady's post-operative experience examined above in that it is narrated not by the recipient of the vision, but by her mother-in-law who only witnessed its effect. Again, it reminds us of the danger of neat categorization of accounts in that it might easily have been placed in the 'shared' category of experience, already examined. And again, it hints strongly at the very positive effect seeing a lightform has upon the witness:

> My husband's mother, in her eighties, came to stay with us after her husband had died a few weeks before.
>
> Just after her favourite radio programme had finished, I heard my husband calling me anxiously. I hurried to the dining room but stood transfixed in the doorway. My mother-in-law had collapsed over the table and was breathing in great gasps. Suddenly she lifted her head, as though her name had been called, a look of bewilderment on her face.
>
> Slowly a light like warm, glowing firelight spread across her. She lifted up her arms to someone invisible to us, smiled with such joy and radiance and fell forward again.
>
> At 7.10 p.m. a doctor staying in the road had certified her dead (angina).
>
> Later, when I told him of my experience he smiled and said 'You saw that lovely miracle doctors and nurses sometimes see, when a good soul passes over.' (51)

Otherworldly 'echoes'

More typical of the pattern of experiencing in this category is the following account: typical inasmuch as it describes an encounter with light in a clearly 'other-worldly' environment. Recalling a wartime incident, the subject writes:

> I was badly injured by a flying bomb & was not expected to survive. I was semi-conscious for several days & at one point found myself travelling down a long dark tunnel. I felt no fear, only a sense of peace. There was a brilliant light at the end & I was looking forward to reaching it. I had reached it & a pair of gates were opening soundlessly & I was about to pass through into a still unseen but what I knew was a peaceful perfect place, when I felt a gentle restraining – I was going to say hand, but it was hardly that. However I was being returned & drawn back down the tunnel, & the gates shut. I felt I was being told that the time wasn't yet. I was told later that the nurses had thought I had died & the doctor had said there was no hope. (2276)

A particularly detailed experience that also appears to have occurred in a place not of this world is reported by a fifty-year-old man who sent an account of it to the RERC in 1970 just over two years after it occurred. Note, in an account written over thirty years ago, the light that is so often reported in contemporary near-death-experience accounts together with the feelings of tranquillity also common to many of them. Note, too, the approach of a comforting, calming presence who, however, never becomes fully visible to the subject:

> While making rapid recovery 14 days after one of [my] heart attacks, I suddenly had a complete cardiac arrest, when, (I was told), the E.C.G reading showed at least a 5 minutes clinical 'death'. (My family have seen the ECG graph taken at the time.)
>
> Eventually a feeble flicker of a heart beat was nurtured electrically until the heart was able to carry on.
>
> During this time, while I was 'out for the count', I recall thinking to myself 'This is *it* – Death.' And 'looked around' to see straight ahead a bright light, sending warmth and benevolence, shaped like a crucifix with an additional cross superimposed diagonally. Elsewhere was darkness, and from my body, which seemed to be on some kind of catafalque, all pain and feeling melted away.
>
> The light did not illuminate much more than my body's length away, but I was aware of a kind of screen to my right. I felt no fear, only a tranquillity I'd never known before, nor did I recall any thought of relatives or life on earth. Only my brain seemed to have feeling, and I relaxed into sheer ecstasy, feeling I did not ever wish to leave this state.
>
> There was no sense of time, no thoughts of anything in particular in my mind.
>
> Then from behind the screen on my right, I heard soft footsteps and as they approached, the light grew brighter, and as it grew, a feeling of great joy grew within me. Was I at last to know the truth and meet the 'Living God'? But, alas, before the footsteps reached the end of the screen, I awoke to see the blurred face of a nurse above me, my wife at my bedside and all the trappings of sudden cardiac failure 'at the ready'.
>
> The feeling as those footsteps approached was as if my 'inner self' was at last to meet someone who understood me, could guarantee tranquillity, judge me correctly and whose integrity I could respect and admire. (427)

The following account also describes an experience that appears to have occurred in a wholly 'other-worldly' location. The writer, an eighty-one-year-old lady, is describing an experience that took place in late February 1919, at the height of the great influenza epidemic:

> I developed pneumonia and as there weren't any special 'tablets', just went on to the crisis.
>
> About this time I must have been delirious on several nights, as I seemed to float into the most beautiful places, and on one occasion I was following

a light set on a hill, and remember thinking if only I could reach it, I should know everything, but *someone was holding me back*. Later I knew it was my husband who sat up with me through the nights.

I also remember feeling I was out of my body, and could go anywhere I wished, and it occurred to me that this was the explanation of Christ's temptation when he was taken up a hill and saw all the countries of the world, and this seemed perfectly natural to me at the time.

Looking back, I feel I was as near dying as could be, and came back because my life was not yet completed, but it was such a lovely experience, I should never be afraid of dying. (3005)

Again, a number of features of this interesting account press for comment. There are two sets of biblical allusions. The writer makes an explicit link between her out-of-body sensation and Christ's temptation in the wilderness in which he was shown 'all the kingdoms of the world and their splendour'. Less obvious, perhaps, is the reference to the 'light set on a hill' which is perhaps redolent of Jesus' injunction to his disciples to be 'the light of the world' which, like 'a city on a hill', clearly 'cannot be hidden'. The light itself may be seen to represent a *potential* turning-point in the experience, for the lady is clearly given to understand that once she reaches it she will receive some kind of momentous insight. Both positive feelings and lasting fruits are suggested by the final line.

The next account once again appears to occur in some other place not of this world. It is narrated by a man, who, 'racked with the most terrible stomach pains' suddenly 'awoke to a spirit of well being'. He continues:

I was standing in a kind of tunnel or cave and ahead of me I could see a disc of light, like an opening to the outside of somewhere. I was clad in only a loose white robe that fell in shapeless folds to my feet which I could not see. I was bareheaded, and my left arm appeared to be quite intact. (I have explained that it was lost in an accident many years ago.)

Yet it was clear that I was like a child, dragging my feet, I did not want to go on through this door to which I was drawing near. Then a male voice somewhere to my right cried out quite loudly: 'Don't go through there, for you can never return. Go back, there is much for you to do.' The power in the voice gave me the strength to stop.

I began to teeter between going ahead and returning, it seemed that two forces were dragging at me. 'Go back', the voice spoke with great authority, 'You have much to do.' It was more an order than a piece of sage advice and I began to back away from that bright gateway if that was what it was, I kept on going back until suddenly I was racked with twinges of the same pain that had swept me into the void.

I was back in my conscious body, the pains tearing through me but with ever decreasing power, and I forced myself to rise from the leather covered couch on which I lay in the semi darkness of the lounge room, where I had fallen (1089)

This account bears interesting comparison with the one that preceded it. In both cases the subject seems prevented from entering the light. The influenza sufferer is held back by her husband's prayers, whilst the man in the tunnel at first drags his own feet, unwilling to proceed towards the light, before he is forcefully deterred by the orders from the 'male voice'. Indeed, it is tempting to speculate upon what would have happened to both subjects had they made it to their implied destinations. In each case, perhaps, would the light have been the ultimate turning-point, the point of no return?

Expectation and experience

What *is* clear from a reading of both accounts is how many features of modern-day near-death experiences they contain. Placed together, they contain the dark tunnel, an out-of-body experience, a meeting with another figure, two descriptions of light (perhaps itself the 'border' or 'limit' described in many NDEs), a removal of all pain, and – in the case of the influenza victim – a transformed view of death. What is most striking about this list of 'typical' NDE features is that it has been compiled from two accounts written in 1971 and 1970 respectively. The significance of these two dates will be obvious to those well acquainted with the literature on NDEs, for they show that both accounts were written some years before the term 'near-death experience' was coined and well before the large public awareness of what constitutes an NDE that exists today. In other words, if some sort of case were to be made to 'explain' NDEs in terms of prior expectation, it would be difficult to reconcile these two experiences with it.

A popular contemporary view of religious experience – including near-death experience – is that it is a product of language and cultural conditioning. Thus, the argument goes, all religious experiences are moulded, shaped and conditioned throughout by the expectations of the experients. In short: we have the experiences we expect to have, and these experiences thus have something of the nature of self-fulfilling prophecies about them. This position goes under various names. Philosophically it is known as 'constructivism'; psychologists talk of 'motivated seeing', whilst philosophers of religion frequently refer to it as the 'vicious circle argument'. Whatever name it goes under, however, this argument might certainly explain some NDEs reported in the closing quarter of the twentieth century and the beginning of the twenty-first: for now there is a huge popular awareness, fuelled by intense media coverage, of the experiences of tunnels, lights and so on reported by near-death experiencers (NDErs). There was none of this before 1975 – the year pioneer NDE researcher Raymond Moody wrote his seminal *Life After Life* and coined the term 'near-death experience'. How, then, do we explain the remarkable similarity of the above accounts, written before 1975, to recent and contemporary NDEs, if expectation alone is the creator of religious experience? Where did these two respondents get the expectations from that shaped their experiences when such experiences were virtually unheard of both when their experiences occurred and when they came to write them down? Indeed, the notion that many of the experiences in this category may confound expectation will be reinforced as we go – for *every one* of them was *experienced* and *reported* before 1975, as we shall see.

The following account, for example, dated 21 January 1972, occurred in June 1944. The subject writes:

> I was severely injured in a flying bomb incident. At the moment of impact I lost consciousness, regaining it only for brief spells during the next few days. Whether or not I was conscious at the particular time I would like to describe to you I cannot say but I felt as if I was slipping away, rather than dying, I mean, & could not hold on to life any longer (if that sounds contradictory, I am sorry, but it does convey how I felt). Suddenly I was aware of a brilliant coloured glow of light & it was as [if] I was somehow being reassured. It was as though something, someone, a presence was reaching out to me but above all I was filled with a feeling of exquisite peace.
>
> When I was able to hold a conversation after the first few days I told my father about my experience & he said that on the day of my accident he received a telegram from the hospital asking him to come at once because I was not expected to live more than a few hours. I mention this because, until my father told me, I had had no idea that I was dying & therefore would have had no preconceived ideas. (2446)

The last sentence is interesting here inasmuch as it suggests that the subject had herself attempted to eliminate conscious expectation as the trigger or shaper of her experience. The light brings with it the typically positive feelings associated with lightforms generally and NDEs in particular. It is not clear, however, that the sense of peace and presence emanates from the light or from some other 'personality' that was with the subject in this strange place between life and its negation. The writer's difficulty in distinguishing her 'slipping away' from 'dying' reveals another typical feature of NDEs generally – their ineffability. The respondent does not describe any fruits arising from her experience, but the next account, dated 20 September 1971, contains some that at first sight may appear surprising:

> After a month of what I call 'unmitigated hell' one day (January 10, 1970), early in the morning, I was sure that I was going to be able to die. During this period I had been sitting up nearly 24 hours each day because of excruciating pain, and then came the day when I could not even sit up straight. So, in a chair, with my left elbow on my knee and my head on my hand, I closed my eyes and I immediately left this earth.
>
> All around me was a soft white light and I felt the presence of someone beside me, on my left and a little in back. So, I did not see, but I thought that God was walking along with me. We were going forward, slowly and steadily, getting closer and nearer with every step, and I kept talking to Him. I was so happy. Real happiness, not of this earth where people and material things are involved. Just pure happiness. Then, all of a sudden, we stopped, and I did not want to stop. So, I pleaded, 'I have such a short distance to go. Only a few steps more.' I could almost see where I was going, but this was indistinct and I cannot describe it. And then I experienced the most wonderful feeling of peace. Not just quietness or serenity, but perfect peace. I immediately thought 'Perhaps this is it' and I hurried to thank God before I died. Of course, I did not know if this feeling of peace would continue. I might just go to sleep. I did not know what it would be like, but I was sure that it was going to be marvelous – so very marvelous.
>
> And then a noise brought me back. I opened my eyes and was so disgusted to discover that there I was. The biggest disappointment of my life. (1792)

Far from dragging her feet, this subject clearly wanted to get to whatever destination awaited her. Compared with the life she was living, this was obviously vastly better. Initially, the fruits appear negative. Compared to the 'perfect peace' of the other place, in the company of 'Him', the world to which she returns disgusts her, presenting her, in fact, with the 'biggest disappointment of my life'. However, on closer examination the situation is rather more complex. Presumably, the world now disgusts her not simply because of the resumption of her pain but because the other world, by comparison, is now disclosed as being so obviously better. This is certainly the case with the following respondent, whose return to the 'world' during a bout of serious illness left her feeling similarly bereft:

> A British subject, unmarried, female, I had just arrived in Naples to take up a new job 3½ years ago, just before my 56th birthday. The morning after my arrival I woke up feeling very ill, and as it turned out, I was to go through a bad illness lasting for the succeeding two months, alone in a pensione, with no-one to look after me or even prepare food, with a doctor who didn't even diagnose the illness till I myself suggested it to him 4 weeks later – in fact, plumbing the depths, physically and emotionally.
>
> That morning, as I was sitting in my room feeling so ill, I suddenly had a vision. High up, as it might be in the sky, there appeared a circle of people wearing long, white, flowing robes; they were looking up towards a large glowing light, like a miniature sun, – almost too bright for me to look at, and they were singing with tremendous fervour and great joy. Although they were looking upwards, away from me, I felt as if they were drawing me up to them – the sense of being drawn upwards as if by a magnet was very strong, and for that instant I shared the joy that was emanating from them.
>
> The vision only lasted a few seconds, but when it faded, it left me with such a feeling of desolation and utter depression – that I was back here instead of being there with them, – that I wept and wept, longing to be away and finished with this life and able to join those people whose company I had shared for those brief seconds. (3132)

A fitter, healthier person might be expected to return to 'life' not merely disgusted and disappointed as in the above two cases but invigorated. A return to normality from a state of sheer bliss – having tasted, perhaps, the 'fervour and great joy' of the heavenly host – might indeed be expected to lead to depression, disgust and desolation, particularly if such normality involves twenty-four-hour suffering or illness endured whilst alone in a foreign land. In such cases it is surely not the experience that creates the fruits, but, rather, the *withdrawal* of the experience that leads to them. If, on the other hand, the 'return' is to a more tolerable state of existence, might we not find the familiar positive fruits already encountered in the accounts of unusual lights that we have examined in our previous 'categories' of experience?

Good fruits

Positive 'fruits' arising from subjects' experiences in this category are strongly implied in the next two accounts. In the first, brief, experience, a person suffering from puerperal septicaemia reports how

> During this unconscious period I saw a large eye of fire in the sky, and kept staring at it for quite sometime. I heard a sound of heavy chains being pulled about, & a huge bell being rung.
>
> Perhaps at this stage I was gaining consciousness, I wondered where I was, what the sound of the chains could be, & what the large eye meant. My baby was kept away from me, as she too was getting malaria & I could not nurse her, & she was crying ever so much as she was only a 4½ pound baby, & all this upset me. Suddenly I got a wonderful shiver & I was wondering what this meant.
>
> Then my inner self said to me, surely this is God saying 'Fear not I am watching over you. Your eldest child is safe with me, & this child will be a comfort to you. Trust in me.' I had a wonderful feeling thereafter.

Later, she adds: 'I kept telling many what I had experienced (1751)'.

A similarly positive after-effect of her experience is reported by the next subject whose experience took place during a difficult childbirth when she was thirty-five years old. In fact, as we will see, it bears comparison with the above account in several interesting ways. It is also interesting in that some sort of communication between the subject and what she understood to be God took place during the experience, later proving to contain information that she could not have known at the time. The subject begins by describing her 'trepidation' as she anticipated her second child's birth. It was to be a home birth, as was customary in those days (1955) if the first birth was unproblematic. In the event, she writes,

> The pains began on Monday morning (10 October 1955), and when the midwife arrived and had examined me she asked when I had last seen the doctor. I said I had seen him on the Thursday, and wondered why.
>
> The doctor arrived soon after but I was already in dreadful pain and I was told that the baby had turned round and that things were going to be a little difficult. I was hardly aware of anything else after that but the pain which seemed to be tearing me apart, and at one time, when it seemed that I could bear it no more for I had reached the end of my endurance I suddenly felt myself uplifted to a great shining light, then a great peace fell upon me and I knew I was in the presence of God. 'I can't bear any more of this pain', I cried 'It's too great. I can't stand any more.' 'There's only one more pain', He answered 'and then no more.'

And that's how it was. I was given the strength to endure the last terrible pain and then I felt the baby being born. I lay back exhausted but wonderfully happy, still full of the wonder and delight of that communion with God. 'That's the worst birth I've had in seven years,' the doctor said, and he went on to explain how the baby had had an arm stuck out one way and a leg the other – as though he'd said 'I've had enough of this, let's get out of here . . .'

Return to normality in this case does not bring a resumption of depression and pain but, rather, clear joy at the new birth. And rather than longing desperately for a return to the heavenly presence, the writer declares that, instead, 'I said to myself that I would never again doubt the existence of God and wanted to shout my discovery from the rooftops.' And as with some of the other accounts already examined, the subject shows clearly that she has considered at least one alternative explanation for her experience – with some doubt as to whether it is adequate to explain it all:

Perhaps you will say that it was the drugs . . . The doctor did give me something to help me (though I don't know what) and he did say to me afterwards 'You didn't feel anything at the end did you?' I just shook my head being still too full of emotion by the experience I had been through to speak. But I had felt everything and knew when the baby was born. And if it was the result of drugs, why was it as God had said – 'Just the one great pain and then no more'[?] (1594)

The fruits of this experience appear to have been wholly positive: certainty that God exists coupled with a desire that everybody else should know this too. And this, as we have been seeing, is a typical reaction to an encounter with a lightform. However, what is *distinctive* about this experience (together, as we shall see, with some other experiences in this category) is the fact that drugs may have played a part in its occurrence. In no other category of lightform so far examined has there been any suggestion that any kind of drug or narcotic was responsible for the subject's experience. However, in this category there were found be a significant number of accounts in which drugs *might* have been responsible for what happened. As we examine these, it will be interesting see how far they resemble or differ from the non-drug-induced 'encounters'.

Drugs and anaesthetics

We begin with the following account. The apparent cause for this twenty-eight-year-old agnostic woman's experience was a life-threatening ectopic pregnancy burst leaving her with a 50 per cent chance of survival as a result of the dramatic blood loss she subsequently endured. She writes:

> They gave me pentothal by injection when their blood tests etc were completed and I went to sleep. The next conscious thought – I knew I had died. I was a mote of light going upward to join a large sphere of light (like the sun). I was filled with a peace that surpasses anything on this earth and had the feeling of going home.
>
> The thought occurred to me that I wished I could ease the path of others in this painful journey called life. A 'communication' from without asked me if I would like to go back and if I would want the same body. I thought this was a perfectly acceptable body and that I would try to help others on earth by telling what I now knew.
>
> When I came out from under the anaesthesia my husband was at my bedside. I told him I had died and what had happened. He quipped 'Maybe that was Hell'. (2453)

Clearly, this account contains many of the features typical of the *non-drug-induced* experiences within this category: it is clearly peaceful and positive throughout, there is a light, and communication from some unspecified presence occurs, resulting in the subject's return to her body. Indeed, this last point suggests that the experience occurred whilst the subject was out of her body – although no direct description of a 'typical' out-of-body experience is given. In addition, it is another example of an experience with 'typical' NDE features – peace, light, other-worldly 'presence', 'return' – that occurred pre-1975: the experience occurred in 1961 and was submitted to the RERC on 4 March 1973.

Another drug-induced experience with 'classic' NDE features is contained in the following account, written in 1971 and describing an episode that occurred during a trip to the dentist in 1958. In it, the subject reports how

> I was given a general anaesthetic (gas) for major dental surgery. It was here in Edinburgh and I was twenty three years old. It was my first experience of this anaesthetic.
>
> Before losing consciousness I seemed to find myself in a great dark tunnel, at the far end, an immense distance away, was a single tiny white light. I was moving towards this and it grew in size and brightness until I

found myself in a large room. It was some kind of course ('Last Judgement'?), various officials were moving about, some with sheets of paper. I was asked my name and age, a long discussion took place between three of these men, at length one came up to me and said 'There has been a mistake, you should not be here.' At which I woke up in the dentists chair.

My actual diary entry reads 'I had the strangest premonition, a kind of "double understanding." I seemed to know that although all I had of the Absolute was one tiny fragment, yet I must hold on to it at all costs for it would be worth more than all "reality". My heart thumped and hammered but I held on, and now it is mine forever.'

Interestingly, the subject adds:

I am not a particularly 'religious' person [but] I try to keep an open mind. I am of pure Scottish ancestry for as far back as I am aware of. I have had several, other general anaesthetics since then, but all were by injection, there were no similar experiences. (2697)

Again, there are a number of by now familiar elements here. There is a tunnel, a light, communication with 'other-worldly' presences, and some kind of life-changing realization or revelation resulting in a strange 'double understanding' that the subject later wrote became 'mine forever'. He also seems to have made an attempt to link his experience with a gas – as opposed to an injected – anaesthetic, noting that only the former produced any kind of unusual experience. Bearing this in mind, consider the following account, in which the subject experienced a most unusual episode after an *injected* anaesthetic:

After the injection my mind became a blank, then after what seemed ages. I found myself surrounded by a translucent deep blue. It was as though everywhere had been a radiance too bright for me, and this had been toned with deep blue so I may see. I felt as though I was in the presence of Almighty God and Christ. I knew I was facing them, but could not see them they were behind the deep blue, in the radiance. Their Holy Presence was not seen but felt. I was wrapped around with it, and spiritually uplifted. A voice – His voice spoke to me, it filled the air, everywhere, completely, yet it was not loud, and addressed me alone. I hardly know how to express the feeling of the Presence, or the healing, which was for me, yet filled the air, I have had no such experience before. He said to me, that Helen [her daughter] & I were to be greatly favoured, Helen was to have the privilege of discovering something of great value to all mankind It was His pleasure that mankind should have this knowledge, & that Helen & I were his chosen instruments; and to this end we were to be spared. I was shewn this benefit, and the good it would do. I felt very humble, and full of gratitude and wonder. I did not see why I should share this privilege, but I was included. He said He was well pleased with us, and again I could not understand, I am so poor a Christian & full of human failings. He told me I must tell Helen she had to become a doctor. This He repeated three times.

After the operation all was clear in my mind except the benefit to be discovered, they had faded. I was uplifted for many days. (686)

We note again the felt Presence, the 'revelation' and the positive 'fruits'. There is a light of sorts too: a 'radiance' that is apparently so bright that it has to be 'toned with deep blue' in order that the subject may see. This is unusual in existing near-death experience studies, where the light is almost always described as being golden or silver. Compare, however, the following account which took place in the British Hertford Hospital in Paris in 1950. The subject, writing twenty-one years later, recalls how:

I all but died of a tachycardia following heart trouble, due, I think, to strain. The nurses had given me up; one dear little French probationer came to say goodbye. I seemed to float away, up and up among huge incandescent globes, so that I wondered if I was catching glimpses of the next world. Then the tachycardia ceased as suddenly as it began, nearly forty hours earlier. The next night I was out of immediate danger and found myself in what I can only call a 'blue heaven'. Everything, including the light itself, was blue, as though seen through blue glass, and it seemed to vibrate with healing, astringent, invigorating qualities.

The door of my room opened and the night-sister, a charming Irishwoman, came in. My only thought was to preserve the vision and I said 'Don't come in now, I'm talking to the Virgin Mary.' I recall saying this so as to make myself understood by a Catholic; she slipped out silently and I resumed the contact. Had she not interrupted I might have had no recollection of it. No presence was clearly visible, but the memory of a conversation with a female presence remains to this day.

This was in fact the turning-point of the illness. I knew I had been told there was some job to return to; possibly I was given some sort of pep-talk, but with a sense of reassurance, purpose and healing. I rate this as a high point in my life even though in terms of vividness and solidity it is the least 'real'. I saw no figure and heard no word. I only knew without doubt that as Sister left the room I returned into the living blue light and resumed the silent exchange. All Sister said next evening was 'And what might you have been getting up to last night?' She gave me an understanding pat. Although I spent six months in a wheel-chair and another six convalescing, there was no serious relapse after this experience. (2575)

These two subjects are clearly trying to describe the same – or a very similar – experience. In each case there is a conversation with an invisible presence, although the second case makes clear that it was feminine. The second case also makes clear that the experience was a 'turning-point'; more, that it was 'a high point in my life'. She talks of no 'revelation' or realization, as in the first account, but in each case there is a strong suggestion that the experience had a positive effect on the subject, leading to lasting positive 'fruits'. It is, however, the blue colour that dominates both descriptions that suggests that something very similar is being described. The first respondent writes of radiance 'toned' with blue; the second writes of the light 'as if seen through blue glass.' Is there a suggestion that this filtering is some kind of 'safety mechanism' designed to protect the subjects from a 'pure' or direct exposure to the light, an exposure that they would have been unable to stand? The first subject implies this when she talks of 'a radiance too bright for me' being toned – toned *down*, perhaps. This might be an accurate interpretation of the second subject's experience also – why else would the light appear to her as if from *behind* blue glass?

If we were to accept that these subjects needed protection from the light, however, this would place both accounts into a very unusual category indeed. Few if any near-death experiencers in other studies report any filtering of the light for their benefit, and we have not encountered any others in this study either. Might another explanation for these accounts be better? There is a temptation to explain them in terms of the effects of drugs on the subjects. As we have seen, the first experience occurred after an injected anaesthetic. The second took place the night after a serious life-threatening episode of tachycardia, and it is very likely that drugs of some sort were given to the subject following this. Is it possible therefore that the medications given to both subjects had side-effects responsible for the unusual lights and colours they saw? I recall the effects of gas given to me at the dentist several years ago when I had a tooth extracted. As I was only having one tooth removed I assume I was only given a small dose. Part-way through the extraction I woke up with the mask still on and looked into the faces of both dentist and anaesthetist. They, together with the light shining down on me, appeared as if viewed through a green lens. Then, suddenly, I started to spin and I felt as if I was shooting up towards the ceiling. It seems probable that both the unusual coloration I saw and the spinning I felt were both due to the effect of the gas on my brain. Might we explain blue experiences of the previous subjects in a similar way?

In fact, no less than four other experiences within this category *also* occurred when drugs had been given during operations. An account submitted to the RERC on 17 June 1974, for example, talks of an experience that the subject had when having 'a back tooth out under "gas"' in which he saw 'A bluish light in which sat my deceased Mother on the right hand side of another person (cannot remember if male or female)' (3105). Two of the remaining cases both occurred when nitrous oxide had been given to ease the discomfort of other tooth extractions. In the first, the writer talks about encountering a blue and gold landscape to the accompaniment of music 'Like Vaughan Williams' "Shepherds of the Delectable Mountains"' before moving 'steadily closer to the source of an all-embracing golden light that seemed to enclose and contain all things' (3415). In the second, the writer speaks of 'proceeding along a dark corridor at the end of which was an ill-fitting door from which radiated beams of light' (18). One final experience that occurred under an unspecified anaesthetic featured a stairway 'shining it seemed from an inner glow' which the subject found himself climbing towards 'a tremendous light which seemed like a flaming cross' (1704).

Of course, the fact that such experiences occur at times when subjects have been given drugs does not necessarily mean that the experiences were caused *by* the drugs. Possibly the experiences would have occurred anyway and were caused by other things – the proximity of death, perhaps, or some undetected threat to life that took place during 'normal' surgical circumstances. However, it is clear that some sort of case could be made for saying that a wide range of NDE features, including unusual lights, can be found in circumstances that imply that they *might* be drug-induced. We even have a clue as to what types of drugs are most likely to cause such effects, for, as we have seen, nitrous oxide consistently appears to create a great many such features. Before we make the oversimplistic conclusion that these experiences are simply *caused* by drugs, however, we would do well to consider the following account:

> I had a second son, who died at birth. For some condition of my health, I was unable to have drugs, and was suffering unbearably, with doctors sisters specialists etc helping all they could. As ill as I was, I was not dreaming, or drugged, or silly, just suffering unbearably! When I felt things had gone beyond endurance, I saw a wonderful bright light, and as I fixed my eyes on it it came nearer, and I knew it was the Christ. I cannot honestly say I could describe the face, but I knew, just like white flowing garments

and the most beautiful brightness. I think I must have been very near to the end, and though I suffered on for an hour or two after, I *knew* I had experienced something given to few. (3323)

We will have more to say about this small but significant number of pre-Moody accounts in the conclusion. For now, however, there is another 'category' of lightform experience to be considered that, like NDEs, appears to occur in an 'other-worldly' realm. Setting it apart from NDEs, however, is the fact that in this category subjects do not appear to have been near death at all. To this 'visionary' category we now turn.

8

Out of this world? Visionary encounters with light

'Visionary' experiences

Whilst staying with her brother and sister-in-law, both famous writers, the subject of the following account underwent a very odd episode. Prior to it, she had been wrestling with the question of whether or not to convert from Protestantism – her existing faith – to Catholicism, and on the day of her experience, her decision still unmade, she was, together with her sister-in-law, writing letters in her room. 'Suddenly', she reports, 'the room faded.' Then:

> Instead I saw a great white light. It was opaque but shone and dazzled me. It was soundless, heatless, shapeless, motionless and yet vividly a live light. The whole impression lasted only a second. It ceased to exist abruptly almost sharply . . . but I was conscious of an enormous change in me. Without volition or action on my part I knew that I believed in the teaching of the Catholic Church . . . All my doubts, my fears, my preoccupations, my arguments had wilted and died in that great light.

She adds: 'Soon afterwards I was received into the Catholic Church' (1382).

This brief account contains a key feature shared by all eighty experiences that were placed into this category. When she writes that 'the room faded' the writer appears to imply that her experience was not of a light that appeared against the 'normal' background of the everyday physical world, but was of a light that was encountered in another, perhaps 'visionary' realm. In fact, this sort of description of an encounter with light was commonly given when the research for the present project was being done, and as a result this category became one of the biggest in the entire study.

Another account may help to make this specific type of experience clearer. In it, the writer describes an experience that took place during a week's retreat in September 1980. Whilst undertaking a complex meditation that included breathing, chanting and visualization, the subject reports how she suddenly began to experience being in a different place altogether with a group of unknown people. She continues:

> Our group seemed to be moving across a green verge towards a Cathedral into which many others were passing. However once we were inside the Cathedral instead of taking our places in the pews in the nave we were led up to the chancel where we stood together before the congregation facing the altar. At the point in the service when the Communion should have been celebrated The Presence stood before us and we received a Blessing.
>
> In a dreamlike manner I found myself alone with the Presence still in a Cathedral but this time there were arches surrounding me and light and happiness seemed to pour through them. I moved across to go through one of these entrancing openings but He stopped me and led me to an archway I had not noticed which was dark and threatening. I felt deeply shocked when he told me this one was for me, but after a moment's hesitation I stepped into the darkness. I began descending as though in a lift, but as I went I found a tunnel of light traced my path and I could look upwards and see a cross of white light over my head at the opening of the tunnel from where I had come. I was not cut off from the Presence in the Cathedral and felt safe. (3913)

Whilst the experience of light is not overwhelming here as it seems to have been in the first account, this writer's description makes clear once again that the light she experienced on two occasions as shining through an arch *and* as a 'tunnel' occurred in some kind of visionary realm. We are not dealing here with a light 'superimposed' on the normal everyday physical background of the subject or with an experience of enveloping or internal light, but with an experience in which *the ordinary physical landscape has been completely replaced as if the subject has 'journeyed' to some kind of visionary realm.* Hence the title of this category: 'Visionary encounters with light'.

Meditative experiences

As with the above account, a significant number of other experiences that fell into this category appear to have occurred when the subject was engaged in some sort of spiritual practice such as prayer, meditation or ritual initiation. Meditation seems to be a practice frequently associated with the sudden appearance of visionary lights, as the following accounts will make clear. The first of these occurred to another female subject. She writes:

> About twenty years ago when I was fifty-two, and living in Norfolk, I was trying to meditate one morning when I had an indescribable experience of being suddenly caught up out of this material world into a sort of circle of radiant light and utter calmness where one was beyond thought but filled with a feeling of complete understanding & joy. It did not last for many minutes but after it was over I felt the effects of it for several days, and although it happened so long ago it has been quite unforgettable. (1585)

Another experience that occurred during meditation is notable for its unusual and dramatic outcome. The subject, a lady aged sixty-five at the time her experience occurred, was diagnosed with an incurable ankle ailment and her pain was severe. She writes:

> I was dumbfounded at . . . the prospect of walking about on sticks for ever perhaps, and so in my prayers each night and morning I included my left ankle, and to help things along, as I thought, I went down to Stokes Bay on every possible occasion to swim in the sea, where I would first swim for an hour or so, and afterwards relax in the chair in my Beach Hut and meditate.
>
> After 5 months of this routine, and on the 15 Oct. 1967, a most wonderful thing happened. After my swim and whilst relaxing and meditating with my eyes closed, I saw what seemed to be a round luminous, somewhat diffused light in a beautiful azure background approaching me, which disappeared on reaching my head. I opened my eyes and wondered for a while at the beautiful colours, but as I was beginning to feel cold I decided to get dressed, lock up and go home. You can imagine my great joy when I saw that there was no swelling, discolouration and no pain in my left ankle.

She adds, almost as a postscript: 'The walking stick is still hanging in the Beach Hut and my belief in the Bible in general and the Four Gospels in particular grows stronger as time passes' (2150).

Two accounts specifically mention yoga as being in some sense associated with an experience of visionary light. The first of these subjects attempts an interpretation of her experience as being of a reality that appears to transcend the narrowness of dogmatic religion, when she writes:

> During meditation at Yoga (1977) I often saw a white light, which is not a purely intellectual colour as the Yoga teacher thought. It is *Life* and contains all intellect, feeling and awareness. Is this what other people call God or Allah? Is this what religious dogma and wars have stemmed from? I find

this inconceivable because of the very positive joy and energy which accompanies this light. (4568)

The second yoga-related experience is unusual in that it describes an experience that seems to have occurred at a time when the subject had ditched the practice in favour of the more traditional 'wordless prayer'. At least, this is the implication, as we will see. The respondent writes:

> About 15 years ago, at a time when, after practicing Yoga for 15 years prior to this, I was in a very sad and almost despondent state of mind through a steady run of 'Bad Luck', I retired into our small box room where I knew I would not be disturbed and withdrawing my mind from all outside objects I lifted up my arms above my head and in a frame of mind of utter helplessness I asked God to help me. I became aware only of darkness as though I were suspended in space, with absolutely nothing around me. Then I saw the light above my head which became larger and larger until it appeared quite clearly to be a hand holding a lighted torch. It rapidly approached my head until the flame touched the top of my head and immediately my whole body was ignited. I remember thinking at this point, 'I am burning' but very soon after this I realised that I was untouched. With this realisation came the feeling that I had received or absorbed into myself a force or power which had removed all my previous feelings of sadness and substituted in their place something similar to the happiness which a condemned man might feel when he discovers he is free. Quickly the whole vision disappeared after I felt this sense of freedom. (3406)

As with the episode in which the subject's ankle was mysteriously healed, we are returned here to our by now familiar pattern of crisis–light–turning-point–fruits, and we are again reminded of how this common sequence cuts across all of our categories of lightform experience. It is also no respecter of religion and/or tradition, for, as we have seen already in this chapter and throughout, unusual lights seem to be reported by persons of a wide variety of various religions and spiritual traditions – or, indeed, by persons of no religion or discernible spiritual background at all.

The next experience was reported by a lady who was forty-seven when it occurred. The mention of breathing exercises in her testimony suggests that some sort of spiritual background may lie behind her experience, although her testimony begins with a disavowal of any conventional religious background or upbringing. Then, she writes:

> It was a September evening about 10:30, I was lying on my back in a darkened room doing my breathing exercise, when I saw above me near the

ceiling a misty cloud of a most wonderful blue, from it a cord of the same misty material hung down towards my body. I felt no fear, only wonder.

I continued with my exercises but now I felt a warmth on the soles of my feet, with each breath this warmth moved up my legs & body until it reached my throat; I now had the strange feeling that all of me was inside my head.

There was a sensation & without any discomfort it felt as if the tip of my head lifted & I rushed out through the opening into space & towards a wonderful white light. In a moment I was surrounded by this light & seemed to lose my identity & become part of it.

At this moment I felt an indescribable sense of peace, love & happiness & a knowledge that everything was united by this light & in fact consisted of this light although we couldn't see it.

These intense emotions were almost more than I could bear & although I wanted to stay in this condition I knew I wasn't ready for it.

I felt as if I were going to sleep when in fact I was coming to, & became aware of my body & the room again. For some time the feeling persisted that what we call life is really a state of sleep & what I had experienced was being awake. (1914)

Experiences during prayer

A number of experiences in this category occurred when the subject was at prayer. A lady whose experience occurred when she was eighty-one years of age reports how

> One day I had a vision. It was absolutely unexpected and not connected with my thoughts at the time. Actually I was kneeling down saying my prayers, and, as is usually during my morning prayers, I was reading the information contained in my Q.O.P. intercession leaflet about the country about which I was intending to pray – my attention was arrested by a voice saying very distinctly 'I am The Father, The Son and The Holy Spirit'. I looked up, startled, and in front me and rather above I saw a Figure surrounded with dazzling light. I bent my head and thought 'Why to me?' then I raised my eyes, but the vision had vanished. This happened over a year ago and I felt it was not meant just for me but to confirm and strengthen the faith of others too. (1037)

Another experience connected with prayer occurred in 1956 and was submitted to the RERC in 1971. In it, the writer describes how

> In 1956 my eldest son was drowned at the age of five years. My love for him was the most wonderful thing in my life. Some few days after his death, in my great sorrow, I was sitting alone in the study of my mother's house and I prayed to God with all my heart, to ask him, when so great a love existed

between two people, to give me some sign of its being eternal and indestructible, as in fact I believed it to be. I also prayed strongly to my son to 'Go on' with his new life and not wait for me to join him. Suddenly I knew that he was standing beside me on the hearthrug, so strong was this feeling that I put my hands to my eyes as though to open them in an effort to see him. I was at once surrounded by such a feeling of peace and happiness that I had never known before or since. At the same time I felt myself lifted up from the chair and my body became quite weightless. Indeed, the walls of the room dissolved themselves and withdrew into the distance as though they were quite unreal like a stage set and my son stood at the end of a great lane of shimmering light with beautiful colours, leading into infinite space and to another dimension which I felt was beyond my earthly eyes to see. It was, as though for a moment or two, I glimpsed the 'other world' in which he now lived. At the same time I was in a way 'sore afraid'. Far from vanishing instantly, this 'vision' faded away very gradually and the walls and things in the room resumed their normal experience, enclosing me once again into their narrow space and it only disappeared entirely on someone entering the room. I would like to say that what happened to me was entirely unexpected and I am convinced that it was no figment of my imagination. One extraordinary thing was the relation of 'light', the light in which I saw my son standing and the lightness (weightlessness) of my own body. (1912)

The ending of this particular account is very interesting, inasmuch as the writer attempts to link the light she saw with the 'lightness' she felt. Is there a sense here in which the outer 'vision' is in some unspecified and unusual way an expression of the inner state? And we note also the occurrence of an experience once again at a time of bereavement with its accompanying mental distress. The following extract from a much larger account also occurred at a time of crisis when a large number of people – but not the subject – were praying for a sick friend, the subject's brother-in-law. On a train *en route* to see him, the writer, aged forty-eight at the time of her account, describes how

I was aware of hazy but very white light. It had a point of origin somewhere to my right. It was not light as I know it but gathered light without bounds, gathered at every point and unconfined (not as in a room). I was aware of movement, purposeful, not within the limits of a body. No bounds or shape to the light or movement . . . There was intense fear. (767)

Wonder and joy

The emotional reaction of the above subject to her experience of light – her 'intense fear' – is unusual. The following account, however, returns us dramatically to the generally overwhelmingly positive feelings evoked by episodes of unusual visionary lights. In it, the subject, a teenage schoolboy, describes how he had been cycling across moorland near his home on a warm summer day. He writes movingly of his state of mind during his ride:

At that time I was wont to spend much time by myself, introspectively. Many factors in my life contributed to this – tension between my father and mother, with me more or less forced to side with my mother out of fear of my father; problems with paying attention to my school work related to the previous situation (I seemed to be emotionally preoccupied by it) and confusion within my first relationship with a girl. A greenstick fracture of the heart – as someone called it! Also, from my mother, I had found myself possessed of a deep interest in religious matters, in particular, the nature of Truth and Love and how to achieve unto them.

So, on the day in point of remembrance, I was alone in unspoilt, wild, natural and open surroundings. At some point I felt in need of a rest. Throwing my bike into some heather I lay down, closed my eyes and began to lap up the warmth of the sun. There was no specific trigger for the experience that followed that I can recall other than the general disposition of my mind and the things it was preoccupied with. But it seemed as if I drifted out into some great light and became aware of some Being or presence which I call God. I found my awareness flooded, however, with a perfect and total realisation of the interdependence of God and my Self. They were, in some absolute and imperative way, necessary to the existence of each other. [The emotions that I felt were more of utter wonder & joy, amazement & delight.] I do not think the time that elapsed during this experience, measured by the clock, could have been more than a minute, if that, but the vision that I had perceived encompassed an awareness of time and space like nothing I had known before.

The realisation was so strong that it stayed with me when I became aware once more of where I was. I was then filled with another imperative – to find a means to write down what had happened. Fortunately I found an old cigarette packet and a stubb of pencil. (4029)

A very similar experience to this was submitted to the RERC on 12 August 1973. As with the above account, the subject was a young man at the time of his experience – a boy of 12. And again in common with the above account, the writer seems to have been undergoing some sort of crisis associated with questions of truth and meaning at the time of his experience, writing:

At the beginning of the summer school holidays, I began to have a number of very disturbing thoughts. These thoughts were based on certain fundamental questions such as, 'Why are we here?', 'What is the purpose of life?' etc., and ultimately distilled themselves into one basic question which, although impossible to express adequately in words, revolved around a doubt of the reality of my own, or anyone else's existence.

Pondering these questions, the subject 'spent many successive days meditating alone in the middle of some grazing land, known as Cliffe marshes, near where I lived at the time'. It was during one of these times that the answer to this young man's question concerning the meaning of his life suddenly came. He writes:

I cannot recall whether or not it came suddenly or gradually. Like the question, the answer was impossible to express adequately in words but implicit in it was the solution to every problem that could ever face mankind. The answer was so overwhelming in its simplicity and completeness, that I was charged with a feeling of such vibrant happiness and contentment that I have not experienced before or since (13 years has passed since this took place).

I was, for the first time in my life, talking with God as to another human being. I spoke to him as though to a friend, and amazingly, for every question I asked (and I asked them aloud, as in normal conversation) he would place the answer in my head with such immediacy that it almost seemed that I heard his reply audibly. I began to grasp, for the first time, exactly what God was; at one level, he was a human being (not of my own age, neither aged, but a young man of 20 to 30); at another level, an all-pervading Energy which encompassed, and was part of, the whole universe, of every living thing, including myself; and also, the Creator of the Universe. It was so amazing that I was communicating with this all-pervading Energy force as an equal – and in doing so, I too was encompassing the universe, becoming a part of everything around me. I found myself liberated from the confines of my body; no longer bound by skin, I saw things so much clearer than before – colours, everything was so vivid, I felt so ecstatic – I soared way up into the blue sky, beyond the clouds and cross the infinite reaches of space. Now, it was all infinite bliss, infinite light – infinity was no longer an enemy but a friend – I had been looking at Hell, a dark threatening universe without God; but now, I was one with God, the life force, light was permeating the universe; God/Life/Light, the three are one – with them, the universe is Heaven; without them, Hell.

The writer continues his account with a description of another experience – although part of the one, single, episode – which bears interesting comparison to the 'oneness-of-everything' sensation described by many of the world's mystics and dubbed by the researcher W. T. Stace as 'extrovertive mysticism':

> I was now at one with everything around me – the sheep, the grass, the water, the sky – we were all part of one harmonious pattern. All conflicts were resolved. It was as if a bridge had been laid across a bottomless canyon in my mind. My bliss was so total, that the smallest fraction of time seemed an Eternity of happiness – Eternal life had become a reality. It seemed that, during these walks on the marshes, I was completely transcending the normal confines of time, I had experienced Eternity in a fraction of a second. I would have been content to die, since there was no greater happiness to be achieved by earthly struggles.

The account closes on a faint note of regret. Whilst the experience continued 'all summer', the subject's return to school made its continuation 'less easy'. Friends failed to understand the significance of it, whilst Christian teaching left him 'progressively alienated'. Adolescence was the 'final blow, since this superimposed a new and very powerful need onto my previous contentment'. None the less, he writes, thirteen years after the experience: 'It is still the most important thing that ever happened to me, and [it] governs my whole attitude to life' (3451).

Wiping away tears

As with the other categories of experience so far examined, several 'visionary' episodes occurred at times of deep and profound life crises not purely philosophical in nature. A lady whose husband's death in 1942 left her in a profound state of despair writes:

> In the early part of 1943 I received a wonderful vision. I had gone to my bedroom and flung myself on my bed and I implored God, if there was a God, to give me a sign. And lo and behold I felt my neck being raised. My tears were streaming down from my eyes, and they were being wiped away. Then the four walls of the bedroom vanished, and in its place was a wonderful golden light such as I have never seen on earth. It so transported me that it has made a great difference to me all my life, for well nigh forty years. So curious, the golden light has stayed with me. And in that golden light I saw five people. They were not angels; they were human beings, but recognized by me; just glorified human beings. And that wonderful vision has never left me. And though I did not see my husband I knew that he was in God's hands. (3948)

Another experience that occurred at a time of bereavement and was sent to the RERC in 1971 contains a similar vision where a wall should have been. The subject writes:

My husband had been killed in action on May 13th 1915. I was pregnant. After announcing the death to my nearest relations I went to bed for 5 days, lay in a darkened room & saw no-one.

On the 5th day, while looking at a bare wall opposite my bed I saw a window open with some figures in it. Then a voice told me 'Get up, everything will be alright' the window was suffused with an unearthly beautiful golden light.

She adds, simply: 'I got up.'

The following experience, also occurring at a clear time of crisis, reminds us how the appearance of a lightform at such a time can produce a turning-point that sets a subject on a new path by providing him or her with a dramatic new insight into the real nature of things. The subject writes:

In 1938 I married a rotter and went to live in London. 7 years and 2 children later I divorced him and returned to live with my parents in the same home I had left. I had tried to live without God and religion for 10 years and now I say at 58, that heaven is where God and Love is and hell is without God.

On my return to a religious home my conscience and my Father started worrying me. I was convinced that I was damned. I knew that God loved sinners but I could find no text in the Bible to say He took people back, though how I missed the 'prodigal son' I don't know, perhaps felt that it did not apply to me. After restless weeks I had my vision! My sister said that nothing less would or could convince me. I was lying in bed but was *not* asleep.

I saw a terrible white light, and knew that it was God on His throne of judgement, and I was cowering in a corner like a frightened mouse. I was then conscious of a shadow between the light and myself and looking up, I saw the figure of a man, very tall and straight with arms outstretched to form a cross and felt that I was safe from that awful light, whilst in His shadow. He then moved his arms so that they were outstretched towards me with open hands (no nail marks) and I heard the words 'Come unto Me all ye that are heavy laden and I will give you rest' *then I saw His face*, and knew not only that it was Jesus but that He is Love! Ever since I have realized that God is Love, that wherever real love is, that is the Spirit of God. (3110)

Is the interesting aside 'no nail marks' attempting to convey the idea here that the experience in some sense differed from expectation? It is clear from a close reading of the testimony that the subject was certainly in a position to 'see' this detail because she describes the man's arms as 'outstretched ... with open hands'. Once again, it seems that we might be dealing with an experience that ran counter to expectation: giving lie to the 'motivated seeing' hypothesis and its central contention that expectation creates much of what passes for experience.

Filled with delight

As we approach the end of this extensive survey of all of the lightforms categories, we are able to remind ourselves of the genuinely positive effects that such experiences leave in the lives of people who have them: both short- and long-term. Another meditation-related episode narrated by male subject describes how

> In the summer of 1969 I began the practice of Buddhist Meditation ... One afternoon about three weeks after I had started the daily practice, my whole being seemed struck down by a blinding flash of light. I was completely overwhelmed by the experience, which occurred shortly after I had begun the day's stint of meditation. My feelings were a combination of ecstasy, terror and awe. The experience came utterly unexpectedly and I felt that God had given me a vision of his power. For two days afterwards everything I did, even what would normally be boring drudgery, filled me with the greatest delight. I felt it didn't matter what happened to me; everything was very good. (3519)

The unexpected nature of the experience is once again a feature here. As is the difficulty of slotting it into a 'neat' category : the context of meditation suggested this episode for inclusion in the 'visionary encounters' chapter, but it might just as easily have been located elsewhere, particularly given the subject's description of being struck by a *flash* of light.

The next experience, also difficult to define with any degree of precision, contains a striking description of the fruits it left. The subject writes:

> [My] first experience of illumination came one evening when I was in London – on top of a bus – suddenly I was in a realm of glory and light and those words were in my mind – 'everything that *is*, is a facet of love'. – (and love was God–)
>
> For many days I was in a sort of exalted state of happiness – everything expressed beauty – I still can see some of the faces of just passing people – they were so beautiful and noble – they were like gods – beauty was everywhere – (3953)

A subject whose visionary experience 'of lights which poured upon me from every direction' occurred as he strolled in his garden in

Staines reports possibly the most interesting and startling after-effects of the entire study. As his experience unfolded, the subject describes how 'it was conveyed to my mind that what was needed for the deliverance of humanity was a servant-nation. It was to the building of this nation to which I was required to address myself.' And he adds as a postscript:

> The outcome of this experience has been the formation of the Mondcivitan Republic as a Servant-Nation, which now has its citizens in some 60 countries . . . The Republic operates as the impartial servant of all nations in the interest of all mankind, and as the working-model of a united world. The Mondcivitan Republic was inaugurated in Cardiff, Wales in 1956 and held its first Parliamentary Assembly in Vienna in 1959. Mondcivitan is from the Esperanto for World Citizen (3438).

Finally, a reminder that, despite the commonality of features across accounts that has emerged throughout this study – a striking conclusion that will be reinforced statistically in the next chapter – not every experience fits the developing pattern. We end with an experience that was so unpleasant that the subject made significant life-changes in order to avoid a repetition of it:

> In our early thirties my husband and I went to various W.E.A classes and were interested in comparative religions. Because of this we investigated spiritualism for a period of 6 Months, and during this period I sat for the so-called 'development' for a few weeks. Nothing happened to me in the class, but just on waking up or going to sleep peculiar things started to happen including a form of catalepsy which was most frightening. Then I had the deepest experience of all – I found 'myself' conscious after going off to sleep in another state and there was a brilliant light and I couldn't look at it – I was frightened and in awe and something made me think it was ultimate reality (whatever that is) or death. It was so powerful that I couldn't bear to look at it, and I said to myself 'not yet, oh not yet' and with a supreme effort I found myself hurtling down a black tunnel to blessed unconsciousness, but I remembered every detail of this frightening experience, but it was difficult to put it into human words. I gave up this class like a hot cake, and we gave up our investigations altogether. (2621)

9

Beams, rays, shafts: penetrations by light

'Lightbeams'

A small number of accounts – thirteen in total – described experiences in which subjects encountered unusual light(s) taking the form of beams, rays or shafts. The fact that they *might* have been trying to use these different words to describe one consistent phenomenon determined that their descriptions be included under one general heading; for, clearly, words like 'beam' and 'ray' might well be used interchangeably to describe very similar experiences. Likewise, a word like 'shaft' could be used to describe a thin beam of light as easily as a word like 'ray'. In the event, as will become clear, the experiences in this category turned out to contain interesting similarities, whatever word subjects chose to use. As will also become clear, the emerging pattern of crisis–light–turning-point–fruits was also encountered frequently, as was the overwhelmingly positive nature of the experiences overall.

Once again, a number of such experiences occurred at times of crisis (a complete statistical breakdown is given in the concluding chapter). One subject, for example, briefly reports: 'I was in my bedroom when my Dad died, & I saw streams of silver light go up, apparently through the ceiling.' Another, longer, unusual account comes from a lady who reports, prior to her experience, 'a generally disturbed and rather unhappy time in our family'. Then,

> One evening, whilst sitting alone in our London flat, after having dined (but not wined) I was reading a book of R. Tagore, when I suddenly began to have what I can best describe as a great upsurge of feeling, which made me put my book down and listen very intently. Then I remember standing up, and realizing how clear and bright everything seemed around me. I felt

very elated and light in myself, and the atmosphere seemed sort of electric and charged with suspense; then I became conscious of this strong visual sensation of a very fast flowing current, or stream of light, way out above me and beneath that a second stream narrower, but flowing in the same direction, with a gap between them. It seemed that I then cognized that this lower and smaller current somehow, symbolically represented my own life stream. Everything was very silent and intense, and I remember feeling extremely peaceful.

Her next sensation appears very strange and almost akin to a 'traditional' out-of-body experience:

> After this there came this very strong physical sensation, as if I was sort of taken out of myself, turned around (or inside out) and was facing myself, but was being carried along in the direction of the smaller stream that was above me, but below the main stream. Like me on two levels, but facing each other and in some way connected.

The next paragraph reminds us both of the ineffability of religious experience, and of the fact that many such experiences – including experiences of light – elude easy classification:

> It is very difficult, practically impossible, to describe such a unique and physical experience. All I knew [was] it was a gripping reality (words scratch). All the time there was this great intensification of light and energy and outline of objects in the room, and this wonderful feeling that I had somehow become part of everything, and attached to something. At the same time I realized that strength and understanding were being given to me together with this new direction I seemed to be flowing in.

The vivid phrase 'words scratch' expresses beautifully the difficulty of putting something so unusual into words and the reference to the intensification of light – perhaps connected with the 'intensification of energy and objects' – reminds us of the difficulties connected with classifying accounts. Indeed, such a description might easily have placed this experience in the 'illumination of landscape' category, save for the fact that it is not entirely clear from the subject's account that the room itself became brighter. Her reference to intensification of light may, in fact, refer back to the stream of light she mentions in her first paragraph. The subject's next paragraph, however, clearly describes the by now familiar fruits of the experience:

> Eventually I felt a settling down and acceptance of what was happening, and after quite a few hours went to my bedroom thinking to get some sleep and rest, but those two streams seemed to follow over and above me wherever I went, and the conviction that I would never truly be alone again

came very forcefully (and it has always remained) as has the memory of that strange but funny two levels, inside out, sort of sensation, which still comes to me if I am thinking intensely or with a lot of people under pressure.

That the fruits were lasting and evident to others is indicated later on in her narrative:

Eventually I suppose I got some sleep, but next morning it was still a very gripping reality, and I could not settle to anything so I remember thinking I would go for a walk and see what happened, but still it all went with me. This lightness, and I felt so free and ridiculously happy and excited. I cannot think looking back on it how one behaved outwardly as usual, but that was the strange thing about it all, it all seemed so NATURAL. The next day I had to go back to my family in the country and keep this enormous secret to myself (though in years to come my daughters all said they had about that time noticed an enormous change in me). (4331)

The subject indicates at the very beginning of this long account that she was training to be a teacher of Transcendental Meditation at the time of her experience and her reference to reading Tagore gives another clue as to her theological and philosophical background. The *following* account is interesting, however, inasmuch as it describes another 'lightbeam' experience but is narrated by a person from within a very different background – a Christian male, whose 'longing to be a better man' provided the context for an experience in which he:

[L]istened to the 'Witness' of a fellow [Church] worker sent to work with me for just that day. While alone for a few minutes thinking of his witness for Christ I suddenly had the sensation of being in a beam of light. An amazing understanding of all my Godly Mother had taught me and what Sunday School Teachers had tried to tell me flooded my whole being and for the rest of that day I bombarded Gods messenger to me with Questions. Finally he said, 'You have a bible at home, read the "Gospel of St. John"'. On my way home I called at the home of my wife's Aunt who had been clearing out some cupboards. She asked me to take all the paper etc into the garden to burn. As she left the room I searched amongst the pile looking for some worldly 'find', and there in gold letters (a sight I shall never forget) were the words 'The Gospel of St. John'. (2134)

The experience appears to have led to a reformation of character and to repentance for past 'sins', for immediately afterwards the writer describes how he generously repaid a shopkeeper's daughter for a deception he had committed at her mother's store some twenty-five years previously. And whilst this account and the one of the trainee TM teacher are obviously very different in content, it is interesting that a stream or beam of light in each case produced both insight and transformation *despite* the differences of theological and philosophical outlook possessed by the subjects prior to their experiences. Once again, it appears that experiences of light containing recognizable consistencies are able to transcend the categories into which they are placed *and* the differing belief-systems of the subjects that report them.

Unusual experiences

The following account provides yet another warning that categorization of experiences containing unusual light is not easy or straightforward. It could, in fact, have been placed in the 'shared' category, save for the interesting detail that one of the witnesses appears to have been a dog. It was submitted to the RERC in 1985 by the daughter of the experient. She writes:

> My mother was a very strong personality with a wonderful sense of humour. She was also one of the most sensitive people I have ever known, and she wrote some beautiful poetry. There was no one more than she who sought answers about the Universe and why all the suffering in the world, even the Ministers could not answer her questions! With a total reverence for living creatures she would not kill even a wasp!
>
> May I explain that since moving to her little pensioner's house six years ago on numerous occasions she had told me that she had sensed that she had company in the house. The final 'out of the ordinary' thing happened just four days before she died on 8th July '85 on a Sunday evening. She was very brave and had a hysterectomy at the age of 73 but had managed to get up and watch T.V. that night. When I arrived her words to me were that she had had a 'strange visitation'. I asked what happened, and she told me that firstly her T.V. screen had gone all ZIG-ZAGY and then black, then through her sitting room window had come a *broad band of silver light*. Mum demonstrated the bridth by holding her hands about 1 foot apart. This band of light passed through the room and out through the kitchen which leads from her sitting room. After it had passed through the room the T.V. came back to normal. My mothers [*sic*] little Border Collie also sat up and saw it.
>
> By the way, there was no lightening about that night as I have thought about that too. We had a very dry summer up here last year, with no thunderstorms. (4165)

Yet another experience that contains unusual detail that might have served to locate it within more than one category is reported by a sixty-one-year-old lady who, on the anniversary of a loved one's death, went to church 'with the intention of thanking God for His care of her ... for her present happiness'. Her experience occurred during the Communion service on that day. She writes:

> After receiving the sacrament, I went back to kneel in my pew. I became aware of a golden ray of light coming down directly at me. It flooded my whole being so utterly that I felt split into millions of atoms, as if each atom was surrounded by this golden light ... like being infiltrated by it. I no longer felt as a body of flesh but as if this 'is' and not me, and yet I 'am' too for I can feel it glowing as if with a living warmth. I looked up the length of light and saw at the top what appeared to be a concentrated mass of itself with about a dozen people standing within. The position of this group was at about half the height of the church and slightly to the right ... as if not to disturb anything going on at the main altar. I went up the path of light. This 'concentration' at the top seemed to hide and blur those in the group so that I could not identify anyone. I was given to know that they are enfolded in the Love of God, that this is their Life force; for a brief moment I felt this too as something indescribably intense and lovely; & it was gloriously beyond my capacity to have imagined, and not of this Earth. I came back suddenly to kneeling in my pew again. I should think only a few seconds of our time had elapsed. (1665)

Detailed and clear as this description is of a most unusual *ray* of light, it is evident that it contains detail reminiscent of some of our other categories of lightforms too. The lady's description of her whole being as 'flooded' with light, 'as if each atom was surrounded' sounds rather like an attempt to describe a *wrapping* with light, whilst her description of being 'infiltrated' by the light is perhaps suggestive of *filling*. Of note too is her description of movement 'up the path of light', suggestive, perhaps of the movement through space reported by some of those in the 'crisis experience' category.

Another unusual account submitted to the RERC in March 1980 is striking in that whilst it contains the familiar motifs of crisis, light, turning-point and transformation, these are witnessed by neither the subject nor the narrator of the account but by a third party. The narrator, the subject's son, relates how

> In the 1930s my mother had an emergency operation in hospital. She was gravely ill for 2/3 days, then began to recover. A patient opposite in the ward spoke to her when she was ready to leave (a complete stranger). She asked my mother's permission to describe a 'vision' she, the stranger, had seen on the night my mother returned to the ward from the operating theatre, unconscious. The stranger said that two figures appeared one each

side of the bed. One, a white haired old lady with steel spectacles, smooth hair and a 'bun' at the back; the other, a soldier in 1914–18 war uniform. The old lady spoke to the soldier, who took off his jacket and the two figures disappeared. Shortly afterwards, a shaft of 'white light' came down from above onto the bed. The stranger, who said she was a 'medium' of some sort, considered that this light strengthened my mother physically and she began to recover from then onwards.

Interestingly, the narrator adds:

The stranger asked whether this vision meant anything to my mother. It certainly did, both to my mother and me. A few years previously, my maternal grandmother had died and her last wish was for the army tunic of her youngest son, who had been killed in the 1914–18 war, to be brought from her wardrobe and laid at the foot of her bed. The stranger's description of the two figures correctly described our relatives.

He also adds a later experience of his own:

It happened in the summer of 1942 when I was in the army stationed in a country village, where I met my wife. We had only known each other for 2/3 months and were almost 'penniless'. However, as we knew I would soon be posted abroad we impulsively decided to get married. On the eve of our wedding whilst talking to her, by a 'slip of the tongue' I found that she had been lying to me about a personal matter we had discussed soon after meeting. I was so shattered, that I returned to the mess son to telephone the priest of the church in which we were to be married, to postpone the wedding for which I had very good grounds for doing. As I approached the telephone my friend, who was to be best man, spoke to me and as I looked into his eyes it seemed as though lightning had struck me, closing my eyes. I then had a vision, clearly seeing the head and shoulders of a 'biblical' type of man, with strong features, piercing eyes, red hair and beard. He did not speak, but raised his fist as though to strike me down. I bowed my head, the figure disappeared. When I opened my eyes and raised my head, I asked the others present what had happened to the lights. No one else had experienced anything, chatting normally. From that moment I felt a great sense of reassurance, and the wedding took place the following day. (3463)

Once again we have an account that is difficult to categorize, yet the description of the light given – 'it seemed as though lightning had struck me' – suggests some sort of beam or shaft that strikes the subject. It resolves his crisis in an immediate and concrete way. From being about to postpone his wedding he decides instead to go through with it, feeling 'a great sense of reassurance'. That the subject and nobody else sees the light is not unusual: as we have already noted, an overwhelming number of cases of unusual lights are seen by single observers. The vision that accompanies the light is strange, though: the 'biblical' man is reported nowhere else in the entire study.

As with the other categories of experience so far examined, this category also contained an interesting description of a blue light. In it, the writer, a Hindu follower of Sri Aurobindo, describes how

> In the night of the 30th–31st January 1970 I was woken up into almost full consciousness and heard someone say to me 'Keep quite still'. I way [was] lying on my back. I think there seemed to be two people near me. I felt no fear or any other emotion. Then it seemed as if a flow passed through the top of my head, went right through my body and out at my feet. I think at the same time I was consious of a vivid pale electric blue light. I say 'I think' because I believe it was only on regaining full consiousness that I realised this, so it maybe that the 'mental' thought this up later, I can't be quite sure. (3491)

As we have been seeing, the fruits of the experiences reported by subjects in this category have been largely positive. We recall, for example, the 'enormous change' wrought by her experience in the life of the reader of Tagore and the 'great sense of reassurance' given to the man whose eve-of-wedding experience persuaded him, after all, to wed. Two further accounts containing clearly positive fruits will serve to close this chapter. In the first, the writer, a fifty-three-year-old married lady, describes how suddenly, one day

> I was aware of knowing I had access to knowledge, that the answers were there and available to me. I was conscious of a sense of tranquillity through some sort of inward strength . . . through an upstairs window (of my old Georgian house) I was vividly aware of an image of strong white light stretching into the far distance between two straight lines – it could almost be described as a shaft of dazzling brightness, but it didn't seem to get any narrower as it went out of my sight. There was no movement in it, it was more like a straight road of blinding white light and with the image of it came the feeling of a new dimension of perception through which I could have confidence in my intuition, and through which I should see everything more clearly. I think I remember thinking this is what people experience when they try to explain why they have a certain unshakeable faith through a religious experience, but that was certainly not the form my 'enlightenment' was taking. It was as if order was being created out of chaos in some part of my mind, and then how soon I can't remember I found my head was crowded with startlingly clear pictures of places and events and people. It was as though floodgates had opened on a vast store of forgotten memories.

Clearly, this lady was undergoing some kind of powerfully transformative experience, and the effects it had on her life are described in similarly powerful and vivid terms as her story continues:

> One realised suddenly that, after all, one had both a vivid imagination and a good memory. Coupled with all this and controlling it all was the strong feeling of having a creative urge to write using all this fascinating and unfamiliar material which seemed to want to flow out of my mind. Strangely it all seemed bottled up somewhere under my diaphragm! It was all too new to me to want to do anything except enjoy it and to try to make some sort of pattern from the myriad pieces. At the same time it was all familiar as if I knew that this was the natural outcome of all my reactions and impressions throughout my life . . . the next day I felt very uplifted in spirit, not unlike being inebriated or perhaps having the unexpected news of a large inheritance. (4141)

Finally, less detailed – but equally dramatic – are the after-effects of an unusual experience described by the following subject whose series of experiences following one upon the other began some time during October 1961 when she was thirty-five and in apparently good health. She writes:

> I was awakened in the night to what appeared to be a light streaming down and a feeling of very great joy. I heard an interior voice telling me three things. 1) that there was nothing to fear, 2) that to die would be the most wonderful thing that would happen to me, 3) that most people had got things the wrong way round. The intense joy continued for about ten days accompanied by a very great love and compassion for everyone, and a complete disregard either for food or sleep. This was followed by a feeling of guilt and unworthiness, but about three weeks later I was suddenly visited with a most great and overwhelming sense of forgiveness which seemed God again. In the third experience of this series, in November 1961, in my garden one day I suddenly 'saw' the world transfigured – not only trees and plants but people as well, impossible to describe but a sort of idyllic Garden of Eden everywhere. (3179)

10

Brighter than the sun: flashes of light

Lights that flash

A small number of all of the accounts examined, only seven in total, contained descriptions of a light that flashed. One subject, in describing such an episode, reports how

> One day I was alone and was busy laying the table for a meal. At the same time I was praying for someone in need of God's help. Suddenly there was a brilliant flash of light brighter than the sun and an audible voice said 'You need not pray any more, your prayers will be answered'. I nearly dropped the plate I was carrying. I thought I was praying for the impossible and was only praying to relieve my feelings because there was nothing else I could do. About a fortnight later God performed a miracle and that prayer was gloriously answered. I have had the experience of hearing God's audible voice twice in my life. Each time followed by a miracle. (2877)

Another subject, writing to the RERC and describing another episode including a clear description of a flash of light, recounts how

> One very dark night I had to pass a desolate, and to me very frightening spot on my way home. So great was my fear that I prayed with my whole being for protection. Suddenly with a vivid flash of light I felt myself lifted and carried in an instant of time to my own doorstep. Surrounding me again I felt the power of a great sustaining love, followed by a spiritual revelation of many days duration. (2880)

Significantly, most of the experiences in this category followed our by now familiar pattern of crisis–light–turning-point–fruits extremely closely. The above account clearly does, as does the following:

> Oct 1964 to Easter 1965 time of great sadness, sickness, etc. (I had known bad times before but this time with division of some of my Family, this I found very hard to take) Sad Christmas 1964, End of January 1965 I took

Young Family Friend to Hosp. Bus Strike on we walked couple-of-miles, after his admission I walked part-way home, bought some Fruit, etc, turned back to Hospital with it, turned again, towards home, it was Snowing I was wearing shoes too-tight as I left Hosp: grounds, feet sore, worried, who would visit boy I had taken to Hosp? (Bus strike, etc.) worried about Home Troubles, Home Sickness, etc. I thought 'got to lift my mind above this or I'll never walk-it' I looked up: Gold Light Flashed across Sky, I was so amazed I walked home forgetting my sore-feet. (1848)

Even where the subject chooses to describe the experience before the events leading up to it – as in the following account – the sequence is still clearly discernible. The respondent, thirty-nine at the time her experience occurred, begins by describing a 'sudden experience of a vivid red double flash . . . as of lightning or "tongues" of fire at the instant of starting to read "No Passing Glory" by Andrew Boyle – A Biography of the Life of Group Captain Leonard Cheshire' before going on to explain why she was reading this particular book at the time of her experience. 'I had bought this book', she writes,

> because I had just been through a spiritual crisis, helped by an R.C. Priest, and thought I would read a book by an R.C. convert and this book was quite definitely waiting for me in W. H. Smith's bookshop across the road from the R.C. Church. The experience took place at a house called Bellair, Madron, Near Penzance, overlooking St. Michael's Mount.

That the experience provided a clear turning-point in the crisis, leading to a sustained and positive outcome, is clear as the writer continues to describe how

> I am deliberately leaving out as much of the emotional impact as possible, but at the same time this was intense. I felt completely uplifted and everything was flooded with light and I found myself in an entirely new level of consciousness. Everything in my life seemed to 'dovetail' and I could discern the hand of Providence in everything. I became increasingly aware as the days went on of being in a pattern and I found myself meeting the right people, reading the right books, as if everything to help me was flowing towards me and into my consciousness.

And she adds, interestingly, that 'The light was so intense for the first few months that I stayed as much as possible in my cottage and garden' (1980).

Notable in the following account is the detail the writer gives concerning the extent (and depth) of the crisis that preceded her experience. I quote it in full:

The story is rather childish, but it was by this I began to know God. I was a member of a large family, and being somewhat irritable of temper was not popular with them. At school, on the other hand, I had friends and was reasonably well liked. I became puzzled, and one question nagged more and more persistently in my brain: 'Which am I? Am I nice, like my friends think? Or am I unpleasant, as my family says? Which am I?'

One Sunday, sitting in a packed church, I was startled by the curate saying in the course of his sermon, 'You are what you are before God.' On the way home I thought, 'God sees me at home as well as at school. I must be at home as I am at school.'

So I tried, and failed. Every night I acknowledged the failure to myself, and made fresh resolves for the next day. Failure was unremitting and worried me increasingly. There was a persistent whisper in my mind, 'Give it up. The others don't worry and they are happy. Give it up.' But I would not. I drew a page of small squares one for each day of a month, and pinned it on my bedroom wall. I thought, 'If I succeed I'll leave the square white. If I fail I'll mark it black. It will help to remind me.' At the end of the month the squares were all black. All the month the whisper persisted, 'Give up, give up, stop worrying.'

One night it was very dark, with no moon or stars gleaming through the window. The bedroom light was duly turned off. As I lay, wide-awake on my bed, the physical dark without was less profound than the darkness within.

'You can't succeed. You only fail. Give up, give up, give up!' urged the whisper. 'All right', I answered within myself 'I'll give up.'

The[n], though lying still and quiet on my bed, I seemed to be sinking down and down, with a sensation that was physical, into a deep, dark pit. I seemed to lie prone on my face at the bottom. Then, though lying quiet and still on my bed, I seemed to myself to lift up my head and cry out, 'Oh I cannot give up. But what shall I do? Across the foot of my bed there flashed a light and in the light the words written 'Blessed are they that hunger and thirst after righteousness, for they shall be filled.'

The darkness and despair left me. (3646)

Finally, an experience that also appears to have occurred at a time of crisis but with an unusual twist: for here, the crisis, a bereavement, affects not only the writer but the writer's pastor as well and the flash of light is interpreted by the writer as the presence of her (and her pastor's) deceased friend:

A dear friend of mine, a Christian woman who had given her time and love in serving the Lord in our church, passed away at a young age. Since her work dealt with youth she and our pastor spent many hours at her home discussing plans. To lose Maybelle was to lose a dear friend and a sister, he was in deep grief at her death.

I tried to take her place, but to carry on with some part of her work and to be a friend, to our dear pastor, to help him.

One day, at his home. He was standing at the door, ready to leave the house, asking his wife if she wanted any errands done while he was out. I went to him, ready to touch his arm, shoulder or hand in a playful way, with a joking remark on my lips – but I didn't touch him, and the words were left unsaid. I felt a force between us. I sensed a flash of light. I've not mentioned this to him and he didn't seem to sense it, unless deep in his sub-conscious he wished I wouldn't do the things Maybelle did. After it happened I felt that she had been there, either protecting him or warning me. The force was real, as physical as a push away. I'll never forget it. (3512)

Part III

11

Throwing light on lightforms – a mystery solved

Statistical analysis

How may we best explain the findings of the lightforms study? Are the accounts examined in Part II genuine evidence of another 'world' existing alongside this one? A world capable, on occasion, of 'breaking through' to our own – perhaps to comfort, to heal, to illuminate or simply to hint at dimensions of reality that transcend our own? Or may science hold the key to the unfolding mystery that we are examining, explaining the unusual encounters with light in terms, for example, of abnormal brain processes, crisis, illness, drugs, fatigue – or even perhaps madness? These are the questions that this chapter will seek to answer. Before we turn to them, however, we need to be clearer about exactly what data it is that we are trying to explain.

To do this, it will be important, firstly, to make an accurate statistical analysis of the entire number of accounts examined in the study. The total numbers of testimonies that fell into each category of experience examined in part II were: (a) Unusual lights with multiple witnesses (chapter 3), 10 cases; (b) Solitary experiences of unusual light (chapter 4), 86 cases; (c) Unusual lights that wrap and fill (chapter 5), 77 cases; (d) Illuminations of landscape and people (chapter 6), 35 accounts; (e) Lights seen during 'near-death experiences' (chapter 7), 48 cases; (f) Visionary 'encounters' with light (chapter 8), 80 cases; (g) Beams, rays, shafts (chapter 9), 13 cases; (h) Flashes of light (chapter 10), 7 cases.

Secondly, it is important to be clear about the percentages of experiences that actually fit the developing 'core' experience that began to emerge throughout part II. What follows, therefore, is a breakdown, for each category of experience, of the percentages of accounts describing lights experienced during times of crisis, lights associated with positive feelings, lights leading to or followed by positive 'fruits', and the colours of lights reported, where these *were* reported. (Under each heading, it will be of note that a distinction is made between each 'type' of experience reproduced in chapter 5 – 'Unusual lights that envelop subjects' and 'Unusual lights that fill subjects' – even though both categories were taken and presented there together.)

Percentage of experiences occurring at times of crisis
Unusual lights with multiple witnesses (chapter 3) 50; Solitary experiences of unusual light (chapter 4) 48.8; Unusual lights that envelop subjects (chapter 5) 50; Unusual lights that fill subjects (chapter 5) 38.1; Illuminations of landscape and people (chapter 6) 25.7; Lights seen during 'near-death experiences' (chapter 7) N/A; Visionary 'encounters' with light (chapter 8) 38.75; Beams, rays, shafts (chapter 9) 44.14; Flashes of light (chapter 10) 57.1.

Percentage of experiences including positive feelings
Unusual lights with multiple witnesses (chapter 3) 30; Solitary experiences of unusual light (chapter 4) 79.2; Unusual lights that envelop subjects (chapter 5) 88.1; Unusual lights that fill subjects (chapter 5) 92.3; Illuminations of landscape and people (chapter 6) 87.5; Lights seen during 'near-death experiences' (chapter 7) 87; 'Visionary' encounters with light (chapter 8) 83.7; Beams, rays, shafts (chapter 9) 91.7; Flashes of light (chapter 10) 100.

Percentage of experiences leading to or followed by positive 'fruits'
Unusual lights with multiple witnesses (chapter 3) 90; Solitary experiences of unusual light (chapter 4) 93.6; Unusual lights that envelop subjects (chapter 5) 88.1; Unusual lights that fill subjects (chapter 5) 90.5; Illuminations of landscape and people (chapter 6) 87.5; Lights seen during 'near-death experiences' (chapter 7) 87; 'Visionary' encounters with light (chapter 8) 83.7; Beams, rays, shafts (chapter 9) 80; Flashes of light (chapter 10) 100.

Number of lights of each colour as represented in all categories of experience
Problematical in this regard was the fact that colour was not specified in each account. Additionally, many colours were reported in only

two or three accounts. The most commonly reported colours were gold (31 accounts), white (28 accounts) and blue (10 accounts).

These figures require some comment. Overall, the manifestation of lights taking various forms at times of (and usually in the depths of) deep crises occurred in 44.1 per cent of the total number of accounts examined. If the category of light experienced in an NDE or similar crisis event is included in the total the figure becomes 51.2, for experiences in this category include, by virtue of when they occur, an obvious crisis 'component'. In sum: *over half of all light experiences contained in the RERC archive across all categories of experience occurred at times of crisis.* This is a significant finding, and one which this chapter will later attempt to explain. Even more striking is the overwhelmingly positive nature of the light experiences in most categories and the positive fruits that almost invariably followed them. Once again, this is a finding that the current chapter must attempt to explore.

Nothing has yet been said about either the *location* of the various experiences within the various categories or the 'personality' ascribed to the lights reported in the various accounts. As regards location, it is of note that analysis revealed few commonalities across reports, save that a significant number of experiences tended to occur when experients were in bed. Whilst this invites charges that some light experiences are dreams or hallucinations occurring on the border between sleeping and waking, it is worth noting that many subjects drew particular attention to the fact that their experiences took place while they were awake. But, overall, few useful conclusions emerged from the analysis of location of experiences. The same may be said for the analysis of personality and/or identity described in the light by some subjects. In fact, comparatively few attempted to identify the light and some were genuinely baffled as to its identity. Much more important, in the vast majority of cases, were the positive feelings accompanying the experience, themselves suggestive of a very benign and loving presence, and the life transformations that usually ensued.

Putting all of this together, it is inviting to turn the above bare statistical analysis into a model that appears to fit a large number of experiences involving unusual lights, as examined in part II. If we were to do so, we would find that, typically, persons in states of deep crisis – both physical and emotional – reach a point of extreme or maximum distress. At this point, when they often feel that they cannot continue, they encounter an unusual light. This light may take various forms and occupy various 'locations'. Sometimes it appears at a specific place within the person's normal environment, such as in a corner of the room. At other times it appears as part of a wholly different, 'visionary' landscape. At yet others it may wrap or fill the subject, and it may also appear as a flash, beam, ray or shaft. Sometimes the light seems to illuminate the entire landscape, like an emanation or an aura. Occasionally the experience of light may even be shared.

The light's appearance, however and wherever it occurs, typically represents a 'turning-point' within the person's crisis, often because of the feelings of peace, comfort, love and joy that accompany it. Sometimes the light can even be identified, but more usually personality is either present but unidentified or inferred by subjects as a result of the overwhelming effects it has upon them. The experience remains unforgettable and may trigger major life-changes in addition to the beginning of recovery from despair. Typical 'fruits' of the experience include a decreased fear of death, a developing awareness of the existence of God or other spiritual realities, or the acquisition of new hobbies and interests.

Care needs to be taken with this model, yet it is useful as a guide to the structure and content of a significant number of experiences that we have encountered. We need to bear in mind, for example, that 48.8 per cent, of all of the experiences examined did *not* occur in a crisis situation. On the other hand, the 51.2 per cent of experiences that *did* amounts to almost 200 experiences in total. And in remembering the diversity of experiences examined in part II, we should not lose sight of the clear patterning of features that emerged clearly and strongly throughout the chapters presented there.

Interestingly, the model bears comparison with some of the 'model' NDEs presented in the work of some of the early near-death experience researchers such as Raymond Moody and Kenneth Ring, as alluded to in chapter 7. In these models, we find a similar structure of crisis–light–turning-point–transformation as detailed in the model above. In view of the clear similarities involved, we are surely led to one of the main conclusions of the current study, one with implications for our understanding of a wide range of experiences involving unusual lights, including NDEs. For now it seems clear that near-death experiences are just one subset of a much wider range of patterned experiences in which loving, benign light-presences appear and transform crisis situations, producing positive, lasting and often spiritual 'fruits' in the lives of people who had previously been on the brink of despair. Perhaps it is time to stop looking for these lights in the midst of death – as much NDE research has done – and to start looking for them in the midst of life: particularly in the midst of life's troughs. What is particularly exciting about this conclusion is the hope it offers us *in this life* for a hope of something loving, spiritual and real beyond it.

Explanations

This tentative, if intriguing, conclusion, is itself open to question, however. For there may be other ways of accounting for the experiences we have been examining that are much more mundane and this-worldly and which do not require notions of 'other worlds' and supernatural presences at all. In 1960, for example, Dewi Rees, a medical doctor practising in Wales, began a study of the effects of bereavement on widows. Concentrating his research on the town of Llanidloes, which he claimed to be a place of diversity both in culture and occupation, Rees was particularly interested to discover the degree to which the bereaved reported things such as weight loss, headaches, insomnia, tearfulness, depression and anxiety. At the beginning of his research in a community of 5,000 people he made no provision for the additional study of reports of the sensed presence of the dead on the part of his subjects. Yet in very many cases this is what he found.

Rees published the first detailed account of his findings in 1971 in a *British Medical Journal* article entitled 'The hallucinations of widowhood'. Discounting any reported nocturnal experiences as dreams – arguably a contentious thing to do, in the light of *this* study's findings – he was still able to report that 46.7 per cent of widows surveyed 'had an experience of the dead spouse that they considered to be significant and real' (Rees 2001: 273).

Most commonly, Rees's subjects reported a sense of the continuing presence of their deceased partners, with 46 per cent of his study group making comments like 'I know she is with me, when I speak to her she goes away' and 'He's always with me'. Fourteen per cent reported visual experiences, with one widow claiming: 'Once he came to the door when I was preparing lunch. It was an awful shock', and another: 'I have only seen him once. He was walking through the gate. He looked very happy. I didn't have a chance to speak to him.' Of Rees's subjects 13.3 per cent reported auditory experiences, typically making comments such as 'I am not lonely because he is with me all the time. I hear him saying "I'm alright Mary". I am very happy.' Tactile experiences, whilst rare – accounting for only 2.7 per cent of cases – were none the less dramatic and not always pleasant. On the one hand some cases were reassuring, with one widow reporting how 'On one occasion in the afternoon, soon after he died, I definitely felt his presence and he kissed my face.' On the other hand, some tactile cases were clearly disturbing, with another claiming of her deceased husband: 'I felt him touch me. It frightened me. Made you think you were going up the wall.' Overwhelmingly, however, Rees found that this apparently ongoing contact with the dead was a positive experience for the living. Whilst 69 per cent of subjects found their experiences helpful, only 6 per cent found them to be unpleasant (Rees 2001: 268–71).

Rees discovered that men and women reported such 'encounters' in roughly equal numbers. Social isolation of subjects was not a factor in determining frequency of occurrence of experiences. Neither change of residence after bereavement nor the religious backgrounds of subjects appeared to have any effect either. Indeed, one of the few factors affecting frequency of experience was whether the prior marriage was happy or not, with unhappy marriages producing fewer post-mortem phenomena. The experiences sometimes occurred long into widowhood, were most common amongst the professional and managerial classes, and tended to leave positive and lasting effects including feelings of comfort and helpfulness.

Overall, Rees concluded that the sense of the presence of a deceased spouse was 'a perfectly normal occurrence and compatible with a favourable outcome to the process of mourning' (2001: 275). But what was the explanation for these extraordinary findings? Both in his original study and subsequently, Rees considered several possibilities. One was that the sensed presence was rather like a phantom limb and therefore a hallucination comparable to those reported by persons who feel the presence of limbs long after they have lost them. He wrote: '[I]t may be argued that the two processes are similar, it is just that the stimuli and neuronal pathways producing the hallucinatory experiences of widowed people have yet to be uncovered' (2001: 277).

Less likely, for Rees, was the possibility that widows were mistaking living people for dead ones. This, he wrote, might be expected if the experiences had taken place in settings generally unfamiliar to subjects. However, this was not at all what he found, discovering instead that 'the bereaved are most likely to perceive their dead partners in and around their own homes where such errors are less likely to occur'. Rees also considered the possibility that yearning and searching on the part of the bereaved might have led some subjects to misinterpret 'mundane' experiences as actual encounters with their deceased loved ones. This thesis, which builds on the work of psychologists John Bowlby and C. M. Parkes, suggests that pining drives the surviving spouse to search for the dead partner: a futile quest but one which assists the grieving process. 'According to this theory', wrote Rees,

> the bereaved pay particular attention to stimuli that suggest the presence of the deceased and ignore those that do not. If ambiguous perceptions happen to fit the image of the deceased, attention is focussed on this data and further evidence is sought to confirm the initial impression. As a consequence, the bereaved person is particularly open to the illusion that the dead person has been perceived (Rees 2001: 277).

As with the other 'explanations' of his findings, Rees was critical of this one – the so-called 'search theory' – as well. For one thing, he wrote, it failed to explain 'why the bereaved should be so prone to misinterpret data when looking so intently for the deceased'. In other words, the intensity of the search should guarantee that the bereaved would be careful *not* to misinterpret mundane or ambiguous stimuli as being evidence of the presence of their deceased loved ones. 'People who are intent on finding a very familiar object' he wrote 'tend to be highly discriminatory' (2001: 278).

There are other problems with the search theory too, as Rees clearly acknowledged. What, he wondered, of experiences that occurred when the bereaved were *not* searching at all? In fact, he wrote, contrary to being a product of expectation and seeking, 'evidence indicates that these events occur unexpectedly and spontaneously.' In this regard, he argued, consider the experience of writer C. S. Lewis after the death of his wife, as reproduced by him in his book *A Grief Observed*:

> Something quite unexpected has happened . . . suddenly, at the very moment when, so far, I mourned H. least, I remembered her best. Indeed, it was something better than a memory; an instantaneous unanswerable impression. . .I said, several notebooks ago, that if I got what seemed like an assurance of H.'s presence, I wouldn't believe it. Easier said than done. (Rees 2001: 279)

Another problem with the 'search theory' came, for Rees, from evolutionary theory. Simply stated: what was the evolutionary point of being able to discern the presence of the dead? Nature, he wrote,

> is 'red in tooth and claw' and is concerned with the survival of the species, not with easing the distress of older members of society whose capacity for reproduction has diminished or ended. Why then has this most subtle of consolations been evolved and enabled to persist? It has no place in a philosophy that confines mankind to a material world, but it does make sense if a spiritual dimension to life is also accepted. (2001: 280).

Indeed, the attempt to explain away such experiences psychologically failed, for Rees, to recognize their overwhelmingly positive nature and the spiritual benefits they brought to the bereaved. By dubbing such experiences 'pathological' and implying that they hindered rather than helped the grieving process, the search theory had, in fact, refused to accept 'the possibility that the widowed may have been enlarged by the experience and their lives thereby enhanced'. By contrast, he wrote, 'A spiritual explanation opens up a new perspective for the bereaved as it implies a continued existence after death which, though it cannot be actually proved, is affirmed by the near presence of the deceased.'

This research, and the issues it raises, have much relevance to this book. Although none of Rees's subjects reported encountering a light, there are many other similarities between his findings and those of the current study that make his work of obvious importance. Most obviously, as with the so-called 'hallucinations' uncovered by Rees, many of the encounters with unusual lights explored in previous chapters occurred at times of crisis (including, often, bereavement), brought with them a sense of presence, were overwhelmingly positive and left lasting, beneficial 'fruits'. Perhaps, then, we should simply conclude that encounters with light after death are just one subset of a much larger group of post-mortem experiences such as those uncovered by Rees that include sensing the presence of the dead, hearing them, or even feeling their touch.

However, Rees's work is also useful because of the possibilities it opens up for accounting for lightforms psychologically. Even though, as we have seen, he rejects many conventional scientific explanations of his own findings, may they have more success in explaining the findings of *this* study?

It is clear that they do not. In fact, many of their weaknesses as uncovered by Rees remain weaknesses as explanations of the unusual lights which previous chapters of this book have explored. It is, for example, surely absurd to argue that 'phantom limb' theories can explain seeing unusual lights at times of crisis. The theory that subjects may be guilty of 'mistaken identity' is equally unlikely. In fact, unlike Rees's study, we have had repeated cause to note that subjects reporting encounters with unusual lights often cannot identify them at all and frequently hesitate to ascribe any identity to them despite the fact that they have been left with a strong sense that they have encountered some sort of personality. This fact also calls into question the ability of the 'search theory' to explain the unusual lights reported by subjects in this study. For if subjects are frequently unsure whom they have encountered, it makes little sense to view their experiences as the result of any kind of grief-driven search. The fact that encounters with unusual lights so often occur spontaneously also calls into question the argument that they are the result of any kind of quest.

In fact, it is tempting simply to share Rees's conclusion that any attempt to explain such anomalous events as evidence of a failed grieving process is itself a failure as it does not explain why such events are frequently so beneficial, even transforming. Of course, the added fact that encounters with unusual lights take place within a variety of different life crises – and not just after bereavement – calls further into question the 'explanation' that they are the outcome of failed or delayed grieving. Thus, the mystery, for now, remains. Perhaps other psychological explanations of the unusual lights encountered in these pages will provide better explanations of them.

Abreaction/rebound

During and immediately after the Second World War, a number of leading psychologists in Great Britain began to develop a series of treatments designed to help soldiers and ex-soldiers suffering from severe traumas suffered in battle, the so-called 'battle neuroses'. Their results make interesting reading, not least because of the insights they promise to provide for our ongoing attempt to account for lightforms psychologically.

Typically, battle neuroses were the result of deeply frightening episodes arising from combat situations, experienced either by soldiers or non-combatants caught up in life-threatening situations such as bombing raids. Frequently subjects would suppress the traumas they suffered, with resulting psychological maladies including mental breakdowns. Working with these patients, psychologists such as William Sargant and J. S. Horsley developed a treatment known as abreaction in which patients were given a combination of drugs and psychotherapy aimed at getting to them to relive the original traumas that had made them ill. Frequently this resulted in a sudden and dramatic cure.

Crucial to the success of the treatment was the actual releasing during therapy of the suppressed and pent-up emotions that had caused the original problems. Sargant wrote:

> Sometimes the episode, or episodes, had been mentally suppressed, and the memory would have to be brought to the surface again. At other times it was fully remembered, but the strong emotions originally attached to it had since been suppressed. The marked improvement in the patient's nervous condition was attributed to the releasing of these original emotions. (Sargant 1957: 17)

Most usually, the emotions released or abreacted were those of fear or anger. By contrast, observed Sargant, 'little could be done by making, say, a melancholic weep and become depressed'. However, when powerful outbursts of anger and fear were brought out, the results were frequently dramatic, with patients suddenly entering widely contrasting states of peace and calm. Sargant wrote:

> Outbursts of fear or anger thus deliberately induced and stimulated to a crescendo by the therapist, would frequently be followed by a sudden emotional collapse. The patient would fall back inert on the couch . . . but he would soon come round. It then often happened that he reported a dramatic disappearance of many nervous symptoms. (Sargant 1957: 18)

Whilst Sargant and his colleagues obtained their results using a combination of psychotherapy and drugs, they were convinced that it was the discharge of powerful emotions that was crucial to the success of the treatment. Sargant was also persuaded that his results might explain other more spontaneous cures of traumas that took place where no therapies were being administered at all. The success of abreaction, he wrote, 'often depends on powerful physiological forces unchained in the process'. These, he noted, can occur in a variety of situations, and thus 'People have been relieved of hysterical blindness by a sudden loud clap of thunder; others have recovered the use of their legs after a strong emotional fright induced by a sudden blow on the head.' Perhaps most controversially of all, Sargant proposed that abreaction was at work when revival preachers gained dramatic conversions at highly emotionally charged religious meetings by stimulating powerful feelings which, when suddenly discharged, resulted in the feelings of peace and 'rebirth' claimed by many converts (Sargant 1957: 18–19).

In recent years the process has been given the label 'rebound' and has been suggested as an explanation of other religious experiences too, such as mysticism. Can the theory of abreaction/rebound therefore be extended yet further in a bid to explain the unusual episodes of light discussed here?

Again, there are problems. On the one hand, the theory might account for the sudden substitution of feelings of calm and peace for those of despair and anxiety which have characterized many of the reports we have been examining. On this reckoning, when, say, a bereaved or troubled person reaches a state in which he or she cannot go on and perhaps prays or cries out loud, the process 'kicks in' and a state of calm and joy suddenly prevails. However, Sargant and his colleagues reported no experiences involving lights. Neither does abreaction or rebound involve any 'presence' other than the therapist and subject. By contrast, as we have been seeing, it is frequently the intervention of the light itself, often embodying a calming, comforting personality, that brings about the transformation of many of the lightforms subjects, and not their sudden articulation of pent-up feelings. In addition, few of the subjects whose experiences of light were transformative were suppressing feelings of anger or fear. Indeed, weeping and melancholy would appear to be the feelings most often associated with these episodes – the very feelings that Sargant and his colleagues were unable to remove. Finally, we recall again the fact that not all encounters with unusual lights take place at times of stress and crisis. As with the theories examined to explain bereavement hallucinations, it appears that the theories of abreaction and rebound cannot adequately explain lightforms either.

Mental dysfunction

Possibly, therefore, we need to ask the question whether or not these unusual episodes of light are evidence of some kind of mental dysfunction on the part of the subjects who report them. To do this, two distinct sets of mental conditions will need to be carefully separated. First, we will need to consider psychological conditions associated with particular types of mental illness. Of course, there is a risk here. It might appear that even to ask such a question amounts to an attempt to ridicule or discredit the testimonies of sincere, genuine people, and as we have already seen, many if not all subjects writing about their experiences of unusual lights sound very sincere and genuine indeed. On the other hand, the literature on subjects such as schizophrenia leaves no doubt that people suffering from such conditions often see, hear and feel the presence of various 'beings' that are not in fact there. Might the experiences in this book be of a similar nature?

In addition, we will also need to consider psychological conditions caused by malfunctions of the brain, malfunctions associated with a range of conditions such as epileptic seizures, drugs, stress and migraine. Once again, various types of vivid hallucinations are frequently reported in association with these. Might these include unusual lights as well?

In an important paper published a few years ago in the *Journal of Neuropsychiatry and Clinical Neurosciences*, J. L. Saver and J. Rabin conducted an analysis of the differences between psychotic hallucinations (such as those of schizophrenics) on the one hand and genuine 'culturally accepted religious-mystical beliefs' on the other. They found three important sets of differences. First, they noted the differences in the feelings and the descriptions of those feelings reported by both groups. Mystics, they asserted, tend to describe their experiences as ecstatic and joyful, frequently highlighting positive feelings of wholeness, transcendence and love. By contrast, psychotic episodes frequently tend to confuse and terrify those who suffer from them. Their experiences often leave them frightened and are described in overwhelmingly negative terms. Secondly, Saver and Rabin drew attention to the differences between both sets of experiences and everyday 'normal' reality. Whilst both mystics and psychotics undergo a break with reality, they argued, mystics yearn for their experiences and when they are over are able to 'emerge' from them back into 'normal' reality where they are usually able to share what happened to them in a coherent way. By contrast, they argued, psychotics frequently experience an *involuntary* withdrawal from reality, are frequently distressed by their experiences and often become progressively isolated from society. Thirdly, Saver and Rabin noted how both sets of experiencers interpreted their experiences differently. Psychotic people, they wrote, frequently develop delusions of grandeur as a result of their experiences, seeing themselves as 'special emissaries from God, blessed with an important message for the world'. By complete contrast, mystics experience a reduction of egocentricity, a quietening of the mind and an emptying of the self (Newberg et al. 2001: 109–10).

As a result of their analysis overall, Saver and Rabin concluded: 'These distinct differences make a very strong case that mysticism is not a product of psychotic delusion', before drawing attention to the fact that other psychological conditions, such as temporal lobe epilepsy, 'can trigger spontaneous hallucinatory events that strongly resemble the experiences described by mystics' (Newberg et al. 2001: 110). We will need to consider this assertion carefully later in the chapter. For now, however, it is clear that Saver and Rabin's findings with regard to mystics and psychotics can be usefully transferred to the current study in various ways. Like mystics, for example, persons experiencing unusual lights talk overwhelmingly of their experiences in positive, not negative, terms, sometimes in fact using the identical language of joy, wholeness and love that mystics use. This has been a consistent finding throughout this book and sets such experiences well apart from the confused and frightening episodes suffered by psychotics. In addition, encounters with unusual lights have been shown to be temporary and lead in virtually all cases to the experiencer's return to normal reality. In fact, far from progressively isolating these people from society, their encounters frequently provide a sort of healing of their lives, sometimes, as we have seen, enabling them to begin to resume more normal functioning after a spell of shock, trauma or mourning. In addition, we have seen no evidence of sudden delusions of grandiosity being triggered by light encounters. On the contrary, many subjects have described what happened to them in ordinary, down-to-earth ways, making no special claims for themselves either before, during or after their experiences. Indeed, the fact that they *do* describe their experiences so clearly and sensibly sets them further apart from the confused, rambling grandiosity of many psychotic episodes, in which claims are made which either make no sense or which elevate the sufferer far above his or her actual status in life.

If the experiences with which we have been dealing are not evidence of conditions such as psychosis, might they be better explained in terms of the hallucinatory effects of things like seizures, stress, exhaustion and drugs? In this regard, part of a recent study of religious experience by Andrew Newberg, Eugene D'Aquili and Vince Rause, *Why God Won't Go Away*, makes interesting reading. In it, the authors have drawn attention to four 'clusters' of differences between such hallucinations and 'genuine' mystical experiences (Newberg et al. 2001: 112). Firstly, they have noted that things like epileptic seizures strike frequently and may even assume a degree of regularity. By contrast, genuine religious experiences such as those of mystics may only occur a handful of times in a lifetime.

Secondly, the authors have noted that hallucinations tend to be repetitious: 'the victim hears the same voice with the same message, for example, or feels the advent of some inexplicable rapture'. By contrast, the spiritual experiences of mystics are variable; 'as variable as ordinary experience', with variations occurring in 'emotional tone' and/or the message delivered by angelic voices.

Thirdly, the authors have drawn attention to the range of senses involved in both sets of experiences, with genuine religious experiences involving a wider range than their pathological counter-parts. Thus, on the one hand, hallucinations 'usually involve only a single sensory system – a person may *see* a vision, *hear* a disembodied voice, or *feel* a sense of presence, but rarely are multiple senses simultaneously involved'. By contrast, mystical experiences 'tend to be rich, coherent, and deeply dimensioned sensory experiences. They are perceived with the same, and in some cases increased, degree of sensory complexity with which we experience "ordinary" states of mind. In plainest terms, they simply *feel* very real.'

Finally, the authors have drawn attention to the after-effects of the different types of experiences. Whilst hallucinations are immediately recognized by subjects *as* hallucinations, due to their 'fragmentary and dreamlike nature', the effects of mystical experiences are very different. In complete contrast to the 'victims' of hallucinations, mystics 'can never be persuaded that their experiences were not real' and, moreover, 'This sense of realness does not fade as they emerge from their mystical states, and it does not dissipate over time.' Overall, therefore, the conclusion drawn is that '[T]his sense of realness strongly suggests that the accounts of the mystics are not indications of minds in disarray, but are the proper, predictable neurological result of a stable, coherent mind willing itself toward a higher spiritual plane' (Newberg et al. 2001: 113).

How might these four 'clusters' of contrasts help us to evaluate the unusual lights with which we are dealing? Are they better classed as hallucinations or as more 'genuine' religious experiences? Like the latter, they appear to occur infrequently. Many subjects, as we have seen, report only one, memorable event within an entire lifetime. They also tend to contain variations, although the common pattern of experiencing that has emerged seems to indicate a degree of repetition. Even here, however, the pattern, where it occurs, seems meaningful, often providing deep support and comfort in the face of overwhelming trauma or upset. In addition, experiences of unusual light tend to be rich in sensory quality. Rarely is something seen without being felt – often profoundly – and sometimes there is a sense of communication also. And far from the fragmentary and dreamlike quality of hallucinations, experiences of unusual light are virtually always recalled and recounted as real – again, often profoundly so – and the memory of them does not fade. Indeed, it is frequently the case that they are recalled to mind with a striking quality and richness years after they occurred. Once again, the conclusion is clear: encounters with light do not resemble 'mere' hallucinations. They are of a very different type and quality altogether.

One further possible condition that sometimes produces experiences of unusual light is migraine, and the whole subject of 'migraine aura' was tackled early on in his fascinating research and writing career by the celebrated neurologist Oliver Sacks. In his book, *Migraine*, Sacks described the types and variation of unusual lights reported by sufferers to him. Some, he wrote, described simple forms including brilliant stars, sparks or flashes. Some reported simple geometric shapes, usually white, but sometimes of other colours too. Sometimes large numbers of lights were reported; 'many hundred' that swarm rapidly across the visual field. Other movement resembled rippling and shimmering, comparable to 'wind-blown water or looking through watered silk' (Sacks 1985: 56). Indeed, so common is the condition of unusual flickering light in migraine attacks that it has a specific term: scintillating scotoma.

Sacks noted a frequent pattern to the phenomenon. 'The majority of migraine scotomata', he wrote,

> present as a sudden brilliant luminosity near the fixation-point in one visual half-field; from here the scotoma gradually expands and moves slowly towards the edge of the visual field, assuming the form of a giant crescent or horseshoe. Its subjective brightness is blinding ... [it has been compared] to that of a white surface in noonday sunlight. (1985: 57–9)

He also noted a pattern to the feelings accompanying the scotomata, with frequent reports of foreboding, dread and the imminence of death. Indeed, this sense of mortal fear was well known in the past, wrote Sacks, and was given the term *angor animi*. By contrast, some patients did report more positive feelings such as mild pleasure, but rarely, he wrote, did this extend to awe or rapture. Feelings of strangeness also sometimes occurred.

In later works, Sacks has continued to explore migraine aura, suggesting that the religious visions of mystics such as Hildegard of Bingen might be explained as episodes of scintillating scotoma and that her experiences were 'indisputably migrainous'. Might the same be said for the lights reported by subjects nearer our own time, recounted earlier?

Yet again, it is doubtful. There seems little sense of purpose to the phenomenon and it is rarely if ever meaningful or positive. On the contrary, as Sacks noted, it is usually fearful and only strange or mildly pleasurable at best. Sacks reports no accounts where a sense of presence is involved and the pattern of experiencing is only temporal and geometrical at best. Scotomata seem rarely to occur when they are needed – indeed, they often appear distressing – and leave subjects with no lasting, positive fruits. As with all of the other 'explanations' explored so far in this chapter, it appears that migraine aura too cannot adequately explain the vast majority of accounts of light in the RERC archive.

Temporal-lobe transients

As this chapter may so far have suggested, religious experience has gained the interest of large numbers of researchers over the years working in a variety of scientific fields. Recent years in particular have seen a significant growth of interest from within neuroscience: so much so that the term 'neurotheology' has been coined to describe the attempts made by numerous neuroscientists to explain religious experiences in terms of what we know of the structure and functioning of the human brain. Foremost amongst these researchers is Laurentian University's Professor Michael Persinger, whose work has centred on the temporal lobe as the place within the brain most likely to produce a rich range of religious and paranormal experiences.

Persinger's overall argument has been that a range of religious, mystical and spiritual experiences may best be explained as arising when the brain's temporal lobe – and, in particular, the right temporal lobe – becomes stimulated and temporarily 'unstable'. These experiences, he suggests, may include a sense of presence, a range of hallucinatory phenomena including smells and strange figures and, most importantly for this book, glowing and bright forms.

In order to explain his position, Persinger has tracked the history and evolutionary development of two particularly interesting areas of the brain: the frontal lobes and the temporal lobes. The frontal lobes are huge, accounting for 50 per cent of our total cerebral capacity. As these developed, human beings began to be able to inhibit their behaviour and to predict likely outcomes of their actions, planting crops in one season, for example, in the expectation that they might be harvested in another. Clearly, both inhibition and anticipation are crucial to the development and maintenance of society. However, Persinger asserts, this societal advantage was double-edged. For in being able as individuals to foresee their own futures, human beings also became able to feel in advance the horror of their own deaths.

However, there was, Persinger argues, a second, 'tandem' evolutionary development that compensated somewhat for this. For at the same time as the frontal lobes developed, the temporal lobes did too. These became the source of memory, evaluation, dreams, fantasies, aggression and the labelling of experiences as rewarding or punishing. With this development came the origin of personhood as well, for, Persinger asserts, the sense of the thinking, introspecting self comes from the left temporal lobe too because thought and introspection both need language in order to occur and language arises within the left hemisphere of the cerebrum. As a result of these developments, the rich range of religious beliefs and practices emerged and was able to counteract our evolved fear of annihilation. However, this was not all. For the experience of a 'sensed presence' and other religious experiences – themselves intensely meaningful and anxiety-assuaging – began to arise from this area of the brain also, particularly when it became prone to seizures, as it does from time to time (Joseph 2002: 273–8).

Persinger makes much of temporal-lobe transients – 'very focal, electrical display[s] within the temporal lobe' in this latter regard. Crucially, he writes, 'People with seizures in this part of the brain experience vivid landscapes or perceive forms of living things. Some of these entities are not human, but are described as little men, *glowing forms or bright, shining sources*' (Joseph 2002: 276–7; emphasis mine).

Both 'soft' and 'hard' 'signs' of unusual temporal-lobe activity may manifest also. 'Soft signs' may include all of the above, plus early morning highs, *déjà vu*, hallucinations upon going to sleep, senses of invisible presences, claimed telepathic experiences and vivid, recurrent dreams. 'Hard signs', on the other hand, may include hypergraphia (the compulsion to write at great length about religious and philosophical topics), a sense of being divinely chosen, extremely altered feelings and a sense of great personal importance. Throughout, both 'soft' and 'hard' signs are experienced as real and intensely meaningful.

These temporal-lobe transients (TLTs), writes Persinger, have occurred throughout history and continue today. Crucial for him, however, is the correct *interpretation* of their origin and significance. Persinger, together with other neurotheologians, prefers to understand them in terms of localized brain seizures. In antiquity and historically, however, the suggestion from within neuroscience is that they were interpreted religiously. Indeed, Persinger argues that context, both historical and cultural, is crucial in determining how TLTs are and have been interpreted and understood. 'Although the content of TLT experiences would reflect a person's learning history', he writes, 'the general pattern of themes would be consistent across every human culture due to the similarities of temporal lobe function' (Joseph 2002: 282).

A number of questions arise from this fascinating research. Foremost among them might be: What sorts of people have these experiences? Who *can* have them? Are they the 'possession' of just a privileged if 'unstable' few? Or are they open to all? Persinger's answer is that we can all have them – and that he even has the means to produce them.

First, he notes, TLTs are not simply epilepsy by another name. For we are all temporal-lobe 'labile': that is to say, everybody can, on occasion, undergo episodes triggered by temporary temporal lobe instability and these need not be accompanied by convulsions or other 'bizarre' behaviours. However, and interestingly in view of what *this* book has uncovered, certain life situations seem to produce TLTs more than others. In particular, he writes, 'These short temporal lobe transients are precipitated by subtle psychological factors such as personal stress, loss of a loved one, and the dilemma of anticipated death.' Given this study's discovery of the link between crisis and the occurrence of unusual lights, this association of TLTs, bereavement and the nearness of death should give serious pause for thought. More interesting still, however – and again in keeping with what this book has found – Persinger adds that other contexts may give rise to TLTs too, including incense, rocking, fasting, lack of oxygen, childbirth and yoga. In addition, he notes:

> The psychophysiological correlates of near-death conditions should be the strongest precipitators of TLTs. Progressive alteration in blood flow and transient vasospasms in key areas, accentuated by the gradual deterioration of the body or by surgical procedures (anesthesia), allow prolonged and optimal temporal lobe conditions. (Persinger 1983: 1258)

In other words, life-threatening conditions and/or surgical procedures including anaesthetics may be particularly expected to produce TLTs. And as we have seen particularly when examining lights associated with crisis experiences, unusual episodes involving lights and presences seem to occur with some regularity at just these times.

The link between crisis and the occurrence of TLTs receives detailed treatment in Persinger's research. He even suggests the 'mechanism' that may explain the link. At times of individual and collective crisis, he argues, right-hemisphere activity in the brain increases. When the crisis becomes intolerable, the left hemisphere may close down almost altogether, leaving only residual activity and allowing the right hemisphere to 'flood' it with its newly released visions, dreams and hallucinations. A right-hemisphere sense of self – a sense of presence which mirrors that 'self' usually located in the language-possessing left hemisphere – may accompany these also. The result of such activity, for Persinger, is to 'kick-start' activity in the left hemisphere, which resumes its normal functioning with new-found feelings of confidence, self-esteem, and even, on occasion, religious bigotry. Indeed, the 'fruits' of TLTs are more varied than this, he writes, for they may in addition produce profound and long-lasting changes in subjects due to their 'profound capacity to evoke pleasurable and meaningful experiences, reduce existential anxiety and generate the security of old parental experiences . . .'. Even a single TLT can do this, he asserts, and we are once again reminded of the lasting, positive fruits reported by the people whose unusual encounters with light have made up the bulk of the current study (Cotton 1995: 208).

As if all of this was not interesting enough, Persinger has taken his research further still with the construction of a laboratory at

Laurentian University that, he claims, will enable subjects to experience TLTs – and hence religious experiences – at will. In 1983, during an EEG study designed to monitor the effects of meditation, a Transcendental Meditation instructor was found to have an electrical anomaly within the vicinity of her right temporal lobe. During this time she reported that she was 'filled with the spirit' and felt the presence of God with her in the laboratory. This prompted Persinger and his colleagues to wonder whether the 'God experience' could be artificially induced at will in experimental subjects. Given that the right temporal lobe might in part or in full be responsible for a range of mystical and religious experiences, could it be 'triggered' within the laboratory in order to produce similar experiences in selected volunteers?

By the late 1980s Persinger had developed a computer-based system in which weak, complex magnetic fields of between ten nanoteslas and one microtesla could be brought to bear on the cerebral hemispheres. Subjects would sit blindfolded while the field was applied to their brains and many reported a 'sensed presence' of some kind of sentient being, even though they were alone. After a number of such studies, Persinger concluded:

> We have been impressed by the common neurophenomenological themes of the experiences reported by the hundreds of university students and special populations (including visiting journalists) we have tested during the last 15 years . . . [T]he themes associated with specific patterns of fields have remained consistent. Each experience, however, has its own special signature that is likely to reflect the beliefs of the experient as well as the cultural labels. (Joseph 2002: 282)

Some of the experiences reported to Persinger by experimental subjects are interesting to compare with 'spontaneous' religious experiences. One twenty-five-year-old volunteer 'exposed to a burst-firing magnetic field' claimed:

> I felt a presence behind me and then along the left side. When I tried to focus on its position the presence moved; every time I tried to sense where it was, it would move around. When it moved to the right side I experienced a deep sense of security like I had not experienced before. I started to cry when I felt it slowly fading away. (Joseph 2002: 281)

The fading is especially interesting here as it occurred at the time that Persinger and his colleagues had 'shifted the field parameters'.

Another thirty-year-old woman who had received 'a frequency-modulated field over the right temporal lobe' reported:

I feel detached from my body ... I am floating ... there is a kind of vibration moving through my sternum ... *there are odd lights* or faces along my left side. My body is becoming very hot ... tingling sensations in my chest and stomach ... now both arms. There's something feeling my ovaries. I can feel my left foot jerk. I feel there is someone in the room behind me. The vibrations are very strong now and I can look down and see myself. (Joseph 2002: 281; emphasis mine)

Finally, a twenty-five-year-old man who received the field over both brain hemispheres reported:

I felt as if there were a *bright white light* in front of me. I saw a black spot that became a kind of funnel ... no tunnel [*sic*] that I felt drawn into ... I felt moving, like spinning forward through it. I began to feel the presence of people, but I could not see them; they were along my sides. They were colourless, grey looking people. I know I was in the chamber but it was very real. I suddenly felt intense fear and felt ice cold. (Joseph 2002: 282; emphasis mine)

Overall, Persinger concludes:

The application of the experimental complex, magnetic fields over the right hemisphere within the laboratory has consistently generated experiences of god or religious entities in people who believe in these experiences ... [Atheists] also report a sensed presence or detachment from their bodies (out of body experience) but attribute the phenomena to their own cognitive processes ... These results strongly suggest that the experience of a 'sentient presence' is an intrinsic property of the human brain and of human experience. (Joseph 2002: 282)

Over the years Persinger and his colleagues have analysed such experiences outside the laboratory as well as inside it, and a number of these findings are interesting in the context of this book. One in particular may be significant given the number of times we have seen that unusual lights are reported at night. 'We have found', Persinger writes,

that the sensed presence whose attributions range from bereavement apparitions to visitations from Gods and Aliens, occurs more frequently between midnight and 06 hr local time and in particular between 02 hr and 04 hr local time. This peak is the same period in which the greatest proportion of overt temporal lobe seizures were recorded during the late nineteenth century before the implementation of effective medications. (Joseph 2002: 286)

Also interesting is the long list of after-effects produced by TLTs and claimed by Persinger and his colleagues to include confusion, disorientation, time loss, partial amnesia, experiences of hearing and knowing information and a sense of intense personal meaningfulness. Over the longer term, they assert, personality changes may also emerge that include 'bouts of automatic behaviour and a sense of the personal' together with a sense of being 'chosen' because of perceived 'patterns of meaning between unrelated experiences'. People may also, they argue, become fixed on specific ideas and/or phrases, may become compelled to write down their philosophical thoughts, and may in some cases become proselytizers, 'to spread the word'.

It is clear that we are dealing here with exciting, cutting-edge, controversial research that promises to enhance significantly our understanding of a range of unusual experiences. How well, then, does it enable us to 'explain' lightforms? A number of insights are clearly useful and thought-provoking. Persinger's assertion that TLTs are more likely to occur at times of crisis fits the pattern we have uncovered. So, too, does his assertion that they occur in significant numbers at night. So too, does his contention that there is a 'common core' underlying the diversity of descriptions of experience that is explainable by the fact that our brains are all, essentially, 'wired' in the same way. So too does his inclusion of unusual lights as one of the phenomena associated with TLTs. Have we therefore finally managed to track down and explain the subject-matter of this book in terms of temporal-lobe transients?

Whilst promising in this regard, Persinger's work still leaves many unanswered questions, and at least two crucial areas leave room for doubt. First, a glance back at the experiences produced 'to order' in the lab at Laurentian reveals how *unlike* the experiences we have been dealing with they are. As we have seen, a large number of unusual experiences of light are rich, coherent and meaningful, and this tends to be reinforced by their occurrence at significant times – often when they are most needed. By contrast, many of the experiences evoked by Persinger and his colleagues appear fragmentary and dreamlike, making them more like the pathological hallucinations isolated by D'Aquili, Newberg and Rause, as already discussed. So, for example, the thirty-year-old woman's out-of-body experience cited by Persinger as an example of an evoked experience includes a range of bizarre and fragmentary features including a vibration in the sternum, a heating of the body, tingling sensations in the chest and stomach and a sense of 'something feeling my ovaries'. To be sure, the experience also includes lights, but they are hardly the meaningful focus of the episode.

Similarly, the twenty-five-year-old male's evoked tunnel and light experience includes apparently invisible but nonetheless grey people, and ends on a note of intense fear and cold: a far cry from the apparently calming, joyful sensations claimed by those whose tunnel and light episodes we examined in chapter 7. Persinger has certainly isolated something vaguely similar to the experiences discussed in this book. But the differences are too great to make his theory a convincing explanation of all – or even most – of these.

Secondly, the 'fruits' of the experiences discussed by Persinger – both laboratory-induced and spontaneous – appear very different from those reported by the subjects of this study. We have seen few examples in previous chapters of light-experiencers becoming confused, disorientated proselytizers, exhibiting automatic behaviour and reporting periods of missing time. On the contrary, many have reported no increase in religious belief, and the reader is often struck by the clarity of their recall of events and the way in which they have incorporated them meaningfully into apparently rich and ongoing lives.

Overall, it is clear that Persinger's neat – some might say *too* neat – framework of explanation of the evolved sense of meaningful experiences to be had as a result of TLTs is able to account for *some* fragmentary episodes involving unusual lights. Yet placed alongside the accounts in the RERC archive it begins to look somewhat artificial, or – worse – it begins to look as if the experiences it is attempting to explain are very unlike those of genuine religious experiencers: including those whose encounters with light make up the subject of this study. Persinger may, in some cases, end up accounting for something vaguely similar. But the differences should make us wary of concluding that he has 'explained' religious experiences – including meaningful encounters with calming, life-transforming lights – wholly in terms of his theory of TLTs.

Divine interventions

Persinger's work ranks as the most recent, foremost and sustained example of a scientific attempt to bring religious experience 'down' to the level of brain processes. If correct – a big 'if', as we have seen – such research threatens to strip religious experience of any claim to put experiencers in touch with 'higher', supernatural, spiritual realities. Instead, it tries to show how subjects are, in fact, misinterpreting unusual but essentially brain-based experiences as transcendent –

even divine – ones. It represents a powerful – if flawed – challenge to the view that something or someone can 'break in' to this world from time to time to bring about healing or change, things that might not be possible in any other way.

Ironically, though, the biggest challenge to this 'interventionist' view comes not from science but from theology. For there are a number of theologians and philosophers of religion who question whether or not God or other transcendent 'powers' should be seen in this way. They also question the very desirability of a universe where such occasional supernatural 'break-ins' can and/or do occur.

Central to their objection is the moral unfairness of a God who acts in this way. The objection is well summed up in the words of Maurice Wiles, who has written critically of miracles viewed as occasional interventions by God to bring about supernatural change. 'If the direct action of God,' he writes,

> independent of secondary causation, is an intelligible concept, then it would appear to have been sparingly and strangely used. Miracles must by definition be relatively infrequent or else the whole idea of laws of nature . . . would be undermined, and ordered life as we know it would be an impossibility. Yet even so it would seem strange that no miraculous intervention prevented Auschwitz or Hiroshima, while the purposes apparently forwarded by some of the miracles acclaimed in traditional Christian faith seem trivial by comparison. (Wiles 1986: 66)

There are several issues surrounding the idea of an interventionist God here. One is that, if overdone, the interventions produced would upset the regularity of a world apparently governed by 'fixed' laws of nature. Theologians such as Wiles and Brian Heblethwaite propose, instead, an alternative scenario, such as that which sees the world as a fixed creation of God that is not subject to any further 'tampering' or correction. For the alternative might be a universe perpetually in danger of having its rules undermined, run by a God who appears virtually arbitrary in his choice of whom he will help and why.

These are powerful objections with obvious relevance to the current study. It is estimated that more people died as a result of suicide after the Falklands War than died during the actual combat. Presumably the majority of these unfortunate people reached rock-bottom despair before they took their own lives. Simply stated: why didn't *they* see a light? Why did nothing appear to them to intervene in their hour of need? Why the 400 or so people in this book and not thousands, even millions, of others?

Of course, the same problem occurs when other types of religious experiences are considered. Why, for example, do less than 20 per cent of people who undergo temporary clinical death have near-death experiences? What about the other 80 per cent? Is there something about them that we do not know or are they just arbitrarily deemed unworthy to get a glimpse of apparent eternity? And, if so, why? And by whom?

Some would argue that there are simply no answers to these and similar questions that may be asked about a range of other religious experiences also, including visions, prophetic dreams, angelic encounters and conversions. Others, such as the philosopher of religion Keith Ward, have suggested that God intervenes occasionally through such things but to build up faith, rather than to reduce suffering (Vardy 1999: 210). As regards the unusual lights with which we have been dealing, very similar issues are raised. We simply do not know why a relative few should be so favoured. This does not, however, mean that they are *not* the recipients of genuinely transforming, life-affirming, spiritual experiences. And possibly the accounts held in the RERC archive are just the tip of a huge iceberg. At present, we do not know what percentage of the population – happy, sad or in despair – experience such things. More research is clearly needed. The large number of experiences in the RERC archive may be indicative of the fact that many, many more encounters with unusual lights occur but go unreported and hence unread.

Pre-Moody NDEs

One fascinating and rather unexpected conclusion that this book has reached is that near-death experiences reported before their massive popularization by Raymond Moody in his book *Life after Life* match to a large extent near-death experiences as defined by him and by researchers who came after him. As we saw in chapter 7, this is a finding with all kinds of interesting implications. Since the term 'near-death experience' passed into popular usage after 1975, when Moody's book first appeared, there have been all kinds of opportunities for people to come to expect experiences at or near the point of death that include such things as out-of-body experiences, trips along tunnels and encounters with bright, benign lights. Pre-1975, as chapter 7 also revealed, there was little popular knowledge or expectation that such experiences might occur.

Yet, as we saw, many pre-1975, pre-Moody NDE accounts held at the RERC archive contain descriptions of unusual lights, feelings of peace and joy, ineffability, tunnels, feelings of great knowledge, out-of-body experiences and lasting, spiritual fruits. Clearly, enough common features across these reports were found that suggested that NDEs are not simply the product of expectation or post-experiential 'shaping' but are instead genuinely mysterious, consistent experiences that have yet to be adequately explained. To be sure, no experience contained every one of the fifteen elements of Moody's original 'model' NDE. Yet this is not really surprising, given that no NDE ever has.

The discovery that pre-Moody NDEs resemble post-Moody NDEs in so many key ways suggests that a more thorough, global search may reveal similar findings. At the very least, more research into NDEs along these lines would surely be welcome. Chapter 7's discoveries occurred as part of a book investigating a much wider range of experiences of light, as this book has, and hence may be said to have been a 'spin-off' from the main project. But a project specifically devoted to a comparison of pre- and post-Moody NDEs, searching further than the RERC archive for such experiences, would enable us to test in a more thorough and systematic way the argument that contends that religious experiences in general – and near-death experiences in particular – are examples of people seeing what they want to or expect to see. The preliminary findings of this book suggest that people's NDEs are *not* examples of what psychologists call 'motivated seeing' or of what philosophers call 'constructivism'. Instead, as we have found, there is a genuinely exciting and strong possibility that at the point of death many people have structured, consistent near-death experiences that they *do not* expect to have. At least, that has been the case in the past. Further research may confirm this finding, and may also reveal that it is equally true of experiences that happen today.

Beings of light

Another finding of this study has been that unusual lights that appear to people are rarely positively and definitively identified. Whilst this is not really surprising in the case of unusual beams, rays or shafts, it is more surprising in instances where lights appear in specific locations, such as in the corner of a room, or where the light is encountered as a personality inhabiting a transcendent or heavenly realm. More surprising still is the almost complete absence of any attempt in any testimony to identify any light as an angel, particularly given the large number of books that currently exist in which real-life encounters with angels are described in terms of episodes including beings clothed in or appearing as a wonderful radiance.

It is tempting to conclude that many more episodes of unusual light in the RERC archive might have concluded that the encounter was one with an angel had the large amount of current literature on angels existed before the late-1990s. We have already seen that people have experiences that they do not expect to have. However, *after* their experiences they may reasonably be expected to reflect upon them and to look around for the best possible way of interpreting them. Clearly these interpretations must be available to subjects, as angel interpretations currently are in ever-increasing numbers. In the early and middle years of the RERC, however, from the late 1960s through to the early 1990s, there was little or no literature dealing with real-life encounters with angels. It is more than tempting to conclude that the lack of such literature is an – or perhaps *the* – explanation of why the identification of unusual lights as angels is missing from the RERC testimonies submitted during these years.

What the study of lightforms has demonstrated beyond doubt is the fact that angelic lights and lights encountered during NDEs must be viewed as part of a much wider variety of unusual experiences involving light. Chapter 2 showed that this variety has existed both historically and cross-culturally. Chapters 3–10 revealed the extent of the diversity of the ways in which persons experience a wide range of unusual lights currently and in a mainly western context. Despite the clear consistency revealed in those chapters, it is clearly also the case that in addition to encountering unusual lights at the end of tunnels, people report light wrapping and filling them, light appearing as a beam, a ray or a shaft, light appearing to illuminate other persons and/or landscapes, light appearing in a heavenly or transcendent realm to which they have suddenly been transported, or light 'superimposed' on the normal everyday environment but given no name. The conclusion to be drawn here is that near-death and angelic experiences involving light are but two 'types' of a much wider range of experiences in which unusual, often benign and transformative lights are encountered.

A mystery remains

This chapter has considered some of the foremost, up-to-date scientific research into religious and spiritual experience and has examined how this research may enable us to account for the lightforms with which this book has been dealing. Interestingly, no single theory that we have examined so far has been able entirely to explain the phenomena under investigation. We are left, then, with a mystery.

Or may we be looking in the wrong place when we look to science to give us explanations of these things? Might we, instead, look elsewhere: to some of the spiritual, religious and paranormal authorities that were examined in chapter 2, perhaps? Some of these authorities, as we saw, see in unusual lights evidence of manifestations from other, higher, spiritual realities. Cultures throughout time and widely separated in space have been generally agreed that this world is not all that there is. That there are other worlds that can interact with this one, and that sometimes that interaction can take the form of unusual but benign lights.

Is this the final conclusion that we can draw; the final lesson we should learn? Should it be? Reading through the accounts that make up this study it is hard to avoid the conclusion that the pattern which many experiences follow may be telling us something. That there are dimensions to reality that extend beyond the physical, perhaps; dimensions and realities that may be able, on occasion, to interact with our own. Interestingly, many of the experiences we have examined throughout these pages have been reported not simply by people in crisis but by people whose crises were no fault of their own: victims of shock, bereavement, tragic illness or desperately bad news. Is this the real lesson of lightforms? That on occasion, when we need it most, when life has dealt us the most terrible of injuries, lights can appear – to comfort, to love, to heal and to guide?

We may call them angels or we may not. Few if any subjects have called them that in these pages. Yet in bringing light into often unspeakable darkness, many of these lights in all their forms seem to behave like them. Did Hardy have evidence of angels sent to him at his Research Centre? Evidence from hundreds of people that has lain largely untouched until now? Or are we dealing with something still stranger?

The main conclusion that I have drawn after almost three years of investigation is that these unusual lights are proof that this world is not all there is. I take great comfort from that fact. Comfort, too, that the other world – if that is the right phrase – seems on occasion to be so close to this one that it can touch it. More, that it can reach out and touch *us*. More still, that it touches us when we need it most. And that its touch brings us comfort, life, love . . . and light.

Bibliography

Barrett, W. (1986), *Deathbed Visions: The Psychical Experiences of the Dying* second edn (Northampton, Aquarian).

Barton, S. and G. Stanton (eds.) (1994), *Resurrection: Essays in Honour of Leslie Houlden* (London, SPCK).

Berman, P. (1996), *The Journey Home: What Near-Death Experiences and Mysticism Tell Us about the Gift of Love* (New York, Simon and Schuster).

Cook, C. and Persinger, M. 'Experimental induction of the "sensed presence" in normal subjects and an exceptional subject', *Motor Skills*, 85: 683.

Corcoran, D. (1996), *When Ego Dies: A Compilation of Near-Death and Mystical Conversion Experiences* (Texas, Emerald Ink).

Cotton, I. (1995), *The Hallelujah Revolution* (London, Warner).

Craig, M. (1988), *Spark from Heaven: The Mystery of the Madonna from Medjugorge* (London, Hodder).

Cupitt, D. (1998), *Mysticism after Modernity* (London, SCM).

Devereux, P. (1982), *Earthlights* (London, Turnstone).

Devereux, P. (2001), *Haunted Land: Investigations into Ancient Mysteries and Modern Day Phenomena* (London, Piatkus).

Devereux, P. and P. Brookesmith (1998), *UFOs and UFOlogy: The First 50 Years* (London, Cassell).

Eckersley, G. (1996), *An Angel at My Shoulder: True Stories of Angelic Experiences* (London, Rider).

Eliade, M. (1962), *The Two and the One* (New York, Harper and Row).

Eliade, M. (1964), *Shamanism: Archaic Techniques of Ecstasy* (London, Routledge).

Fenwick, P. and E. Fenwick (1995), *The Truth in the Light: An Investigation of over 300 Near-Death Experiences* (London, Headline).

Fox, M. (2003), *Religion, Spirituality and the Near-Death Experience* (London, Routledge).

Green, C. and C. McCreery (1989), *Apparitions* (London, Hamilton).

Guggenheim, B. and J. Guggenheim (1997), *Hello from Heaven* (New York, Bantam).

Harris, R. (1999), *Lourdes: Body and Spirit in the Secular Age* (Harmondsworth, Penguin).

Hay, D. (1987), *Exploring Inner Space* (London, Mowbray).

Hay, D. (1990), *Religious Experience Today: Studying the Facts* (London, Mowbray).

Heathcote-James, E. (2001), *Seeing Angels: True Contemporary Accounts of Hundreds of Angelic Experiences* (London, John Blake).

Hollenback, J. (1996), *Mycticism: Experience, Response and Empowerment* (Philadelphia, Pennsylvania State University Press).

Hynek, J. (1972), *The UFO Experience* (New York, Abelard Schuman).

James, W. (1902), *The Varieties of Religious Experience* (London, Collins).

Joseph, R. (ed.) (2002), *Neurotheology: Brain, Science, Spirituality, Religious Experience* (California University Press).

Katz, S. (1978), *Mysticism and Philosophical Analysis* (London, Sheldon).

Laski, M. (1961), *Ecstasy: A Study of Some Secular and Religious Experiences* (London, Cresset).

Lindbeck, G. (1984), *The Nature of Doctrine* (London, SPCK).

Maxwell, M. and V. Tschudin (1990), *Seeing the Invisible: Modern Religious and Other Transcendent Experiences* (Harmondsworth, Penguin).

Moody, R. (1975) *Life after Life* (Atlanta, Mockingbird).

Moody, R. (2001), *Life after Loss* (London, Rider).

Moody, R. and P. Perry (1988), *The Light Beyond: The Transforming Power of Near-Death Experiences* (London, Macmillan).

Morse, M. (1992), *Transformed by the Light: The Powerful Effect of Near-Death Experiences on People's Lives* (London, Macmillan).

Newberg, A., E. D'Aquili and V. Rause (2001), *Why God Won't Go Away* (New York, Ballantine).

Osis, K. and E. Haraldsson (1997), *At The Hour of Death*, third edn (Norwalk, Hastings House).

Persinger, M. A. (1983), 'Religious and mystical experiences as artefacts of temporal lobe function: a general hypothesis', *Perceptual and Motor Skills*, 57, 1255–1262.

Rees, D. (2001), *Death and Bereavement: The psychological, religious and cultural influences* (London, Whurr).

Ring, K. (1984), *Heading toward Omega: In Search of the Meaning of the Near-Death Experience* (New York, William Morrow).

Ring, K. and E. Valarino (1998), *Lessons from the Light: What We Can Learn from the Near-Death Experience* (Massachusetts, Persius).

Rinpoche, S. (1992), *The Tibetan Book of Living and Dying* (London, Rider).

Sabom, M. (1998), *Light and Death: One Doctor's Fascinating Account of Near-Death Experiences* (Michigan, Zondervan).

Sacks, O. (1985), *The Man Who Mistook His Wife For a Hat* (London, Macmillan).

Sacks, O. (1995), *Migraine* (London, Macmillan).

Sargant, W. (1957), *Battle for the Mind: A Physiology of Conversion and Brainwashing* (London, Heinemann).

Sutherland, C. (2000), *In the Company of Angels: Welcoming Angels into Your Life* (Australia, Doubleday).

Thouless, R. (1923), *The Psychology of Religion* (London, Cambridge University Press).

Underhill, E. (1993), *Mysticism: The Nature and Development of Spiritual Consciousness* (Oxford, Oneworld).

Vallee, J. (1970), *Passport to Magonia: From Folklore to Flying Saucers* (London, Neville Spearman).

Van Hien, G. (1963), *What Is Subud?* (London, Rider).

Vardy, P. (1999), *The Puzzle of Evil* (London, Fount)

Warren, L. and P. Robbins (1997), *Left at East Gate* (London, Michael O'Mara).

Wiebe, P. (1997), *Visions of Jesus: Direct Encounters from the New Testament to Today* (Oxford, Oxford University Press).

Wiles, M. (1986), *God's Action in the World* (London, SCM).

Index